The Rampant God

NIGEL DAVIES

The Rampant God
Eros Throughout the World

WILLIAM MORROW AND COMPANY, INC.

NEW YORK 1984

Library of Congress Catalog Card Number: 84-60201

ISBN: 0-688-03094-7

Printed in the United States of America

First Edition

1 2 3 4 5 6 7 8 9 10

BOOK DESIGN BY ROBERT FREESE

Contents

Foreword

A few years ago I wrote a book on human sacrifice, practiced at one time or another in almost every corner of the globe. Having tackled such a fascinating but grisly subject, I wanted to examine some aspect of human behavior that was more conducive to pleasure than to pain.

So much has been written about human sexuality that in some respects there may be little left to say. Most books on the subject, however, are concerned almost exclusively with sex in Western society. Those that deal with its historical aspects mainly confine themselves to the endless struggle of European man to reconcile his more natural urges with the dictates of that most sex-negative of all religions, Christianity.

Accordingly, I felt that much more remained to be said about the sex life, past and present, of other cultures, both of tribal societies in various stages of development and of the world's other higher civilizations. For while nearly all peoples now strive to acquire the technology of the West, many are far less eager to adopt its present-day attitudes to sex; some have reacted strongly against them.

The West, since the sexual revolution of the 1970s, now tends to accept the viewpoint, almost universal among other peoples, that sex is something not merely to be tolerated but also to be enjoyed. But in other respects we surely still have much to learn from the customs of some of those non-Western cultures, so different from our own, and I therefore hope that this study will prove both useful and interesting.

CHAPTER ONE

The Birth of Sexuality

At the Beginning

In the long history of our planet, sex appears only toward the end. Life on Earth began about 2.5 billion years ago, but its earlier forms were celibate; they could multiply by themselves and had no need to mate. For countless aeons the world teamed with organisms, such as algae, whose single cell would simply divide into two. Thus each new creation was the split image of its forebear, and the tempo of change was limited.

Then about six hundred million years ago the tranquillity of this sexless world was shattered; a new kind of being had evolved that could not multiply in the same simple way because it had only half the necessary equipment and needed a separate partner to supply the other half. This was the beginning of sex.

Its advent was a watershed, since each offspring of such unions is distinct, produced by a different blend of two sets of genes. Sex thus became the dynamic force in evolution and brought forth a whole series of new species, culminating in our own. The presence of male and female, both among humans and animals, may appear to us earthlings an imperative necessity. But while asexual, or single-sex, beings have obvious limitations, it is not impossible that one of the other hundred million stars of our own galaxy might have a planet where things were different; three or even four sexes could conceivably exist, all in some way needed for procreation.

Viewed impartially, sex may seem an absurd mechanism, a mere generator of unnecessary strife. Eventually, however, it produced *Homo sapiens,* whose changing forms of sexuality are the subject of this book. Such forms can be seen in perspective only by retracing the first stages of human sex life, or sexuality —a term that implies a relationship between male and female that goes beyond random copulation as performed, say, by mice or stoats.

Though it is far from clear from which of the apes man is most directly descended, a consensus exists among scientists that evolution did take place. The process is still questioned by many humans loath to admit that their deepest emotions and finest aspirations stem from an animal heritage. However, those who reject evolution outright do so now for reasons that are more religious or emotional than scientific. The story has often been told of the wife of Bishop Wilberforce, dumbfounded when Charles Darwin first published his theory of man's origin over a century ago. "Descended from monkeys," she said with a sigh. "Let us hope that it isn't true. But if it is true, let us hope that it doesn't become widely known."

However wide the acceptance of evolution, it offers few clues as to the love life of the first humans. Until recently, their sexual customs were more often related to those of Western culture and thus were commendable to nineteenth-century anthropologists. Most of these scholars thus were imbued with the notion of early man as the guardian of the home and breadwinner of a monogamous family unit, an intrepid hunter, prepared also to kill his own kind in defense of his loved ones; the female in this context is cast in the role of nest builder and adoring mother. The image of "man the hunter," popularized much later by writers in the 1960s, was all-pervasive—until it dawned upon scientists who studied man's earliest remains in more detail that hunting played a lesser role in the lives of the first humans, who were not great meat eaters. The latest research on animals, whether primate apes or others, also serves to question the role of the dominant male; for instance, it was discovered that a beaver colony is organized around the adult female; she, not the male, not only repairs dams and obtains food but also guards her offspring from attack.

The question of early man's hunting skills is thus open to question. Equally, the argument as to whether he was promiscuous or monogamous has generated much heat and is far from resolved. The argument is not new. In the first century A.D., a Roman philosopher, Lucretius, wrote: "At first men lived like beasts. . . . Lacking the institution of marriage, they followed a career of sexual promiscuity." In contrast, nineteenth-century students of the problem preferred to think of primitive families more in terms of a model working-class household in Victorian England; they still accepted the biblical view that sexual license developed only after the fall of man.

However, in 1877, the leading American anthropologist of the time, Lewis Henry Morgan, revived the notion of early man's promiscuity, since no concept of physical paternity can have existed (a concept also lacking among most Australian aborigines and Polynesians). Based on studies of surviving groups, he concluded that primitive families were in effect matriarchies in which people took their ancestry from their mother, who produced offspring after pairing with various males. However, at the beginning of the twentieth century, the wheel once more took a full turn with the publication of Edward Westermarck's *History of Human Marriage,* in which the author devoted no less than 234 pages to refuting Morgan's theory of primeval permissiveness. Nowadays many anthropologists adopt a middle stance: They may doubt the existence of any true form of marriage, but they tend to favor the adoption of some kind of pair bonding at an early stage as a prime factor in the emergence of man. Sexuality then becomes crucial to the very existence of the human species.

However, a basic problem inhibits the study of prehistoric sex life. Immense strides have been made in collecting data on early man and on the tools he made, but such vestiges give no inkling as to whether he was monogamous, polygamous, or merely promiscuous in a general sense. Bones and teeth tell us much about locomotion and diet but nothing of sharing patterns and mating habits.

Although primeval man's own remains offer few clues as to his sexual relations, two alternative approaches to the problem remain: We can either study his eventual successors, the more primitive surviving human groups of today, or we can investigate the habits of his precursors, the anthropoid apes. Both approaches have many snags.

In contrast to early man, fairly plentiful data exist on the sex life of the more primitive groups and tribes encountered over the centuries by European pioneers. Nonetheless, these people offer a most imperfect model for the customs of our remoter ancestors millions of years ago; their members belong exclusively to the *Homo sapiens* species that appeared only in the past hundred thousand years, as the end product of millions of years of evolution since the first hominids. Not only is modern man's technology different; many such tribes have domesticated animals, while others rely on sea and river fishing as a major source of food, developments that occur very late in the archaeological record. In addition, the religious beliefs and social structure of such ostensibly simple groups as the Australian aborigines are complex in the extreme, and the search for a race or tribe whose mentality and way of life remotely corresponded to those of the first humans is a hopeless quest. We cannot find the key to primordial religion by studying Australian beliefs any more than we can rediscover the mating habits of early man by recording those of present-day New Guinea.

The Irritating Apes

Since neither the remains of early man himself, nor the customs of primitive tribes that survive can solve the problem, scientists logically turned to the only alternative approach and studied the animal kingdom. But such studies also resolve few doubts concerning the family life of our first forebears. For instance, Morgan's belief in human promiscuity is not nullified by the mere fact that in the case of many insects, as well as toads, the eggs are deposited in the back of the male, who thus becomes the model parent, loaded with the full responsibility of caring for the young.

Primatology, or the study of man's nearest relations, the primate apes, has made immense strides in recent years, and a wealth of data on nonhuman primates have been gathered. For instance, it used to be thought that apes were entirely vegetarian, until they were more closely watched in their own habitat; moreover, scientists long supposed that it made little difference which primate species was used as a basis for speculation about human origins. But the habits of those most closely related to man have now been found to be bewilderingly diverse. Most unobligingly, the various species conduct their male-female relations in such utterly different ways that they can be used to prove or disprove every conceivable theory about our own ancestors.

On the one hand, the gibbons of Southeast Asia are so strictly monogamous that the missionaries intent upon mending human ways could have taught them nothing in that respect. Males and females bond for life, and children are their joint responsibility. Gibbon fathers spend much of their time defending the family territory, to an extent unknown among other primates. Nonetheless, the male obtains his own food, which he does not share with his family.

In total contrast, if the gibbons are the Calvinists, the baboons are the Moslems of the primate realm. The Gelada baboons from the North of Ethiopia move in large herds, composed of a number of separate harems, each consisting of a single male and three to five females, together with their children. In one colony of baboons observed in captivity there were twenty-five males and twenty-five females. Five males purloined all the females, and the remaining twenty were unmated; of the five privileged apes, one had seven wives, while a few had only one, a situation not unlike that of polygamous human societies. The number of females in each group is determined by the male's ability to satisfy their wants, both sexual and material, including periodical grooming. If the male does not groom his wives regularly, they are apt to desert him and join the harem of one of his rivals; such a desertion by one wife may lead to a chain reaction, and a mass exodus follows, as other wives also choose to join the new challenger, who previously may have had none. Unlike the occupants of a human harem, female baboons are free to change husbands, and the male therefore faces an inescapable dilemma: The harem is his status symbol but if he grabs too many wives, he may, by virtue of neglect, lose them to an usurper. The Indian macaque monkeys present an exaggerated version of the baboon pattern. They live in large groups consisting mostly of females, accompanied by few males. Other males are simply expelled and forced to form bachelor groups.

Polygamy is not confined to baboons, and a comparable form is favored by the thirteen thousand sea elephants on the Punta Norte Peninsula in Patagonia. Harems of up to twenty females surround a hulking male sultan, who measures up to twenty feet in length and four tons in weight. They loll together on the shore with their offspring in groups spaced about every hundred yards.

Orangutans in their turn follow a totally different pattern. For much of the time they live as solitary individuals. When a male meets a female, they often copulate on the spur of the moment, but no lasting relationship ensues. Hence psychologist Glen Wilson describes them as the rapists of the jungle, since the male often takes the female by force; the latter, when first assaulted, struggles and emits distress signals, but once she is pinned down she submits cheerfully to her fate.

The chimpanzees have been more closely observed than any other primate species in the search for clues to early human behavior. Nancy Makepeace Tanner in *On Becoming Human* tries to relate known chimpanzee behavior to the available data on early humans. Her case is in some respects convincing; central to her theme is the close genetic link between chimpanzee and man revealed by recent research. Nonetheless, the chimpanzee was not a forebear of *Homo sapiens,* and the question as to why the chimpanzee should serve as a model rather than any other primate remains open. In support of her thesis, Tanner stresses their cleverness, shown by recent field studies, in selecting raw materials and fashioning them into tools. Such talents may have little to do with their sex life, but she insists that chimpanzees also remind us of ourselves in their greeting patterns and gestures, such as kissing and embracing. For Tanner, accordingly, they offer a more specific model for the behavior of man's most immediate ancestors. Moreover, while the gorillas are vegetarians, the chimpanzees kill and eat small animals, though the term "hunting" hardly applies to such killings, for which tools or implements are not used. They do employ certain simple implements for gathering, and particularly for collecting termites. Chimpanzees will modify an inanimate object so that it serves better as a tool, as, for instance, the leaf "sponges" they use for sucking up water in tree holes. In addition, they can learn aspects of human linguistic codes.

Among the primates, the chimpanzees have the most free-and-easy approach to sex and form no enduring bonds. They live in loose communities, consisting usually of between thirty and eighty individuals. The males seldom fight over the females, who copulate with many partners; mating may be initiated by either sex.

The Human Problem

The contrasting behavior of the various primates thus offers no yardstick with which to reconstruct early human conduct, though human mating habits certainly seem to have something in common both with the permissive chimpanzees and the strait-laced gorillas. Primates as a whole, moreover, have certain customs almost certainly shared by early man. For intercourse the female turns her back to the male, a coital position probably also used by the transitional hominids. Delousing before copulation is practiced by most apes; for instance, among rhesus monkeys grooming amounts to a kind of secondary sexual activity, causing a certain erotic stimulation. Grooming previous to coitus is also known among surviving tribal peoples and was almost certainly part of the original human mating procedure. Even the courting songs of humans have their counterpart in recognizable sexual calls of many animals, including apes. Another likely common trait is the exposure of the genitals by receptive females, shared by all subhuman primates.

Even some variant forms of human sexual behavior are present among monkeys. Submissiveness on the part of the weaker or passive partner is basic to certain forms of homosexuality; but observers of monkeys have found that if one male is cowed by another, he may adopt a typically female gesture of submission by bending over and offering his backside as an invitation to copulate. Some monkeys thus temporarily adopt a feminine role; this trait is hardly surprising in the case, for instance, of the macaque monkeys, among whom large bachelor groups are deprived of all female company. Another human sexual variant, sadism, involving the giving or receiving of pain as a form of sexual arousal, is practiced by many species who engage in some sort of mock fight or struggle before copulation.

Despite these common traits, the disparities in primate mating habits are so wide that clear-cut evidence as to the mores of early man cannot be gained from a study of his nearest relatives. Though he evolved from these, both physically as well as mentally, he represented a radical departure. Moreover, man is capable of great diversity; demonstrably, the diet of very early human groups varied enormously from one region to another, and their sex life was not necessarily uniform.

Compared to monkeys and apes, the physical differences between men and women (known to specialists as "dimorphism") are on the whole smaller. For instance, baboon males are nearly twice the size of females, and males have long, daggerlike canine teeth. Exceptions to this rule, however, are gibbons and marmosets, whose males and females are almost of identical size and are hardly distinguishable, except to a trained observer.

Physical differences between man and ape may be obvious, but their respective role in man's mental progress is less clear. Bipedalism, the habit of walking upright using only the two feet, was long accepted as the critical factor that made humans out of nonhumans. However, this insistence lost much of its force following the discovery in Ethiopia in 1974 of parts of the skeleton of a tiny female, 3.5 feet tall, who was christened Lucy by her discoverer, Don Johanson. Lucy, who suffered from arthritis, died in her early twenties some 3.3 million years ago; it was evident from her hip, knee, and ankle bones that she walked totally erect. In spite of this most human trait, however, she had buck teeth, protruding snout, and no chin; in addition to these animal traits, her tiny brain made it impossible for her to qualify as human, although she walked upright and had pelvis and leg bones almost identical in function to those of modern man. Johanson also found larger bones that led him and his colleagues to conclude that the variations between Lucy and her menfolk were greater than among latter-day humans; this sexual dimorphism in the fossils led them to suggest that some kind of male-female division of labor had existed more than three million years ago.

Anthropologists have been plagued by this problem of bipedalism for over a century. It was first thought that brain development had preceded bipedalism, and many specialists refused to accept the evidence that Java man (approximately 500,000 B.C.), discovered in 1891, walked erect, because his skull was rather primitive. Since that time, however, a general consensus developed that bipedalism, brain enlargement, and regular tool use were part of the same process and had arisen more or less simultaneously. Tool use would have stimulated the development of a larger brain, better suited to devising implements, and also would have encouraged erect walking to be able to carry them around and to employ them effectively.

This notion was already called into question by the discovery of different varieties of Australopithecus, a near-man with a comparatively large brain, who lived in southern and eastern Africa about two million to three million years ago; for though he certainly walked erect, he seems to have been little more than a casual user of tools. The theory was further eroded by the discovery of Lucy who, notwithstanding her tiny brain, also walked erect nearly two million years before the existence of the earliest beings (named *Homo habilis* by their discoverer, Richard Leakey) who can more truly be called human, since they were constant tool users and even killed large animals. Although in the past attention was mainly focused on toolmaking as the main factor in the emergence of man, more stress is now being laid on social and sexual factors than on mere implements as the spur to the growth of the human brain; some scholars go so far as to suggest that the key to man's evolutionary breakthrough lies in the growth of a pair-bonding relation between male and female, whereby man undertook to feed and protect his women and children to a degree unknown among apes. This change of emphasis led to sexuality being regarded no longer as a result but as a motivator in the rise of the human species.

The Sexual Athlete

Bipedalism was far from being the only physical trait that distinguished man from the animals; other marked differences have more bearing on sex. The sexual performance of the human female sets her apart from the apes. Anthropologist Helen Fisher has aptly called her the sexual athlete of the primate world, since by a remarkable evolutionary twist, occurring millions of years ago, she became capable of constant and continuous arousal. In no species, whether elephant or insect, can the females make love so regularly; the others have a period of heat, or estrus, during which they copulate, while for the rest of the time they avoid sexual contact; in many mammals this occurs only once a year, during the annual mating season. Moreover, a female's period can be very brief, since once she has conceived, the estrus ends. Monkeys are somewhat more like humans than other animals, since the female primates have a monthly menstrual cycle and a period of heat that lasts for about ten days. Female primates thus enjoy sexual activity for more than a third of the time; chimpanzees in particular make the most of this, and while in heat they will copulate indiscriminately with every available male. A female gorilla has a period lasting only four days; according to observations made in the Yerkes Regional Primate Research Center, during those four days she will track down the male and force him to copulate several times. In addition, humans are literally forced to have intercourse more often than monkeys in order to produce children; since a woman has no period of heat, a couple cannot tell when the female is ready to conceive; unlike the apes, the woman's genitals do not swell at ovulation, and no pungent odor proclaims her ripeness.

A reasoned explanation as to how human females became sexual athletes is given by Helen Fisher in *The Sex Contract.* In tracing man's origins she recalls how the jungle, which then covered much of Africa, receded. About fourteen million years ago the climate began to change. Man's forebears slowly came to live in places where the woodland trees were interspersed with stretches of savannah grass. In these surroundings they lived partly by gathering, using sticks and stones to pry edible foods from the ground, and partly by eating small animals, such as lizards and turtles, that they learned to catch.

Africa continued to dry up, and about ten million years ago the woodlands in certain places began to disapper altogether; these protohominids were then forced to face the unfamiliar challenge of the open savannah, which became very arid in the dry season. Though they might search the hillside for herbs, nuts, and fruit, these often were scarce, and catching animals became vital to survival. This need called for more implements; but such makeshift implements, or weapons, had to be carried when on the move, not only to dispatch any available quarry but also to protect their owner against larger beasts of prey, such as lions; only those who could carry them survived, and they could do this only if they walked on two feet. Lucy was an early example of such beings; she was thereby the product of an innovation that offered protection but in itself did not require a larger brain, since it only involved the use of torn-off branches or of suitably shaped stones, a process that modified the body but hardly taxed the mind.

According to Fisher, however, the new stance, adopted simply to carry useful things, then led to a second decisive development that did raise man above the beasts. On the one hand, bipedalism enabled people to roam farther afield and bring more booty back to a central place, where they could congregate as a group and eat in safety. But if the two-legged stance solved certain problems, it created others. In particular, it led to a reshaping of the pelvis, involving a reduction in size of the female birth canal. Evolution took care of this challenge as best it could; the only solution was for the female to bear her children much sooner than the apes, at a stage when the head was still small enough to navigate the shrinking birth passage. But if nature thereby solved this problem, it created yet another: Females now had to care for their infants for a much longer period, and because they walked upright, were forced to carry them or strap them to their backs. This in turn made it harder for them to catch their own small animals, and they became incapable of providing for their young without recourse to the male population, the only unused source of manpower. Males then had to be enticed into cooperating with females in a way unknown among animals and that Fisher calls the sex contract.

But the task of recruiting this untapped work force was not easy and led to the third great change, which would at least permit the survival of the fittest females, who could somehow gain from the males the support that now became a necessity. The latter were reluctant helpers; mammals had existed for sixty million years, and invariably the males had simply fended for themselves, obliging the females by copulating with them during their short periods of heat. If males were to do more for the females and stay with them all the time, they demanded some return for their services in the form of a richer sex life. According to the general primate pattern, after a few monthly cycles the female would become pregnant: Not only during pregnancy, but also for some time after the infant was born, she would refuse to copulate, a pattern followed by our prehuman ancestors and by which the male's coital quota was severely rationed. But Fisher stresses, as part of her theory, that variations in sexual performance always exist between members of a species and among the female protohominids—a few were sexier than others and could have had longer cycles; remaining in heat for several weeks on end, they were perhaps even able to copulate during part of their pregnancy, and they came back into heat soon after delivery. Natural selection favored this type of sexy female, who alone was able to provide a more constant measure of satisfaction to suitors, as the only way to survive the long infancy of her "premature" babies, because those suitors, in return for sexual favors, provided food that she could not get for herself. Over the course of countless generations, natural selection produced more and more of these female prodigies, whose availability was further prolonged until a point was reached where it was continuous. As they began to lose their periods of heat altogether, these sexual athletes were the ones who prospered and survived.

The outcome of such physical changes, according to the same theory, was a turning point in the process whereby one species of apes gradually became human, as members of a well-defined social unit. Linked by constant copulation, the theory assumes that pairs of males and females began to divide their labors and to share their daily food, the plants and fruit gathered by the woman and the animals caught by the man. At first the sex contract was a loose arrangement. The bond was not necessarily monogamous. Some males supported more than one female, and (for instance, among the Australian aborigines) one female could pair with several males. Some such bonds may have endured a lifetime, but for many couples pairing only lasted long enough for the mother to care for her young during infancy.

At a later stage, further physical changes cemented the bonds of pairing: Unlike all other primates, the human female came to possess a forward-tilting vaginal canal, designed for frontal intercourse. Face-to-face copulation was a further crucial factor, leading to a new degree of intimacy and communication between partners. To reinforce this intimacy, other anatomical features, absent among the primates, made human females more seductive; they all appear on the front of the body, including fleshy earlobes, everted red lips, and swelling breasts. The human male for his part developed the largest penis of all the primates.

Certain tenets of the "sex contract" are widely accepted, while others remain contentious. But at least it offers a more coherent explanation of the mystery of human origins than others that carry less conviction, since it was discovered that man walked on his two feet two million years before he began to be a regular user of stone tools. In effect, the theory reverses the previous order of priorities; the revolution in female sexuality and its social consequences are seen as the decisive factors in setting man apart from the apes; bipedalism and the casual use of implements serve as mere preliminaries.

The most valid criticism of this and all other explanations is that the quest for logical, as opposed to chance, causes for the emergence of man is in itself problematical. Although Fisher establishes a logical sequence for human development, neither she nor any other specialist does much to clarify the sexual evolution of other primate species or to explain, for instance, just why the gorillas evolved a pattern that was sternly monogamous while the chimpanzees remained happily promiscuous.

Among birds such differences are even more pronounced and defy any logical hypothesis. For instance, as with chickens, a cock pheasant will serve a given number of hens who hatch their eggs and rear their young, a process in which he shows no interest. But partridges behave in the opposite way: They form a monogamous bond, and a hen will not sit on eggs unless supported by her husband, who takes turns in sitting and helps to find food. At the opposite end of the scale, among the crested tinamou of Patagonia, the male incubates the eggs by himself.

The element of chance seems to be inseparable from the evolution of such contrasting habits. Man's adoption of a two-legged stance may be equally fortuitous. Owen Lovejoy, a prominent researcher in the field of hominid origins, also believes that once upright walking developed, subsequent changes were more sexual and social than technical. He describes early man as a socially and sexually innovative ape who became a biped; Lovejoy accepts fully the role of chance in the process and describes as sheer luck the fact that this biped much later made systematic use of tools and developed the much larger human brain. For Lovejoy, the transformation of the otiose male into a family food provider was vital to the whole process; bipedalism is viewed as a starting point not only for food sharing but also for pair bonding so close that it was virtually monogamous—a conclusion that seems much more uncertain.

The Hunter Downgraded

Assuming that some form of sharing labor existed among the early hominids, the question still remains: Was this an arrangement between equals, or were men the dominant partners from the outset? Recent studies give scant support to the notion that at this stage men had attained the mastery over women that men later achieved. The notion of male supremacy had pervaded early thinking on evolution. Then in the 1960s and early 1970s the matter became further confused by the myth of man the killer, the great *macho*, who at the protohuman stage—two million or three million years ago—learned how to hunt big game and even took to killing his own kind to eliminate rivals and lord it over the females of the group, who depended on him for supplies of protein.

It all started with Raymond Dart, a South African anatomist, who wrote in 1954 of "this common bloodlust differentiator, this predacious habit, this mark of Cain, that separates man dietetically from his anthropoid relatives and allies him rather with the deadliest of carnivora." Nobel laureate Konrad Lorenz was the first to popularize Dart's ideas when Lorenz published in 1966 *On Aggression,* whose sales reached blockbuster proportions. This gruesome vision of early man spread like wildfire; it owed much of its popular appeal to the convenient excuses provided for horrors perpetrated in this century by early man's descendants. Finally, Robert Ardrey, a playwright turned amateur anthropologist, perfected this dogma when he dubbed man "The Killer Ape." The dramatist, when he accidentally met Dart, was spellbound by his vision of ancestors whose monstrous propensity to kill set them apart from all other living creatures. He vividly traced the worst instincts of modern man to his reputed forebears, Australopithecus. In his elegant but misleading best seller *African Genesis,* Ardrey outdid Lorenz when Ardrey wrote, "While we are members of the intelligent primate family, we are uniquely human even in the noblest sense, because for untold millions of years we alone killed for a living."

From the very first, anthropologists shook their heads, since serious proof was lacking. Such crude carnivores would have in any case made abysmal hunters and have doomed themselves, rather than game animals, to extinction. On the contrary, protohuman remains bore few signs of violence; admittedly some of the bones associated with Peking man, some five hun-

dred thousand years ago, were charred and broken and suggested that two groups might have come to blows a very long
time ago. Evidence, however, soon came to light that the holes
in an Australopithecus skull, according to Ardrey the most telling proof of man's aggression against his own kind, were not
man-made, since they exactly fitted the standard tooth gap of a
leopard. Furthermore, recent research shows that if Australopithecus used violence, he was far from unique in that respect
among the primates; chimpanzees sometimes kill intruders,
while gorillas can murder their own kind.

In contrast to this killer ape theory, much stress is now laid
on food sharing as a driving force in human evolution. Prehis-
torians are now able to prove that for the early hominids gathering played a critical role, while full-scale hunting, on which the
popularizers had based their case, was unlikely. Hunting thus
was downgraded but not altogether eliminated as a factor in
early human evolution. Initially, before sharing began, mothers
still fed their young single-handed and had to collect and carry
their plant food. Males were basically foragers, eating whatever
was available. This was the practice among the Australopithecus, 90 percent of whose diet was probably plant food and
for whom evidence of hunting skills is entirely lacking; no hunting implements connected with this species have ever been
located. No herds of elephants were at this time driven over
cliffs, and no giant carcasses have been found near these
protohuman bones of, say, two million years ago. Proteins could
be more easily obtained from nuts, ants, and birds' eggs than
from mammoths.

Morgan had insisted a hundred years ago that the first human
societies were matriarchies, but he could not prove his case.
Now, however, his theories gain strong support from the work
of archaeologists who search for protohuman remains, of social
anthropologists who study surviving tribes, and of primatolo-
gists who observe the anthropoid apes. Although they differ in
their pairing habits, females have been found to be the center
of social life, whether among gorillas, baboons, or even chimpanzees. The first human males were not great hunters, and, as
we shall see, primitive surviving groups in today's world are not
always man-dominated. Most authors now conclude that in

foraging groups as a whole, the roles of the two sexes are separate but fairly equal. Hence the long-held theories of man the breadwinner in the first human societies have been exploded. Gradually and grudgingly, as we have seen, the male was induced to obtain food for women and children. But such a step, however basic to human progress, could not make the male supreme at a time when his role in fathering children was still unrecognized.

A situation of this kind survives today among the Kalahari desert's Kung bushmen, one of the few hunting-gathering groups that still exist. Until they recently adopted newer techniques, the men went out in the morning and captured porcupines, rabbits, and birds; however, their efforts provided only 30 percent of the group's annual diet, while the remaining 70 percent came from the women, who also went out on foraging expeditions and returned loaded with an assortment of nuts, fruits, and vegetables. Equally, among the Agta, a primitive Negrito tribe in the Philippines, women not only make an important contribution to the daily food supply but also control its distribution. Apart from gathering, the women make their own bows and arrows and hunt wild pig and even deer. Far from being subordinate, women among the Agta are as vocal and critical as the men when decisions have to be made. Anthropologist Colin Turnbull describes another primitive group, the Mbuti Pygmies of Zaïre, as egalitarian: Women do almost all the things that men do, including hunting and gathering; division of labor involves no kind of sexual subordination. Admittedly, men hit women more often than women hit men, but the huts belong to the women.

Assuming that at the outset of human history the male already helped to feed the children, his share of the work was surely less than among the Agta and Mbuti, and he could lay few claims to dominance in a matriarchal society and in which his contribution to the family larder was strictly limited.

The Road to Subjection

The question then arises: How did it come about that so many of those tribal societies, including a few of the more primitive that survive today, or that have been described by explorers and anthropologists over the past four centuries, should be male-dominated? Admittedly this process was often far from complete, since anthropologists have studied many peoples who were matrilineal, descent being traced through the mother, while the role of father and head of family was occupied by the mother's brother. Nonetheless, male domination came to be a feature of human society as a whole, a trend that war intensified among the world's higher civilizations, such as those of India, China, and Islam.

To assume that his greatly superior physical strength led automatically to domination of male over female is a common fallacy, though it obviously played some part in the process. Sexual dimorphism (the physical differences between the two sexes) is, as we have seen, limited in humans as opposed, say, to baboons, whose males are not only very much bigger but have larger teeth. If hunting later became everywhere a monopoly of the males, this was less due to their strength than to superior mobility, since they took no part in the care of the children, to whom the mother was inseparably bound. Females were physically capable of going on hunting expeditions, but they were anchored by family ties and were in no position to take off for days on end in pursuit of antelopes or bears. Consequently, a natural division of labor was established as the man became a hunter and devised weapons for the purpose, while woman did the gathering and, very much later, tended cultivated crops. The process was gradual from the moment when, over a million years ago, man finally did learn to hunt bigger animals, something Australopithecus and other early hominids had not done. This larger-scale hunting reinforced the division of labor but did not initially lead to male domination in a society in which the woman bore most of the responsibility and still produced much of the food.

A state of relative equality between the sexes still existed, and only for a mere fraction of human history, measured in tens of thousands, not millions, of years, has man been the lord and master over woman. Gradually, however, the dice became loaded in favor of the man; as the population increased, more

food was needed, and intensified hunting called for the development of new tools and weapons not needed for gathering. Man's
superiority was thus based not on brute strength but on technology. French anthropologist Paola Tabet effectively demonstrates that man began to gain the upper hand only when he
took charge of mechanical progress and devised instruments
such as the sling, the bow, and the trap, which applied the
principle of leverage or the use of springs, whose force exceeds
the strength of the human arm and body. Man seized control not
through his own musclepower but because he vastly increased
his physical capacity with the help of such inventions, while the
fairer sex was still limited to manual tasks, aided by the simplest
tools. Women were henceforth left with tasks that might be
termed residual, while men took charge of the production of
new instruments.

This kind of situation is no mere armchair hypothesis but has
been observed in recent times among the Aruntas of central
Australia, who are among the most primitive people to survive
into the present age. A report by Baldwin Spencer and F. J.
Gillen, written in 1927, states: "Early in the morning the occupants of the camp are astir. . . . If food be required, then the
women will go out, accompanied by the children, and armed
with digging sticks and *pitchis* (a kind of wooden trough used to
carry things) and the day will be spent in the bush in search of
small burrowing animals, such as lizards and marsupials. The
men will perhaps set off armed with spears, spear throwers,
boomerangs and shields in search of larger game, such as emus
and kangaroos." In a coastal aboriginal tribe, the Murngin, the
men were in complete charge of technical developments, which
included making and operating canoes, and the construction of
harpoons to catch turtles. In Australia, as we shall later see,
aboriginal man was partly but not wholly the woman's master.
In tribal societies throughout the world, fishing as well as hunting techniques had become a male preserve, though at times the
women would merely pull fish out of the water with their hands
but without any kind of tackle.

As technology improved, not only did men monopolize the
making of weapons, they also invented types that women were

physically incapable of using. For instance, among the Hazda of Tanzania hunting is today an all-male activity, and the men use large and powerful bows that cannot be drawn by women; smaller bows, which are equally efficient, could be used by women, but they are not allowed to do so. In other respects, however, relations between the sexes have more in common with those postulated by certain specialists for early man; Hazda marriage basically consists of the woman according sexual favors to a man in exchange for meat. She does not even have a formal obligation to cook for her husband. For the Hazda, the arrangement assumes a collective role; the women need protection for themselves and their children from wild animals and hostile neighbors, but it is afforded by the men of the camp as a whole rather than on an individual basis by husband to wife.

After the invention of agriculture some ten thousand years ago, the need for technology carried male dominance a stage further: The women performed the simpler and more laborious tasks in the fields, while plowing was done by the men. (The plow itself was an ingenious invention of the Old World, never made in the New World.) Equally, when pottery was first used, the women would make the pots, but with the invention of the potter's wheel (also unknown in the Americas), men took charge of its manufacture. At an even later stage in human development, stone carving and metalworking were everywhere a male monopoly.

The use of arms, not only against animals but also for warfare among human groups, set the seal on the supremacy of the adult male, on whom the tribe's safety now depended. To quote Paola Tabet: "The exclusive working of hard materials by men . . . demonstrates the solid rock on which male domination is based; the ban on arms production by women and their dependence on males for almost all the instruments of production. The control by men of the production and use of tools and arms becomes the necessary precondition of their supremacy over women, based on violence (due to a monopoly of arms) and the under-equipment of women (male monopoly of tools). Without such conditions man would have found it hard to attain such a total appropriation of women and such a degree of exploitation in work, in sexuality and the reproduction of the species."

The Decisive Steps

Specialists may still argue as to the decisive steps in man's development: whether tool use led to upright walking or vice versa. Present evidence favors upright walking as coming first, but it is by no means conclusive, and further startling finds surely will be made by archaeologists. The third major development that distinguishes man from the beasts is now increasingly stressed: a radically altered relationship between the sexes, as the human female was freed from the estrous cycle and became constantly available for intercourse.

Helen Fisher offers one logical explanation of how it all happened: The use of rough-and-ready implements favored upright walking; the modified pelvis in turn produced "premature" babies and forced the female to recruit male help to feed them. Thus the division of labor arose, even if man's initial contribution was modest—the provision of meat for extended sexual favors on the part of females who came to shed their heat period.

So far, so good. But the precise nature of any new relationship between the sexes is hard to determine. Lovejoy sees male provisioning of women and children as the real breakthrough in human development, but to treat Australopithecus as in effect monogamous and to write of "pair bonding" at such an early stage may be stretching a point by making too much of what were probably casual and short-term relationships. The term "pairing" in this context surely should imply more a temporary or *ad hoc* relationship rather than a primitive form of "marriage."

In contrast, Nancy Tanner believes (though she cannot prove) that the promiscuous chimpanzee is a truer model for early man's behavior than the monogamous gorilla. Certainly no student of history could deny that throughout the ages, irrespective of race or creed, humans have tended to have a roving eye, regardless of rules. Moreover, among many tribes that survived into modern times, couples were not wholly deprived of alternative outlets. The infinite variety of marriage regulations and taboos devised by different groups represents their attempts, however vain, to keep any penchant for promiscuity under control; if it did not exist, such rules would not be needed.

Nonetheless, man does seem to display a stronger tendency than most other primates to form both sexual and social partnerships, though their nature may vary from place to place. However, even a limited form of interdependence, leading to a division of labor but not initially to male domination, was important. Such partnerships that, unlike the gibbon ménage, involved food sharing and perhaps even a degree of affection between partners who embraced in frontal coitus, had far-reaching implications and mark the birth of sexuality as opposed to mere sex or indiscriminate copulation. Sexuality becomes a driving force in human relations, leading to the establishment of the family unit as the basis of society; as a pervasive urge, the source of so much good and evil, it underlies the human condition and permeates human culture.

CHAPTER TWO

The Nubile Savage

Explorers and Anthropologists

On the mating habits of early man, theories may multiply but doubts persist. They are neither resolved by studying his anatomy, nor removed by observing his cousins, the anthropoid apes. Primitive surviving groups offer only tenuous clues, as we have seen; even those who grew no crops and made no pots when first discovered were subject to complex tribal lore, hard to relate to the first humans.

But the study of existing tribes, whether backward or advanced, has a much more direct bearing on the habits of the earliest members of our own species, *Homo sapiens,* about a hundred thousand years ago. Such studies inevitably focus on the first observers' reports of these tribes and chiefdoms. Some, such as those of West Africa and parts of America, became known to Europeans in the fourteenth and fifteenth centuries, while others, including the Australian aborigines and the peoples of central Africa, were left to their own devices until the nineteenth century.

It would be useless to infer that nomad groups encountered, say, in Australia offer a carbon copy of how our remoter ancestors existed fifty thousand years before the present, or to suppose that farming peoples in Africa provide a blueprint for the society of the first farmers ten thousand years ago. Nonetheless, they may serve as a useful pointer to the sex life of early *Homo sapiens,* about which archaeological data solve few riddles. Large numbers of fertility symbols, the "Venus" figurines dating from between 30,000 and 20,000 B.C., have been dug up all over Europe, and specimens from many places are remarkably alike, with bulbous bodies and small arms folded over low breasts, which drop like sacks to far below the waist. But while they may demonstrate the obvious fact that the people who made them were interested in sex, attempts to relate them more closely to their social customs lead nowhere.

Studies of tribes observed by modern man offer more meaningful clues. Some of the materially most backward known to science, such as those of New Guinea, came from Asia, though there is no sure way of learning whether their complex social and sexual patterns had evolved before they moved south, or whether they were formed after they reached their final destination. The aborigines have a few customs unknown elsewhere, but these also might have Asian origins, even if they were later abandoned on that continent. More striking, perhaps, is the near-identity between many sexual practices and taboos of the Old World and the New, which suggests that their origins are very ancient and may precede the peopling of America. The Bering land bridge that joined Asia to America finally sank beneath the waves about twelve thousand years ago, but most of the migrants from Asia into the New World had arrived well before this, starting as early as 40,000 to 50,000 B.C., not long before the time when the first groups were also heading for Australia.

While reports of tribal sex life may therefore be relevant to those of our own species from its very origins, they are seldom very complete or accurate. At least some record survives of the mores of nearly two hundred human groups in every corner of the globe, some spread over vast deserts and jungles, others confined to tiny islands. But only in a few cases does this record tell in any detail of sexual customs, and often simple but fundamental questions remain unanswered.

In the first place, matters are complicated by the close ties between primitive religion and sex, both intrinsic to the cult of fertility (of which the Venus figurines offer early evidence). Sexual practices are intertwined with myths, magic, and dreams, of small concern to early explorers and anathema to missionaries, who described these peoples before their way of life had been eroded by Western influences. The anthropologists later sought to piece together vestiges of this sex-linked mythology, profound also in its implications for psychiatric theory. Their findings, the product of this fieldwork, have been open to two interpretations, one favored by psychiatrists and the other by anthropologists.

The fragmentary record of tribal sex life thus derives from a series of visitors: from conquerors and explorers, such as the Spaniards in the New World or Captain James Cook and other voyagers in Oceania; from missionaries, together with a few colonial administrators; and last, from trained anthropologists.

The earliest European visitors, such as the South Seas explorers, were less concerned with fact-finding than with fornication, enchanted to find themselves besieged by a bevy of eager sleeping partners. This euphoric welcome gave them no insight into local religion, and their understanding of the social hierarchy was meager. For instance, in Polynesia they jumped to the inevitable conclusion that *all* women were clamoring for their favors, blithely unaware that a chief would not dream of offering his daughter to a common sailor except in some dire emergency, such as the exhaustion of his supplies of rum after he had developed an unquenchable thirst for European liquor. Explorers, moreover, mainly describe those people, such as Polynesians, whom they themselves found attractive, and ignored the (by European standards) uglier Australian aborigines.

The copious nineteenth-century accounts of native customs from all over the world were mostly the work of missionaries. Hence two early viewpoints survive, diametrically opposed; one comes from people who made the most of native permissiveness, and the other from those who were out to suppress it. For the explorers, the islanders of the Pacific were the denizens of an earthly paradise. But for the unrelenting missionaries this so-called paradise was more akin to hell, and such happy-go-lucky devotees of free love were nothing but deceitful and disgusting debauchees. These men of God abhorred the native religions as works of the devil and abominated the local sex cults of which they were an intrinsic part. At times they were themselves reduced to a psychopathic state when, using the only means known to appease such all-powerful white shamans, people would press them to sleep with their own wives and daughters.

Finally, the anthropologists arrived in force, but not before customs had already been modified by decades, if not centuries, of European penetration, in the course of which native sex life had first been corrupted by adventurers (prostitution in the strict sense of the word was unknown in pre-European times) and then constricted by missionaries. Many of the best accounts by anthropologists date from the early twentieth century, and opportunities for close study today grow daily fewer as Western influences obliterate the last traces of former sexual patterns. If tacit resistance to the bleak tenets of the missionaries was widespread, the garish trappings of the consumer society are more alluring and act as potent instruments of change.

Great gaps exist in the reports of the earlier anthropologists, whose spiritual background was late Victorian and who usually were too bashful to ask the most obvious questions. Some were hardly more liberal-minded than the missionaries themselves, and their reports on sexual customs are laced with such adjectives as "depraved," "disgusting," and "unthinkable." Accordingly, if they mention sex at all, they seldom do so with complete objectivity.

To this limitation, exceptions fortunately exist, such as Bronislaw Malinowski's study in 1917–18 of the sex life of the Trobriand Islands. And even Malinowski is not immune from the tendency to use such derogatory terms as "lower races" and even "depraved habits."

Other anthropologists of his time were more reticent; they feared the reactions not only of the general public but also of their own colleagues, who were apt to regard as lechers any whose writings savored too much of sex. As late as the 1930s, descriptions of coital positions and techniques were considered unfit to print in a modern language; instead, Latin was used to convey not only the more salacious passages of the Chinese erotic novels translated at that time, but even quite down-to-earth details of sexual practices in Africa, included in reports by anthropologists.

But if these trained observers were coy about describing the *ars amatoria* in their own tongue, they could at least have left a record of more innocuous details, such as the physical traits in women that most attracted the men of a given tribe (preferences differ from one people to another to an astonishing degree). In most cases even such basic facts are lacking in their accounts. For instance, in A. L. Kroeber's great compendium *Anthropology Today,* published in 1953, sex scarcely raises its ugly head; the words "sex" and "sexual" do not even figure in the long index. Certain German scholars, however, were less inhibited and wrote comparative studies of peoples all over the world, not only about their general customs but also devoted specifically to sex. Among these may be cited H. Fehlinger's *The Sexual Life of Primitive Peoples,* written in 1921 and therefore contemporary with Malinowski's study, together with a work with a very similar title, *The Love Life of Nature Peoples,* written a generation later (in 1961) by Adolf Tullmann. Incomparable also as a source of general information is the classic compendium by Clennan S. Ford and Frank A. Beach, *Patterns of Sexual Behavior,* published in 1952, which contains a rich and revealing fund of statistics on 185 tribal societies.

Universal Customs

The following three chapters will treat the customs of a few tribal peoples for whom, unlike most others, studies are more informative: the Australian aborigines; certain American Indian tribes, such as those of California; and Malinowski's Trobrianders, together with certain other islanders of Oceania.

Within the context of tribal life, these peoples stood at different cultural levels. Nonetheless, whether settled or nomad, they shared many common traits usually modified or even discarded by higher civilizations. As a general rule, the domination of man over woman is far from absolute, though in the more advanced tribal societies, or chiefdoms, such as the Polynesians, a greater degree of male supremacy is already present. In these the well-to-do were polygamous, and women's status was inferior, since their sexual license was curtailed by rules that did not apply to husbands.

These groups also shed light on certain specific ingredients of human sexuality that constantly reappear in almost every society ranging from the most primitive to the most advanced. Of these the first, circumcision or genital mutilation in some form or other, will be considered in connection with the Australian aborigines, where the practice took peculiar forms. The second, the incest taboo, was carried to extraordinary lengths among the peoples of Oceania, who form the subject of Chapter 3. A third intrinsic trait, a strongly bisexual element in human erotics, is well illustrated by the customs of certain American Indian tribes.

Sexologists and psychiatrists ever since Freud have been obsessed with these primordial factors, particularly castration anxiety, with which they associate circumcision, and the incest taboo, ascribed to the Oedipus complex but plainly arising aeons before the age of King Oedipus. Clinical studies of their patients reinforce the link between tribal mores and those of our own society; for psychiatry, unlike anthropology, is less concerned with tribal rituals and taboos for their own sake than as means of understanding those of modern groups and individuals.

Among the most riveting traits of tribal life—not irrelevant to our own times—is the active encouragement of premarital sexual relations between the ages of puberty and marriage, almost amounting at times to a form of compulsion. Paradoxically, this mandatory premarital intercourse usually was accompanied by a deep disapproval of childbirth out of wedlock; if allowed to live, such offspring grew up as social outcasts. No one has yet given a plausible explanation of the apparent fact that such unflagging teenage copulation produced relatively few of these unwanted offspring. In contrast to premarital sex on a prodigious scale, much stricter rules invariably applied to both men and women once they married. Such rules, designed as safeguards to the married state and to the family unit, usually left certain alternative sexual outlets open to both men and women, as concessions to human frailty, though these fell far short of the state of free love enjoyed by teenagers. Wife-lending was a widespread custom; another such outlet often involved orgiastic rites on special feast days, a sexual safety valve that was retained in a number of higher civilizations. But concessions of this kind were temporary and based on mutual consent between spouses; if wife-lending was tolerated, wife-stealing was not.

In 61 percent of the peoples studied by Ford and Beach, marriage did not exclude certain forms of controlled promiscuity. The rules were somewhat loaded in the man's favor, since in 155 of the 185 societies for which evidence is available men were permitted by custom to have more than one mate, if they could afford the luxury. In most of these 155 societies, married men were also at liberty to seek temporary partners, but these were often hard to find. If they seduced other men's wives, they were liable to be punished; though technically free to seek intercourse with unmarried girls, in many instances husbands on the loose had to compete for their favors with young and eager bachelors. In some of these societies, wives also enjoyed a certain license, if only as instructors in coitus to young boys.

Intercourse with a member of one's own sex was another fairly common option both for adolescent and adult. Of the 185 societies studied by Ford and Beach, only in seventy-six cases were data available on homosexual activities; in other instances their absence was perhaps due less to native reticence than to the Victorian inhibitions of those who made the studies and for whom such questions simply were unaskable. In twenty-eight of these seventy-six societies, homosexual acts on the part of adults of either sex are reported to be wholly absent, rare, or, as Ford and Beach suggest, they were more probably carried out in secret.

As examples of absence or disapproval among these twenty-eight tribes they cite the Kwoma of New Guinea, who treat sodomy as revolting, while among the Chiricahua of the southwestern United States, children were whipped if they indulged in any form of homosexual play (most neighbors of the Chiricahua, as we shall see, took a very different view of such matters).

In the remaining forty-eight (64 percent) of the seventy-six societies in question, homosexual activities are socially acceptable, at least for certain people. In its most common form, institutionalized homosexuality was centered upon the transvestite, a male who dresses like a woman, performs women's tasks, and adopts the passive role in sexual behavior with male partners; less frequently, a woman dresses like a man and seeks to adopt the male sex role.

Male homosexual behavior in tribal societies most frequently involves anal intercourse. Although for most it was an optional outlet, in others it was compulsory; among the Siwans of North Africa, for example, all men and boys indulged in this practice. Siwans are not transvestites and adopt the feminine role only in a strictly sexual context; males who do not take part in these activities are treated as peculiar. Prominent Siwan men even lend their sons to each other and talk about masculine love affairs as openly as they discuss liaisons with women. Married men as well as adolescents would have affairs with both men and women.

In contrast to permissive attitudes toward homosexuality, the ban on incest was almost always absolute. Rules made to ward off this evil were inflexible; in many cases prohibitions against incest with near relations were stretched to include a ban on marrying anyone who belonged to one's own group or clan. This rule of exogamy was widespread in tribal society.

Marriage à la Mode

If judged by their meager technology, the Australian aborigines must rank among the most primitive peoples ever studied by European scientists and explorers. They descend from a band of migrants from Southeast Asia over thirty-thousand years ago and reached Australia, where they lived for endless millennia cut off from the rest of humanity. In those days they could have made the journey by land, except for the Torres Strait, which already divided the Asian landmass from that of Australasia and which they contrived to cross. When first visited by Captain

Cook, they were still living in their own Stone Age; they made no pottery and grew no crops. Unlike most peoples, they had no hereditary leaders. In contrast, however, these tribes, whose material progress was negligible, had evolved a social structure so intricate that even trained anthropologists were baffled by its complexities. The rites that marked the initiation of the young in each tribe or clan, and their passage from adolescence to the adult state, were among the most elaborate in the world and included bizarre forms of genital mutilation unknown elsewhere. These were still practiced at the turn of the century, and the best reports date from that period. Fortunately, since they had no sex appeal for traders, lived in remote regions, and were not an early target for reforming missionaries, their institutions survived until then.

The Australians practiced unusual forms of polygamy that have often been described in terms of group marriage, supposedly favored by those earliest bands of humans; certainly aboriginal customs offer no support to those who insist that early man was monogamous. Marital relations were complicated by the fact that in many regions two forms of sexual union existed side by side. A young girl would be given in marriage to one man, often much older than she, and without regard for personal sympathies; such unions served practical ends, since the wife took care of the home and was as much a housekeeper as a sexual partner. But in addition to this house-sharing arrangement, a man might make a formal bond with one or more other married females, purely for the purpose of sexual intercourse, which usually took place when the woman's own regular husband was absent.

This second form of pairing is often termed *pirauru*, after the name used by the Dieri tribe, where it was first studied in the 1860s. Unlike the first form (known as *tippa maru* among the Dieri), pirauru normally did not last a lifetime, and pirauru relationships could be switched at intervals. From time to time special ceremonies were held at which a kind of general post took place, involving a reallotment of pirauru wives to new partners.

This dual form of coupling was far from simple. The leading

men of a tribe usually had a whole string of pirauru wives and also several regular, or tippa maru, spouses. Hence, in addition to their own regular wives, they had the right to sleep on a pirauru basis with those of a number of different men; by the same token, their sexual rights over their own regular wives were shared by others. A man with several pirauru wives might also lend them to unmarried males in exchange for presents.

Australia differed from more advanced tribal societies in that women were not merely an item of male property. They were themselves entitled to take the initiative over pirauru relationships, and a woman could even ask her tippa maru husband to give her as a pirauru wife to some important individual. She had no right to insist if he refused, though he would normally agree; on the other hand, the man could force his wife to become another man's pirauru.

Such peculiar arrangements are hard to define. Some anthropologists have insisted that, since no man had the exclusive right to one or more women, the word "marriage" in its usual sense did not apply. The system differs from recognizable forms of polygamous union, since if a man had several wives, the women also had several husbands. Equally, it cannot properly be described as group marriage, which implies a free-for-all between male and female, whereas in the typical Australian tribe the question of who slept with whom was subject to formal, if flexible, rules. The nearest approach to group marriage occurred in those cases where two men shared the same quarters and each had as pirauru wife the tippa maru wife of the other; this sometimes occurred between two brothers.

Since a woman might have the right to sleep with two or more different men, who were sometimes brothers, the system has alternatively been described as a kind of polyandry, a relationship in which one woman has several husbands. A well-documented example of this form of marriage, which has survived into the twentieth century, is the Toda tribe from the Nilgiri hills in southern India. Among the Todas, whenever a woman marries a man, it is understood that she also becomes the wife of his brothers at the same time; even a brother born to the bridegroom after he had married the girl grew up to inherit the right to join her coterie of husbands. The brothers and their single wife would live together, and when a child was born they were all equally regarded as its fathers. In rare cases, where a woman was married to two or more men who were not brothers, one of the husbands claimed the right to perform the baptismal ceremony of giving the bow and arrow to her sons, and he then became their father for all social purposes. Fraternal polyandry also existed in Kashmir and among certain peoples of the Punjab mountains.

The Australian system may be seen less a group marriage than as a kind of halfway house between polygamy, whereby one man may have several wives, and its opposite, polyandry. Sometimes, among the Todas, two brothers living together would take not one wife but two, whom they shared in common, creating a situation not unlike that of two or more Australian couples who lived together and shared wives. But if they did not exactly amount to group marriage, the customs of the primitive tribes of Australia serve as a pointer to the notion, though they cannot be cited as proof, that much earlier generations of mankind were promiscuous rather than monogamous.

Sex for Nine-Year-Olds

As occurred in more advanced tribal societies than their own, Australian aboriginal adolescents led a hyperactive sex life before they were married. For boys the period of premarital experience was uncommonly long; they usually had their first intercourse between the ages of twelve and fourteen, after their initiation ceremony, while the age for marriage varied from seventeen to twenty-two years.

Even before initiation, some boys would pair off with girls of nine or ten years. However, after these early experiments, both sexes would turn to older partners to gain wider experience and improved techniques. A youth won prestige by copulating with mature women weary of their official mates and eager for the embraces of lusty juveniles. Girls were allowed a shorter period of premarital license than boys. After their first experiences, sometimes as nine-year-olds, when barely in their teens they would be sent for a trial period to a future husband; as soon as they qualified for the role, they would become his pirauru wife.

In Australia as elsewhere, information is scanty as to how often premarital sex produced offspring. Among the aborigines an alleviating factor was the tendency for a young man, during the long years between initiation and marriage, to copulate mainly with older women, since any progeny could be credited to their husbands. The sexual act was not directly associated with childbirth; if a feeling existed that the male partner had something to do with conception, such notions remained vague among peoples who had no understanding of the physical processes involved.

Most anthropologists assert that the Australians ignored entirely that intercourse produced children. It has even been proposed that though at one time they had been aware of the relationship, this awareness gradually became obfuscated or lost. According to a more plausible theory, the aborigines believed that while the people who had coitus normally produced children, childbirth was not tied to a single specific sexual act. Baldwin Spencer and F. J. Gillen, who wrote copiously at the end of the nineteenth century on the Arunta and other tribes of central Australia, held that intercourse was thought to prepare the mother for the reception and birth of an already formed spirit child. As British anthropologist M. F. Ashley Montagu puts it: "I have pointed out *ad nauseam* that the aborigines are aware of the fact that intercourse is a necessary factor in the production of childbirth, but that they do not consider it to be of any great importance in the production of such a condition. Intercourse is not a cause of childbirth; it is merely a preparative act for the reception of a spirit baby."

Nonetheless, the question is unresolved, and Ashley Montagu points out that even today no one knows exactly what those Australian tribes, allegedly ignorant of facts of procreation, do and do not know about this.

Alternative Outlets

Given the propensity of tribal leaders not only to take several wives but to wed girls much younger than themselves, men of

marriageable age were often at a loss to obtain a suitable partner. Institutionalized homosexuality, widespread in Australia,
served to ease their predicament.

Among the Arunta of central Australia, pederasty was a recognized custom, and a young man who was not yet married would
take a boy of ten or twelve years old to live with him as a "wife"
for several years until he found a female bride. Such boys were
not yet circumcized and initiated; they did not become transvestites. Social proprieties were observed, and a man's prestige
would suffer if he formed a liaison with a boy whose social
standing was lower than his own.

Inhabitants of nearby New Guinea went even farther than the
Australians; among the Keraki of southwestern New Guinea,
sodomy was universal. In contrast to Australia, the passive partners had already attained puberty and undergone initiation;
inseparable from such rites was tuition in the practice of anal
intercourse with older males. After a year or two as the passive
partner, roles would be reversed and until they married they in
turn would sodomize the newly initiated. Such practices supposedly were kept secret from the women. Far from incurring
censure, they were held to be not only desirable but even essential for the health and development of a growing boy. Unlike the
Australians, Papuans sensed the connection between the sex act
and childbirth; consequently they were haunted by fears that
their catamites might become pregnant. Public ceremonies were
held at which the boys were fed with limes, whose contraceptive
powers in such cases were demonstrably efficient.

According to Margaret Mead, in another New Guinea tribe,
the Marind-Anim, unmarried males found homosexual intercourse more enjoyable than any other form; to settle for heterosexual relations and for marriage was regarded as a sacrifice. To
mark this act of renunciation by a group of males, a rite was held
at which they formally renounced their former habits.

In parts of Australia and New Guinea, as well as among certain
tribes in Africa where transvestism was also absent, institutionalized homosexuality did not mainly cater to hardened pederasts.
On the contrary, it was a stage through which all passed, thus
providing an accepted outlet for young men who had few others,
because the boys married later than the girls. In certain higher

civilizations, as we shall see, a similar situation arose in cases where the important men took the lion's share of the women.

Bizarre Mutilations

While institutionalized homosexuality is a very common tribal trait, a more unique aspect of Australian sex life is to be found in their bizarre forms of male genital mutilation. These formed part of the complex initiation rites to which boys were subjected on reaching puberty. The first and least painful mutilation was a standard form of circumcision. This practise, treated as a solemn rite among so many primitive and advanced peoples, is both ancient and widespread and clearly springs from needs more profound than a mere quest for hygiene, though admittedly the custom of circumcising newborn babes survives today among peoples for whom it has lost all religious significance and serves purely as an aid to cleanliness. Nowadays, except where it remains a religious rite, circumcision becomes necessary, as opposed to merely cosmetic, only in cases of phimosis, a condition in which the foreskin cannot be retracted to uncover the glans, a complaint that impedes both urination and intercourse.

In Australia, between the ages of twelve and fourteen boys underwent the more ordinary form of circumcision, an act involving, as in other regions, a most complex ceremonial. First a boy was told of all the secret rites, the knowledge of which was forbidden to women and children; his instructors were the older men of the village, often his own father and uncles. Next he would be painted with red and yellow ocher, and on the appointed day was taken to the place where he would be circumcized. Here three of his male relatives would lie close together on the ground to form a kind of table, on which the initiate was then laid. A leather pad was stuffed into his mouth, since cries of pain were totally taboo. Another relative held him down by sitting on his belly, and the operation was then performed by his maternal grandfather with a stone knife. After the grandfather had made the first cut, he handed the knife to the boy's eldest uncle, who completed the removal of the foreskin. This was then seized by the victim's eldest brother, who ran around in a circle, touching with it the bellies of the boy's adult sisters. The disposal of the foreskin varied from tribe to tribe: In some cases it was eaten by a younger brother, to give him strength and make him grow; among the western Aruntas, the foreskin was given to one of the boy's sisters, who dried it, smeared it with red ocher, and wore it around her neck. The Anula tribe buries the foreskin beside a pool to make the water lilies grow.

Circumcision was followed by the incision, or subincision, of the penis, an excruciating performance peculiar to that of the Australian aborigines and called ariltha in several of their languages. Ariltha took place five to six weeks after circumcision, when the first wound was fully healed. It was considered just as indispensable as the first rite, from which it differed in that women were forbidden to attend the ceremony.

The procedure for the two operations was similar; once more a few of the boy's relatives lay on the earth to form a human operating table, while another sat upon his belly. On this occasion, however, the initiate suffered agonies; the operation consisted in slitting open all or part of the penile urethra along the under surface of the penis. The initial cut was about one inch long, but this often was later enlarged, until the incision extended all the way from the glans to the scrotum, thus laying open the whole of the under part of the urethra. Such additional cuts were made when, after the novice had undergone his subincision, one or more of the young men present, already subincised, would volunteer for a second operation, whereby the whole length of the penis thus was laid open.

The healing of the wound was slow and painful. During convalescence the youth would be allotted three women, known as "mothers," to attend him. He was supposed to lie only on his back, since otherwise his organ would grow crooked. Until completely healed, he was forbidden to eat the flesh of opossum, snakes, and all lizards, since this was supposed to retard his recovery. In some cases the wound became badly infected and the patient died.

Once they had been subincised, young men could marry; they were also allowed to go naked, whereas their sexual organs previously had to be covered. The nature of the cut made it necessary for men to urinate in a squatting position like women, holding up the penis and allowing the fluid to flow from the under part. When they had an erection, their member would become wide and flat; nonetheless, the effect on coitus and on fertility seems to have been small. Sometimes it has been alleged that procreation was effected because the sperm were apt to leak out instead of entering the vagina, but in fact most subincized males were able to father children.

Female circumcision, still practiced in many parts of Africa, can have more damaging side effects. One form only was present in Australia, known as introcision, involving the cutting open of the vagina; it was practiced among those tribes that also performed ariltha. A girl, on reaching puberty, would have her vagina enlarged by a male relative who tore the vaginal orifice downward, using three fingers bound together with opossum gut; among other tribes an old man would slit the vagina with a stone knife, after which he would sweep three fingers around inside the orifice. When the operation had been performed, the victim was immediately forced to have intercourse with a series of young men; the bloody semen was collected and drunk by the sick and aged to give them strength.

Introcision is mainly confined to Australia; however, other operations, for which "female circumcision" is an inaccurate term, still are common in Africa. The most drastic version, known as infibulation, is today practiced in seven African states, most particularly Sudan. Infibulation involves the removal of the entire clitoris, the labia minora, and part of the labia majora, sometimes by burning but more often with the help of a rusty razor; the two sides of the vulva are then partially sliced off or scraped raw and sewn together again, mostly with catgut; in Sudan and Somalia, acacia thorns usually are employed to hold the two bleeding sides of the vagina together. The entrance to the vagina is thus closed, except for a tiny hole left to allow urine and menstrual blood to drain through a tube.

Infibulation makes sexual intercourse impossible until the woman's vagina has been cut open again to allow penetration, and it thus offers to the man a sure guarantee that his bride is inviolate. The custom is also known as "pharaonic circumcision" because it has always been practiced in Upper Egypt and was known to the ancient Egyptians. In Latin *fibula* means "clasp" or "pin," and the term derives from the Roman practice of fastening a "fibule" through the labia majora of slave women to prevent childbearing, which would hamper their work.

The various forms of female circumcision are not only agonizingly painful, they also bristle with health hazards and offer no compensating advantage. Of these, a cruel if less drastic operation, called excision or clitoridectomy, is the most common. Nowadays in some countries (for instance in Somalia and Mali), excisions are carried out in hospitals. However, under less favorable circumstances—as when a father simply seizes his daughter and cuts out her clitoris in the bathroom—uncontrolled bleeding and shock still can bring about immediate death. Urinary problems due to chronic infection also may lead to infertility; sometimes they even cause incontinence, and a woman may become an outcast of society because she constantly dribbles urine and feces.

According to *The Hosken report,* published in 1979, excision was still practiced in twenty-three of the forty states of Africa listed in the text. It involves the removal of the entire clitoris, usually together with the adjacent parts of the labia minora. In some cases the operation follows the Australian pattern by also making cuts to enlarge the opening of the vagina. Most Africans who favor the operation believe that excision was decreed by their ancestors, and many myths support such beliefs. Since it brings no conceivable health benefits, its origins are clearly ritual, though particularly in Islamic countries it may also serve a more practical purpose, as an aid to the process of male sexual supremacy. Although in many places the procedure is nowadays more clinical than magic, it was originally an important element in female initiation rites. For instance, among the Nandi of Uganda, elaborate ceremony still accompanies the burning away of the clitoris with a firebrand; this is regarded as the most sacred moment of a girl's life, and if she cries out, her father or a near male relative must kill her with a spear. To heal the wound, the girl had to go into retreat for four months, which she would spend not with her mother but with an aunt.

A Deep-Seated Imperative

Female circumcision, so painful, so harmful, and even danger-ous, raises an obvious question: Why did sexual mutilation be-come so widespread in human societies? Intrinsic to initiation ceremonies, it served few practical ends. Sir James Frazer, who in *The Golden Bough* provided a catalog of rituals and myths, concluded that these initiation rites were "the central mystery of human society," essential to the cohesion of the tribe. For Frazer, genital mutilation is a basic ingredient in such rites, linked to those first rudiments of religion conjured up by the human mind when it began to range beyond thoughts of mere earthly survival.

Circumcision and genital mutilation obviously spread by a process of diffusion from one people to another. Found among the most primitive and most civilized people of all continents, their practice seems to obey some deep-seated imperative basic to the problems of human sexuality. The best analysis of the problem has been made in *Symbolic Wounds* by Bruno Bettel-heim. As Bettelheim (a psychiatrist) stresses, anthropologists generally view male circumcision, and female circumcision where it exists, as a clearcut step to separate the initiate from his or her old group and, after a period of isolation, introduce the person into a new adult life. This step cuts off a youth from his past, after which he is reborn, or resurrected, to an entirely fresh existence as a fully fledged member of society. In some places the initiate was forced to imitate the actions of a newborn babe as part of the process of rebirth. For instance, among the Pap-uans of New Guinea, a youth would first behave as a worn-out old man, growing progressively weaker, until he finally col-lapsed and lay down at the bottom of a canoe. He was then lifted up and immersed in the sea. After this act he was "reborn" and played out the reverse roles, first of a baby and then of a growing child who did not yet know how to handle the paddle.

Psychoanalytic interpretations of circumcision, questioned by many anthropologists (though based upon their fieldwork), explain matters differently. Inevitably such views still tend to fall beneath the long shadow cast by Freud's Oedipus complex, whereby the boy's first genital affections attach to the mother who takes care of him and his first sexual rivalry is directed against the father, whom he sees as her owner.

Taking as their point of departure castration anxiety (already stressed by Freud) and the Oedipal conflict, psychiatrists tend to view circumcision as an act of simulated castration; it reinforces the incest taboo because it symbolizes the father's revenge on his covetous sons and serves as a token of their submission to his will. Circumcision is seen as a symbolic substitute stemming from a true act of castration actually performed by an avenging father on his hostile son, a prey to the Oedipus complex.

On the basis of more recent field research, anthropologists today tend to question any close association between circumcision and castration, though they agree that castration anxiety itself is no mere figment of the psychiatric imagination; in countless recorded cases patients have suffered from a ravaging complex of this kind, inspired by an overpowering father figure. Moreover, savage ceremonies involving not symbolic but real castration were widespread among the higher civilizations of the ancient Near East; even the Greeks performed brutal acts of self-mutilation in honor of the mother goddess Cybele.

Although they may differ as to its links with castration, anthropologists and psychiatrists do concur in another respect: Both view circumcision as a step that enhances biological differences between man and woman. To stress the contrast, the male loses his foreskin, the part of his sexual anatomy that most recalls the vagina; most forms of female circumcision eliminate the clitoris, which also recalls the penile glans.

Freud himself was among the first to insist that males and females were born with bisexual tendencies, and he wrote of "the great enigma of the fact of the duality of the sexes." He further observed that not until puberty (the age at which initiation rites were performed) did many biological differences between male and female become sharply defined. (Even with modern techniques, physical anthropologists find it hard to tell the difference between skeletons of males and females who died before puberty.) Initiation rites for Freud, and for most anthropologists today, thus ended the span of life in which such distinctions were less clearly marked; genital mutilation further enhanced them.

The rites of circumcision thus serve in the more orthodox sense as an act to set apart the male from the female. Boys, if not inhibited, often like to show off their penis as a display of what may be called "phallic pride," and the phallus, in India and elsewhere, was to become a religious symbol of deep significance. The ability to exhibit the glans freed of its foreskin furthers such efforts to assert manliness, and in this respect the circumcised boy is at an advantage. His glans always shows and is taken as a sign of masculinity. In initiation rites, as part of the process of rebirth, a new penis is born that looks more like a phallus in erection, and its owner becomes more sharply differentiated from the opposite sex.

Such explanations of the rites of circumcision, while basically correct, ignore one factor: In both sexes the desire to be set apart from the other is not unqualified and is beset by deep-rooted inhibitions. Psychologists insist on the great number of cases of penis envy in female patients; conversely, a certain number of boys suffer from vagina envy, though this has received less attention in psychiatric literature. Bettelheim writes of the many cases of mentally disturbed boys who insist that they have a vagina, refusing to accept the fact that girls have two lower-body openings. In addition, the bleeding caused by male circumcision in a sense recalls female menstruation; in many cases the blood that flowed from the penis was treated with the same veneration as that produced by the deflowering of virgins.

Bettelheim tries tentatively to account for this apparent paradox in circumcision: the ostensible aim of sharpening the distinction between the sexes, and the more subtle but contradictory desire in certain victims, not necessarily homosexuals, that their organs should be made more, rather than less, like those of the other sex.

The underlying purpose of circumcision is thus seen as serving two related ends: first as a strong reassertion of sexual identity and second as a drastic extirpation of any latent envy of the organs of the other sex. The emblems most apt to inspire such envy, the foreskin and in the girl's case, the clitoris, simply are excised. If the effort succeeds, blurred distinctions between the two sexes, present in their organs, are eradicated, and they are able to live together in greater harmony as more sharply defined entities. Circumcision seen in this light is the opposite of male castration, a mutilation that, far from accentuating distinctively male traits, forcibly removes them.

The strange rite of ariltha in Australia seems at first sight to run counter to such explanations. Though it involves radical surgery, its origins are seldom discussed. Subincision makes men more, not less, like women; moreover, in many aboriginal myths, women had performed the first acts of male circumcision. Just as in fantasy girls are apt to dream that they have acquired a penis, among certain Australian tribes the bleeding penis after subincision was likened to a vulva; the Arunta employed the same term for the subincision wound as for the vulva. This use of the same word is most suggestive, implying that ariltha, unlike circumcision, was conceived as a symbolic attempt to reproduce the female sex organ; the reopening of the wound to make further cuts then recalls the periodic phenomenon of menstruation.

The absence of subincision except among the primitive aboriginals is significant. Like their dual form of marriage, it might have been more prevalent at an earlier stage in man's cultural history; if it ever existed elsewhere (as explained above, the aborigines stemmed from Asia), it had long since been abandoned. At this early stage, marked by a greater equality between the sexes, bisexual tendencies would have posed fewer social problems, and perhaps the urge was lacking to adopt those forms of mutilation that made sexual distinctions sharper. On the contrary, concessions were made to latent male vagina envy, and the distinction between the sexes was, if anything, underplayed rather than overstressed.

Alternatively, ariltha might be explained as an attempt to universalize a rare deformity, whose victims were held in awe by other members of the tribe. There are, as we shall later see, various categories of physical hermaphrodites, whose organs are part male and part female. One such deformity is known as hypospadias, a condition in which fetal development of the penis remains incomplete. As a result, the skin does not wrap around the shaft of the organ and fuse on the under side to form the urethral tube. Instead of a tube there is an open gutter, with an orifice between the base of the penis and the scrotum. This orifice houses the urinary opening, which may be situated anywhere between the scrotum and the tip of the penis. Prior to surgical repair, which is nowadays possible, urination can be performed only by squatting, just as for victims of ariltha.

To our modern way of thinking, deformities or abnormalities are to be remedied. But to the primitive mind, deformed people, and in particular hermaphrodites, can become an object of awe. Possibly one or more such beings suffering from hypospadias might have become a tribal hero, venerated by virtue of this peculiarity. Under such circumstances, the custom could then have developed (whose origins were later forgotten) of performing surgery not to cure the "complaint" but, on the contrary, to produce a similar condition in as many healthy males as possible.

CHAPTER THREE

The Permissive
Islanders

Back to Malinowski

The role of Bronislaw Malinowski in modern social anthropology is unique. In 1929 he published *The Sexual Life of Savages: An Ethnographic Study of Courtship, Marriage, and Family Life Among the Natives of the Trobriand Islands, British New Guinea.* The book was based on his work in the islands in 1917 and 1918, when the impact of Western culture was still limited there. No one has written a comparable study for any other part of the world, and it could hardly be done today, when customs have so greatly changed.

The title tells only part of the story, since the book's more fascinating pages relate less to marriage and family life than to the insatiable hunger for sex of the unmarried teenagers, and to the wide variety of ways in which it could be assuaged.

Because Malinowski offers us such a copious account of the love life of the Trobrianders and of their unstinted devotion to the cult of Eros, one might easily suppose that they were the world's only sexual gluttons. But, as we shall see, the erotic urges of the Polynesians of the Pacific Ocean were, by all accounts, just as intense, though, thanks to Malinowski, more is known of the Trobrianders in that respect; comparable systems, moreover, probably existed in other regions apart from Oceania, though our knowledge of them may be fragmentary.

For the inhabitants of the Trobriand Islands, situated off the southeastern tip of New Guinea, sex implied pleasure rather than procreation; husbands, for instance, would extend a joyous welcome to children born to their wives after they had been absent for a year. They had an odd theory to explain the sexual functions of the body: The eyes were the seat of desire and lust; from the eyes, such sensations passed to the brain and thence to the male or female organs via the kidneys, causing an erection in the case of the male. The theory was summed up in the saying "A man with his eyes closed will have no erection."

The Trobrianders took the opposite view to Christians and Muslims, obsessed with the notion that a bride should be delivered intact. From the outset of puberty, the virgin state was virtually unknown and, had it existed, would have been a source of scandal. On the contrary, the more sexual experience a girl could acquire with a whole string of partners before marriage, the better fitted she would be to become a good wife.

Malinowski gives an exhaustive account of the "bachelors' houses" dedicated solely to teenage copulation and also found in so many other regions of the world. In addition to alternative opportunities for fornication, such as special games and raiding parties, adolescent boys and girls normally would pair off and cohabit for a period. This was a socially accepted relationship but not one that usually led to the marriage bed. This bond between lovers was easily dissolved and imposed no legal obligations; it differed from an affair between teenagers today, since it applied exclusively to copulation; the couple shared a bed and nothing else. They never ate meals together; had they done so, the girl would have been disgraced in the eyes of the whole village.

For such liaisons between boys and girls a place had to be provided where they could be alone. For this purpose, tribal custom (in the Trobriands and elsewhere) provided them with bachelors' and unmarried girls' houses. In each of these, three or four couples would cohabit for a period; they also served as brief love nests for even younger couples, sexual novices in their early teens, who sought amorous privacy for an hour or two but who had not yet reached an age at which boys and girls regularly began to live together. Mating arrangements were not confined to people from the same place; if a boy had an affair with a girl from another village, he would be made a temporary citizen of that group and would take up residence with the girl in one of its bachelors' houses.

The typical Trobriand village was divided into several distinct parts. The center had no dwellings, since cooking there was taboo, and contained only the chief's mansion, yam storage huts, and the bachelors' houses. Cooking was confined to the outer ring of dwellings, where married couples and their families lived; no food was needed in the bachelors' houses, since the couples would spend much of the day with their families in the outer ring.

Malinowski relates that in his day there were still five of these houses in the center of the village of Omarakana; the number had already shrunk owing to the implacable opposition of the missionaries, to whom such establishments were the work of Satan. For fear of those meddlesome clerics the older tradition was being abandoned, and some bachelors' houses were tucked away in the outer ring of dwellings, where they were less conspicuous and harder to recognize. Only ten years earlier there had been fifteen bachelors' houses in Omarakana, and the older inhabitants remembered a time when no less than thirty had existed (owing to the recent practice of camouflaging them, more may have still existed in Malinowski's time than he was able to locate). By the 1920s, timeless traditions were swept away and many young men and girls lived with their parents; however, this in no way changed their attitudes to sex out of wedlock but merely created a need for new subterfuges to achieve the same ends.

The bachelors' houses had been designed more for constant copulation than for gracious living. There was hardly a stick of furniture, except for bunks with mat covering. The buildings usually belonged to the boys, who used them for the sole purpose of fornication with their temporary mistresses. Each couple had its own bunk; when a pair separated, the girl left the house and went in search of another lover and another sleeping place. At first sight such an arrangement might be confused with group marriage, since a number of couples were involved. Nothing was farther from the truth: A strict decorum was observed, the occupants never indulged in orgies, and it was considered the worst possible form to watch another couple performing. Relationships were conducted on a strictly one-to-one basis; poaching or exchange of partners was not allowed. On the contrary, couples sought the maximum privacy and even tried to make love as quietly as possible to avoid waking the others.

Obvious questions arise: Were many children produced as a result of such liaisons? If so, what happened to them? Children born out of wedlock were most unwelcome; they were not killed, as on many Polynesian islands, but from birth onward they were social outcasts and suffered every conceivable handicap in a society that spurned them. For the Trobrianders themselves, the answer was quite simple: They insisted that semen did not make children, who were brought by the spirits. This Trobriand ignorance of the process of conception, rather implausible at first sight, is confirmed by their attitudes to pig breeding. In certain villages all male pigs were castrated; the sows were allowed to wander freely on the outskirts of the village to improve their condition. Under such circumstances they could become pregnant only when inseminated by wild bush pigs; but the islanders denied this patent fact, and a strange taboo even forbade people on the largest island, Buyowa, from eating the flesh both of bush pigs and their offspring.

Why so few children resulted from these teenage liaisons fascinated the European residents in the Trobriands and other islands. Malinowski quotes an informant from Teyava who states with concise logic: "Copulation alone cannot produce a child. Night after night for years girls copulate. No child comes." The author himself, during his long stay on the islands, was not able to locate more than a dozen illegitimate offspring. He and other anthropologists have toyed with the notion that after puberty a few years followed in which a girl who had intercourse was not likely to conceive; he asks: "Can there be any physiological law that makes conception less likely when women begin their sex life young, lead it indefatigably, and mix their lovers freely?" In addition, Malinowski mentions the belief among the whites on the islands that the natives had secret and potent ways of preventing pregnancy. But such precautions would have seemed absurd to a people who failed to connect copulation with conception and who thought that seminal flow was without effect. Moreover, modern science, while conceding that for a fairly brief period girls may begin to menstruate before they ovulate and can therefore conceive, discounts the notion that promiscuous teenagers do not produce offspring just like anyone else. Natural means of contraception undoubtedly existed among certain tribes (for instance, in Africa), but their efficacity was limited. The problem, therefore, remains unresolved.

Sex Games and Feasts

The bachelors' houses were a perfect setting for fornication, both as dormitories for adolescent couples and as lovenests for even younger novices. But these facilities were merely one of a number of erotic options. Feasts to mark the change of seasons offered further delights, of a kind that varied from one village to another. Grouped by Malinowski under the heading "Customary forms of license" were certain "games," including excursions, picnics, and bathing parties.

On the last few days before the full moon, young children would sit up late and play in the central plaza of the village. Older boys and girls would join them, followed by the more mature teenagers of both sexes. The children were gradually edged out, and once the adolescents were the main players, the real fun began; often by then the whole village would be gathered in the square to watch the proceedings. Toward the end of the evening ribald songs and ditties began to be chanted. A free translation of a fairly typical ditty reads:

> O the rapidly growing *taytu* yams, O the stout *taytu* yams,
> Men with enormous penises sit on food house platforms
> [that is, they keep away from women]
> They are pederasts.

(Notwithstanding these lines, Malinowski denied that pederasty existed in the islands.) Another ditty, sung by the girls, reads:

> O men, you use *duwaku* strips for your pubic leaves;
> They are short strips, far too short!
> Nothing so short will induce us to fornicate with you!

Such moonlight games in the village center were not an automatic prelude to copulation. They did, however, involve physical contacts that often led to lovemaking. Games of a different kind, played on other occasions, were more directly erotic. In one of these, in which boys and girls participated, the players stood in a long chain, holding hands. Chanting lewd chants, they would then walk around those who were placed at one end of the line. Thus, while some stood immobile, the others moved around them in a circle that grew progressively narrower until eventually all the players were pressed together in a knot. The fun lay in squeezing the knot so tight as to bring about the closest physical contact, followed by the obvious consequences.

Another game served as the perfect preamble to copulation. It began by two of the players sitting back to back; two more sat between the thighs of each, then two more between the legs of the second pair, and so on. So seated, they all sang and began to push backward. The row of bodies that pushed the other out of its sitting position won the game.

Late at night, as a climax to other games, a form of hide-and-seek was a popular pastime, ideally suited to erotic pairing. Participants would start out from the middle of the village but would do their hiding outside, in the bush. Some players would contrive not to be found for a conveniently long time, and in the interval had coitus in the seclusion of some cozy nook. The tug-of-war also was popular, since in the end all the players would fall to the ground in one heap. In certain places, the winning side would mock the vanquished; this would end in a public display of copulation. It was not thought proper for married women to partake of these frolics, but in another ceremony, called the *kasaya,* they were allowed to join the adolescents. Boys in gala dress would walk around the central plaza, singing songs. The women, who on this occasion took the initiative, would start by merely teasing them; from teasing they would pass to scratching and would finally attack them with mussel shells and bamboo knives, or with small obsidian axes. If a boy was attracted to his assailant, her attack would be taken as an invitation to copulate. The ambition of each woman was to slash as many males as she could; the latter were proud to bear the scars of many cuts and to reap a rich sexual reward for their wounds. The kasaya was notable for the relaxation of established taboos. Its sexual acts were thus carried out in the main plaza; married people not only took part but even behaved without restraint in the sight of brothers and sisters, with regard to whom the strictest incest taboos otherwise prevailed.

The women of certain islands indulged in another bizarre form of sexual violence, directed at passing strangers from other villages. The women would gather together for the ostensible purpose of weeding the village garden; if a stranger was sighted, they would first tear off his pubic leaf; then by masturbation they would try to produce an erection in the victim. Once this was achieved, one woman would squat over him and insert his penis into her vagina. While this was going on, others would defecate and urinate over his body, to pollute it as thoroughly as possible, while a few more would rub their genitals against his nose and mouth. Far from being ashamed at such a performance, it was treated as a display of virility on the part of the village women.

The *ulatile* (literally "male youth") may best be described as a lovemaking expedition. There were several forms of ulatile; in one of these, a group of boys from one village would go in a body to a neighboring settlement to seek temporary lovers. Secrecy was essential, since such forays encroached on the rights of two other groups, the regular sleeping partners of the ulatile boys themselves, and the youths of the other village, whose girls were their quarry.

Another kind of expedition was called a *katayausi.* Unlike the ulatile, it was carried out openly. The girls of a village would proceed to the communal grove and sit down outside its perimeter, where they would be met at nightfall by a group of boys from another place. There was no pretense at secrecy, and the whole community would sit facing the group of girls, with the exception of their own sweethearts, who were spared the indignity and merely sulked at home, since custom forbade them to interfere with the proceedings. After some joking and banter, the visiting boys would approach the girls, and the process of pairing began. According to custom, the choice was left to the girls, and each boy was bound by etiquette to accept any offer; he would produce a small gift for his suitor, a comb or a bundle of beetlenut; if she accepted, she became his lover for the night. After all the boys and girls were happily paired off, they would go out into the jungle together to do their night's work.

The Married State

One might wonder what ever induced the young to abandon this idyllic state of free love for marriage. This, however, was mandatory for a man, since until he took this step, he had no true status in the community.

Among the Trobrianders, as in most tribal societies, the contrast is marked between teenage freedom and the strict rules for married couples. Except on specific occasions when such rules were relaxed, marital fidelity was enforced, and if a wife committed adultery in a way that did not fall within the permitted range, the husband had the right to kill her. Nonetheless, his control over his wife was far from absolute. Trobriand women, as we have seen, tended to be aggressive, and in certain cases the men even complained of being henpecked; wife-beating was unknown.

Malinowski, moreover, revealed a vital aspect of marriage in the Trobriands. At first sight, the structure of their families seemed not unlike, say, our own; but on closer study, it proved to be quite distinct; society was organized on a matrilineal basis, a system now known to have existed not only in the South Seas but also in many other parts of the world. By virtue of this system, a child inherits not from his natural father but from his mother's brother. The true father, whose role in the conception of the child is discounted, is treated more as a benevolent family friend than as the parent of his offspring; all authority over children is vested in the mother's brother, who in effect becomes their father figure. The true father is nonetheless an indispensable member of the household; paradoxically, though not credited with any part in conceiving the infant, his marriage to the mother alone confers legitimacy on her children, who would otherwise be bastards and outcasts.

Anthropologists have known of matrilineal societies for some decades, and their existence has often been taken for granted. However, Dr. John Hartung, posing the problem in sociobiological terms, has more recently claimed that matriarchy is the logical product of frequent extramarital copulation. In societies where such liaisons are common, Hartung argues, a man cannot be absolutely sure of any connection between himself and his own children (even if he *does* associate sex with procreation). He is, however, positive that he and his brothers and sisters share the same mother and that he is therefore related to them. Thus he can only be sure that he is passing his wealth to true blood relations if he leaves it to his sister's son or to his younger brothers. Hartung's reasoning is supported by the fact that in many of the 186 societies of the Ford and Beach investigation, frequent extramarital sex coincides with inheritance by sister's sons.

Techniques and Taboos

Sadism was a marked trait in Trobriand sex life, particularly on the part of women. *Kimali,* meaning "erotic scratching," played the same part in lovemaking as does kissing in other societies; moreover, female wooing as a preliminary to sex, involving beating and even wounding prospective partners with sharp instruments, went far beyond mere scratching.

Although the sheer quantity of opportunities for intercourse was remarkable, its quality is less noteworthy. In the most usual form of coitus, the man squats in front of the woman; with hands resting on the ground he moves toward her, taking hold of her legs and gradually pulling her toward him, until their genitals touch and insertion can take place. The islanders despised the standard European coital position and made fun of cook boys and other servants who spied on the copulating methods of their masters and copied them.

As described by Malinowski, the Trobrianders were certainly among the most sex-orientated peoples in the world, though other candidates for that distinction are not hard to find. Even their funerary rites were a pretext for sex. When a man died, people of other villages would come and take part in the singing and dancing, which lasted for most of the night. When the visitors eventually left, some of the girls customarily stayed behind to sleep with boys from the bereaved community. On other occasions the situation was reversed, and the girls of a particular village would be duty-bound to sleep with a group of male mourners. Moreover, eroticism was not confined to life on earth; in Trobriand accounts of Paradise, other aspects would fade into the background, and sex inevitably came to the fore. For the people of the small island of Tuma, heaven was a place where stunningly beautiful women toiled tirelessly all day but were still eager for a night spent dancing and lovemaking (presumably Malinowski's informants on this point were men). By a mechanism hard to explain, all commoners became chiefs, waited upon by bevies of beauties.

Nonetheless, Malinowski ceaselessly insists that sex was subject to well-defined rules; license was never absolute, and he denies that freedom was the equivalent of "immorality, debased or perverted though it may be." He goes on to stress: "As a matter of fact, the Trobrianders have as many rules of decency and decorum as they have liberties and indulgences. Among all the customs of sexual liberty so far described, there is not one warrant of license which does not imply definite limits; not one concession to the sexual impulse but imposes new restrictions; not one relaxation of the usual tabus but exacts compensation in one way or another."

If Europeans found the Trobrianders licentious, the latter were just as shocked by certain Western customs, such as dancing with bodies pressed together, showing tenderness to one's wife in public, or making a ribald jest in one's sister's company, a major breach of their incest taboos. Malinowski sums up matters by saying that in some respects their moral regulations were biologically sounder than ours, as more refined and subtle and as offering a more efficient safeguard to marriage and to family life: "The best way to approach sexual morality in an entirely different culture is to remember that the sexual impulse is never entirely free, neither can it ever be completely enslaved by social imperatives. The limits of freedom vary; but there is always a sphere within which it is determined by biological and physiological motives only, and also a sphere in which the control of custom and convention is paramount."

Paradise Lost

Far to the east of the Trobriands, on islands scattered over the boundless Pacific Ocean, live the lighter-skinned Polynesians. Although no accounts of the mores of these people match up to Malinowski's work, enough data survive to show that the Polynesians were equally sex-orientated. In Polynesia, inhibitions that restrained other races simply did not exist; to quote Captain James Cook's observations after he had first landed in Tahiti in 1769: "There is a scale in dissolute sensuality which these people have ascended, wholly unknown among other nations whose manners have been recorded from the beginning of the world to the present hour, and which no imagination could possibly conceive."

In countless islands sex and sex play, enjoyed by both kings and commoners, were simply the leading sport or pastime, adding color and excitement to the otherwise humdrum existence typical of a small island. Failing other topics, people talked about sex in much the same way as elsewhere they might discuss eating and drinking. Although certain taboos were strict, any sense of modesty was unknown: a nose or a penis, an anus or a knee joint would be talked of in the same way.

French scientist and explorer Louis Antoine de Bougainville had landed in Tahiti a year before Cook's visit. Householders produced a girl for each of his crew, and if the white man accepted the offer, a crowd of onlookers would gather and behave much as if they were in a theater. The audience was highly critical, since Polynesians regarded the European approach to coitus as clumsy and amateurish. Captain Cook's men encountered the same nonchalant curiosity: "A young man, nearly six feet high, performed the rites of Venus with a little girl about eleven or twelve years of age before several of our people, and a great number of natives, without the least sense of its being improper or indecent, but as appeared, in perfect conformity with the customs of the place. Among the spectators were several women of superior rank, particularly Oberea, who may be said to have assisted at the ceremony, for they gave instructions to the girl how to perform her part, which, young as she was, she didn't seem to stand much in need of."

Famous naturalist Joseph Banks, who accompanied Cook's expedition, was honored by a special welcome. Two girls marched solemnly toward him; first one and then the other lifted her skirt and exposed her genitals, at the same time offering him a banana, a gesture whose symbolism was unmistakable. They then embraced him in such a way as to banish any remaining doubts as to the object of their visit.

Class distinctions were scrupulously observed in these approaches. Although a chieftainess might fling herself at an explorer captain, a lady of rank would have shunned an ordinary seaman or even a petty officer. But the crew was never short of girls who felt no shame or embarrassment at being seen copulating with a sailor.

The lack of inhibitions applied to children, who were encouraged to indulge in sex games; older people, if troubled by their shouting, would tell their offspring to go off and masturbate, rather as a parent today might pack them off to an ice cream store. Males began at the precocious age of three, and some could masturbate almost before they could talk; young boys of six or seven would disappear into the bush for masturbation contests.

In such a society celibacy was unknown. The inhabitants of the Cook Islands, west of the Society Islands, were so puzzled by the sexlessness of Roman Catholic priests that they would ask them if their genitals had been sewn up. The Maoris of New Zealand, the largest islands of Polynesia, were equally baffled by Protestant clerics. Early in the nineteenth century one of the first bishops to arrive from England was received in a remote village. After a gargantuan banquet followed by long speeches, the prelate was about to retire for the night when the native chief bawled jovially to his staff: "A woman for the bishop." When the bishop's English attendant angrily demurred, the chief, flabbergasted at such uncouth behavior, could think of only one explanation and shouted even more loudly: "Two women for the bishop."

The virgin state was untenable beyond infancy in most islands, since the competition among men was intense to deflower girls at the earliest possible age. Moreover, coitus was held to be mandatory for a girl's healthy growth; for instance, in the Tuamoto Archipelago, even in recent times, when a virgin girl was systematically raped by a group of boys in series, everyone thought that this was for her own good. (No one, as we have seen in the case of the Trobrianders, has yet accounted for the reportedly low rate of pregnancy resulting from such encounters.) Only after the arrival of the Europeans was any premium placed on virginity, because it then became a marketable commodity; mothers on the Tonga Islands would bring their virgin daughters onto whalers' ships and trade the first honors for goods.

The amazement of the European explorers at the permissive society of Polynesia knew no bounds, and they provide an endless fund of anecdotes describing the joys of this earthly Paradise. Such accounts tend to confuse the issue, since they tell nothing about what the natives did among themselves and simply describe how they behaved toward these visitors at whose lechery they were equally astonished. Some even concluded that sexual relations must be unknown in the homeland of these libidinous seafarers and that they came to the islands solely for that purpose.

Students of Polynesian customs inevitably fall back on these fabulous stories of early explorers. But although their accounts lack inhibitions of latter-day visitors, they mainly reflect the

Europeans' own relations with the lower classes, whose conduct was laxer and less hedged in by rules than that of the princely elite. Explorers ignored such rules and were thereby apt to overstate the admittedly high level of promiscuity.

Olden Times

In writing of the sex life of Oceania, we face two distinct worlds: a life guided by traditional concepts, and a second phase, after these had been mutilated by Europeans. Malinowski describes a situation not too remote from the original, or unchanged, ways of a corner of Oceania. Not only were Europeans few in number in the Trobriands sixty years ago, but they also were physically unattracted to the dark-skinned inhabitants; some of the customs he describes survive today in remoter islands of the group. And yet even Malinowski has to admit that times had already changed. The bachelors' houses were disappearing; and in describing the ulatile expeditions, he states that they had not taken place for the past twenty years. Apart from the rapturous stories of the pioneers, enough data exist on earlier customs to show that in many archipelagoes Polynesian teenagers had enjoyed liberties comparable to those of the Trobrianders. In pre-European times (for instance, in the Society Islands), the girls rather than the boys built the bachelors' house, and it was the girl who chose the boy with whom she wanted to share her mat; the boys were prohibited by custom from expressing a preference for a particular girl. The system presented no problems, since in the eyes of the average male one vagina was as good for copulation as another. In Tahiti, the main island of the group, as an alternative to bachelors' house pairings (before they were abolished), three or four couples might go off on moonlight picnics. Fairly early in the proceedings, each boy would have coitus with his chosen girl; quite often, however, this might be followed by a change of partners for a second session.

For the nobility, the rules were very different. The daughters of chiefs were closely guarded, and for them such activities were banned. Polynesian princesses were expected to remain virgins until wedded to a man of equal rank. For instance, in Samoa, a chief's daughter had to be intact when she became a bride. She was deflowered by her husband's first two fingers as she stood naked before a vast assembly; if no blood was visible, she was promptly clubbed to death by her relatives. In Tahiti also, at the end of the wedding ceremony the bridegroom would deflower the bride in front of a critical audience.

Once married, the sexual outlets of a high-born girl were less restricted, and the husband's conjugal rights were at once extended to his cousins and certain other relatives. Even his guests could claim such rights unless he specifically objected, a course that would normally be taken as a sign of overt hostility. Chiefs might also allow males of their household to have intercourse with one of their wives to compensate for services about the house. The allure of such a dazzling reward would serve as an inducement for ordinary citizens to enter a chief's service.

In the Marquesas, the order of deflowering was reversed. At the wedding feast of a young noble, not he, but his relatives, were the first to initiate the bride. She would lie down with her head on her husband's knee. A line was formed up in strict order of rank, the oldest leading the way; in that order each copulated with the bride, and the husband was the last to do so. After this marathon performance the poor girl often had to take to her bed for several days, though the more men she satisfied in this way, the prouder she felt.

Such practices should not be taken as a mere concession to the lusts of those who attended weddings; a princely marriage was a solemn occasion, and it seemed only natural that sexual intercourse should form part of the religious rite, inseparable from female fertility.

A most peculiar institution in Tahiti and other of the Society Islands also illustrates the close ties between sex and religion in pre-European Polynesia. Some of the elite spurned marriage but chose a way of life affording boundless opportunities for intercourse. Known as *arioi,* they were a kind of religious lodge, dedicated to travel from village to village and from island to island; wherever they set foot they would stage more or less obscene performances and encourage onlookers to join in the wild orgies that followed. Membership in this itinerant sex show was a great honor, open to the highest-born men and women. Members renounced parenthood and swore a solemn oath to kill all children born of their activities; pregnancy was not un-common, since one of the strictest rules ordained that no member of either sex could decline a colleague's advances. In effect, by abjuring marriage, they contrived to perpetuate the carefree promiscuity of the teenager.

In contrast to these arioi, the common people always married (apart from certain transvestites). Formal rules defined the married state, though they were much less strict than for princely families. Polygamy was the privilege of the upper classes, and monogamy was normal for the remainder; an ordinary wedding entailed few ceremonies, and unions were in effect based on common-law consent, formalized by an exchange of gifts.

Marriage was, however, not an exclusive state, and, as among the Australian aborigines, forms of secondary union were practiced in many islands by commoners but not by the nobles. Such additional partnerships could be formed by either husband or wife, with the consent of the other spouse. Secondary mates could cohabit for a time; alternatively, the male would visit the secondary wife at her home. Thus it was more frequent for women to have several "husbands" than for men to have several "wives."

These secondary marriages have been erroneously described as a form of polyandry, whereby a woman could have an exclusive right on several husbands. While polygamy was practiced by the chiefs, who claimed sole rights over several wives, the reverse situation, polyandry, did not exist. In no case did a woman ‚enjoy an exclusive claim over several men; such partners were only secondary husbands, who also had their own wives.

Although marriage offered both spouses alternative outlets, these bore no comparison to teenage promiscuity. For married women extramarital coitus was taboo without the husband's consent. Wives who were secretly unfaithful faced dire penalties, and husbands had the right to kill both offending wives and their seducers; sometimes women caught *in flagrante* would commit suicide to escape such a fate.

But if the married state was subject to certain rules, in practice it was not easy for an ordinary husband to prevent his wife from copulating with other males, even if he wanted to. Wife-lending was a compliment hard to withhold; apart from guests, anyone wanting to sleep with another man's wife had to ask leave of her husband, but both in Tahiti and Hawaii any rebuttal would have been looked upon as mean and insulting. Apart from such voluntary pairings, a wife could even be lent without her consent, and her spouse might force her to have relations in return for merchandise. (In Hawaii, a custom known as *punalua* provided further opportunities for changing partners; it gave a husband presumptive rights not only over his wife's sisters but also over all female cousins, even if they were married.)

Such extramarital outlets were made simpler by a general refusal to recognize that intercourse caused pregnancy. Even on those islands where the facts of life were better understood, people were convinced that if a wife had intercourse with her husband within a day of sleeping with another man, not the causal partner but the husband would be the true father of any child.

Children were in any case treated as a rather mixed blessing and were not necessarily reared by their own parents. For instance, in the Solomon Islands of Melanesia the custom prevailed for the richer people to kill off their infants and then to purchase older children from a neighboring tribe, since the care of the very young was a tiresome chore best left to others. In Tahiti, people would have no compunction telling foreigners how they had killed their children and would calmly visit missionaries' houses even before their hands were cleansed of their infants' blood. In Hawaii infanticide served as a kind of family planning; parents were entitled to kill their children and often exercised this right after two or three had been born, to save themselves the trouble of raising a large family. A certain reluctance to having sons arose from a belief that a newborn babe was the reincarnation of a revered ancestor; hence from the day of his birth he took precedence over his father and was treated as the rightful owner of his property.

The Missionaries

Oceania, before the white man's assault on their customs, embraced a series of societies, permissive in many respects, that had developed over many millennia independently of the rest of mankind. On the whole they worked well under a special combination of circumstances.

Although it may be hard to recapture in detail the old way of life, nowhere did the European presence destroy this traditional balance of sex as much as in Polynesia. The Christians fought a bitter battle against the islanders' free-and-easy approach to the subject, but after initial successes the Christians tended to defeat their own ends. Part of the initial attack on sexual customs was directed against the old religions, for in the pre-Christian cults, sex and religion went hand in hand. Polynesia was a warrior society, and copulation often took place in temple premises so that the offspring would be good fighters. From the moment that the missionaries arrived, accounts of Polynesian mores relate to a quite different world in which sex, if still eagerly pursued, assumes a furtive aspect, remote from the libidinous frolics witnessed by Cook and Bougainville. Intent upon mending the wicked ways of their flock, the most pressing task of the missionaries was the suppression of the bachelors' houses, or pleasure houses, as Bengdt Danielsson aptly calls them in his writing on Polynesia.

Although this was a clear-cut objective, their success in other fields was more qualified and they were apt themselves to become the targets of the still uninhibited Polynesians. For instance, in the Marquesas Islands the tale is told of a middle-aged male evangelist named Harris who gladly accepted a native chief's offer of accommodation. After he had been living in the royal hut for several days without making any advances to the chief's wife, as custom demanded, it seemed obvious that he must be impotent. To banish all doubt, the chief's wife and two women friends crept into his room while he was asleep and began to examine his penis. Their inquisitive fingering woke the evangelist; he panicked and fled from the house, horrified and ashamed. The crew of the mission ship found him on the beach the next morning, wandering like a man who had lost his reason. He was hastily embarked and never set foot in the Marquesas again.

The missionaries' efforts at times backfired. Like nineteenth-century English schoolmasters, they were convinced that idleness inspired wicked thoughts. They therefore also promoted soccer, usually played after church on Sundays, hoping that the participants would then be too weary to plan nocturnal prowlings in search of lovers.

Such schemes, whatever their use in England, did not work among inhabitants of the Marquesas Islands, who treated the games themselves as the ideal setting for preliminary sex play; just as the Trobrianders' tug-of-war games, soccer, after the usual exchange of jokes and innuendos, served as an occasion for picking sexual partners from the opposing team, since both boys and girls took part. Boys, in anticipation of more alluring sports, often became sexually aroused and would then continue to play soccer without the slightest attempt to hide an almost constant erection.

In their attempts to impose their moral code, the missionaries overplayed their hand in other ways. As part of their campaign to instill Christian morals, native pastors would form vice patrols to search for any successful suitors who had penetrated the defenses of their flock. On the Ellice Islands in Micronesia, dogs were at one time used by would-be fornicators to sniff out girls confined to parents' homes; as a result, the missionaries on Funafuti Island forbade all dog owning and the island remained dogless for the latter part of the nineteenth century.

The clerics not only fought ancient beliefs but even set their face against perfectly natural efforts to make oneself physically attractive as an aid to the pursuit of love. For instance, in the Cook Islands, in support of their (to the natives) outlandish view that intercourse without marriage was vile, they banned body adornments that might appeal to the opposite sex. Not only could flowers no longer be worn behind the ear, but boys were even forbidden to appear in public with girls. Church deacons tried to impose a curfew and would fine offenders; until very recently all unmarried people had to stay home after 9:00 P.M. or face prosecution. Now, however, such disciplines are losing their force. Young unmarried men still can be temporarily expelled from the Boys' Brigade for fathering a child, but local clergy have ceased in schools and sermons to fulminate against masturbation, unorthodox coital positions, and oral-genital contact.

The Anthropologists

The anthropologists appeared upon the scene much later. But if their aims differed from those of the missionaries, their reports on Polynesian sex life leave many gaps and do scant justice to such a rich and riveting topic. Most accounts dating from before the past decade, when scholars finally shed the enduring inhibitions of Victorianism, are permeated by notions of "higher" and "lower" races, from whom decent behavior could hardly be expected.

Even the great Malinowski was not altogether free of such limitations in spite of his fine work on the subject. The one scholar who was an exception to the rule and supposedly had a special way with the natives in fact cordially detested them. Malinowski left a private diary that was—perhaps unfortunately —published in 1967. This extraordinary document contains such phrases as: "I am glad that the Oboraku niggers are behind me, and I'll never again live in their village," or, "at bottom, I am living outside of Kiriwina, although strongly hating the niggers." He adds that he consoled himself by reading Racine's *Phèdre*. At times he goes even further in voicing his innermost thoughts on Melanesians: "On the whole my feelings towards the natives are decidedly tending to 'exterminate the brutes.' " He complains of how his informants lied to him and of how he would then get angry and shout at them. Moreover, he felt none of the earlier visitors' physical attraction for Pacific islanders; on the contrary, he would yearn for contact with the wives and daughters of white settlers: "Am gripped with amorous desire for Mrs. N.," or (on the same page), "My erotic feelings are exclusively reserved for T." He modestly describes his own work as an opiate rather than a creative expression.

Unlike early explorers, other anthropologists who studied Polynesian customs would often recoil from showing too overt an interest in sex, on the odd pretext that such inquiries were an invasion of "individual privacy." Reports tend to display a contrived detachment; passing references are made to Polynesian sex customs, but they seldom figure as the specific subject of a monograph. Due to such reticence, even data that must automatically have been acquired were never revealed.

In contrast to her more prudish precursors, the celebrated Margaret Mead went to Samoa in 1925, and in 1928 she published *Coming of Age in Samoa,* in which she went out of her way to extol the stress-free sex life of the easygoing Samoans. Mead, then aged twenty-three, had set off for Samoa after a short pep talk from her mentor, Franz Boas, the leading anthropologist of his time. Boas was the impassioned leader of the school of cultural determinism, convinced that people were born as a kind of blank slate, their personality shaped by the environment in which they were raised; for Boas, adolescent *Angst* was the product of upbringing rather than heredity. Mead obliged him with the news that Samoa had a culture that seemed to fit his theory like a glove. As quoted by one of her admirers, Mead said of Boas: "He told us what to look for and we went and found it." Her book became an immediate best seller.

Forty-two years later, and four years after Mead's death, Dr. Derek Freeman of Canberra University set out to burst her South Seas bubble in *Margaret Mead and Samoa: The Making and Unmaking of an Anthropological Myth.* As the leading expert on Samoa and the adopted son of a village chief, Freeman's qualifications are impeccable. But as long ago as 1964 he met Mead and told her personally of his doubts, and this has prompted critics to suggest that he might have published his work earlier, before her death.

Few would deny Mead's achievement as a pioneer spokesperson for the science of anthropology and her success in arousing public interest in the subject. Millions of people, including many who have never heard of her, have been affected by her reasoning, originally based on Samoa, and which served as a spearhead for women's liberation and for the sexual revolution. Her stress on the absence of jealousy among the islanders was taken up by the counterculture of the 1960s.

Nonetheless, Freeman is on firm ground in faulting Mead's fieldwork, which showed little of Malinowski's objectivity. Her data are mainly based on the views of twenty-five young Samoan girls; emerging from the seclusion of the American home in which she lodged, she plied them with questions in her very halting Samoan and accepted without reserve as much as she understood of their replies. Perhaps the worst disservice Freeman could do to her memory is to send people back to study *Coming of Age in Samoa,* rich in purple passages that now read like a parody of a student's flights of fancy: "As the dawn begins to fall among the soft brown roofs and the slender palm trees stand out against a colorless, gleaming sea, lovers slip home from trysts beneath the palm trees or in the shadow of beached canoes, that the light may find each sleeper in his appointed place."

The current furor over Mead's work underlines the contrast between two Polynesian worlds, that of today and that of yesterday. By an odd paradox, her work reflects the spirit of a Samoan society that already in 1925 had almost vanished. Teenage sexual liberty had been a standard feature of Polynesian life in the days of the bachelors' houses, as attested to in innumerable accounts. Mead's juvenile informants, all females, seem to have been primed by their grandmothers to convey to the visitor the essence of a Samoa that she sought, gleaned from memories of a bygone age. Mead admits that much of the adolescent fornication by the time of her visit took place when young men sneaked into the houses of girls' parents, though she does not explain how they got past the dogs she mentions, which served as sentinels.

Mead is most probably right in implying that a great deal of teenage fornication took place in Samoa, but this surely no longer amounted to institutionalized and unrestrained free love of a kind described by Malinowski in the Trobriands, as yet not as greatly changed as in Samoa. However, where she is obviously wrong is in her conclusion that just because the Samoans remained more tolerant toward adolescent promiscuity their society was *ipso facto* stress-free.

Sexual tolerance, past or present, has never produced in Polynesia a society where tensions were absent. One has only to consider the case of tiny Easter Island, whose original inhabitants were pure Polynesian and spoke the dialect of East

Polynesia. For centuries before Captain Cook's arrival the inhabitants, numbering about six thousand, had been engaged in endless warfare between two rival factions, in which women and children were freely slaughtered; by the time the Europeans appeared, Easter Island civilization lay in ruins, and most of the famous statues had already been overturned and lay flat on their faces. Throughout "stress-free" Polynesia warfare was endemic and human sacrifice frequent; a painting in the British Museum portrays Cook as he watches a sacrifice to which he had been invited in Tahiti.

The myth of the noble savage had been exploded long before Mead's day. Sexual permissiveness was an unreliable antidote to aggressiveness, whether in Polynesia or among Western teenagers. In Oceania people were not stress-free; their tensions were merely different and found partial release in their addiction to war, often for the purpose of capturing enemies to eat them (as, for instance, among the Maoris).

On the other hand, when Freeman and others go to the opposite extreme and call Samoa a puritanical society, they greatly overstate their case; to judge from accounts of other island groups, the missionaries did not make the people into puritans except on the surface; they merely forced them into adopting different tactics to achieve the same amorous ends as before. Anthropologist Brad Shore of Emory University in Atlanta is surely right in taking a middle stance: He maintains that Freeman exaggerates the supposed Samoan cult of virginity and points out that it may be prized as an ideal but is widely violated. By all accounts, premarital virginity was only an ideal or, more precisely, a rule for the nobles of long ago.

On a different plane is the more recent work of American anthropologist Robert C. Suggs, who wrote in the 1970s on the Marquesas Islands and who gives a more factual and less motivated account of an important archipelago fifty years after Margaret Mead's day. Suggs readily admits that he is studying a society that had already been torn apart, but he, unlike Freeman, insists that certain underlying attitudes defied reform. Admittedly in the Marquesas they probably changed less rapidly than in American Samoa, but the life he describes is the reverse of "puritanical." Invaluable as a general guide on sex customs of Polynesia in recent times are also the writings of Swedish Bengdt Danielsson, who first came to the islands on board Thor Heyerdahl's famous *Kon-tiki* raft; he equally fails to detect in the present-day islanders a vein of prudery.

By the time Suggs produced his invaluable study of the Marquesas Islands (*Marquesan Sexual Behavior,* published in 1966), the bachelors' houses, already disappearing in the Trobriands in 1918, were a thing of the past. In some places they were formerly the grandest buildings of a village; for instance, Yap Island in the Caroline Islands had been famous for the splendor of such structures, whose gabled roofs, fifteen to twenty meters high, towered over all the other buildings of the community. The tradition of sexual hospitality has also waned. Suggs, in the whole course of his stay on Nuku Hiva, was offered only two women and one boy as a gesture of hospitality.

Studies of recent times show that the rules of the game may have been forcibly changed but that fundamental aims have altered less. What are now described are not so much the original institutions on which sex life was based, as the subterfuges since adopted to achieve similar ends by different means. Passive resistance to missionary repression has remained strong, and even today nothing is apt to delight the natives more than to pass off on an unwitting Westerner the village slut, fresh from a serial encounter with five or even ten local boys.

Despite the missionaries' preaching, the accepted rules for adolescents and married couples still differ widely. The idea that teenagers of either sex should remain virginal has never taken root. In the Marquesas, most boys and girls, having already indulged in sex play for several years, begin to copulate at the age of eleven or twelve, often with a mature partner. A girl's first experience may occur when she is caught alone in the bush, or while bathing; if she shows the slightest reluctance to gain this first experience, she may be raped, supposedly for her own good. Girls on reaching puberty usually receive instruction on intercourse from their grandmother, including the different positions for coitus and techniques for stimulating their partner. Suggs, writing in 1963, relates that many girls on the island of

Atuona would lose their virginity when picking coffee on the land of the Mission of the Sacrés Coeurs de Picpus, which maintains a convent school. During the season, when the girls were sent out to harvest the crop, sex-hungry men would wait in the dense brush around the coffee bushes, in the hopes of picking off a willing virgin.

Suggs shows how, already in the 1960s, the original pattern of Marquesan sex life had been greatly modified and how different means were employed to achieve the same ends. Boys would have their first heterosexual experience when a year or two older than the girls. The boys' initiation often consisted of serial intercourse with an older woman in her husband's absence; she would take special pains to please, and most adult men would look back fondly on their first partner. In turn, the married women in the Marquesas looked upon this process of deflowering as a special delight. Once the first step had been taken, the average boy led a hyperactive sex life. He would quickly be drawn into one of a number of male groups. After the abolition of the bachelors' houses, the boys would prowl at night, visiting the houses of unmarried girls and of women whose husbands were absent. Preparation for such forays were most elaborate, and the hunters were at great pains to attract their quarry. After careful bathing and the generous application of perfume and pomade, flowers were pinned behind the ear; an indispensable item of equipment was a large flashlight, and guitars were often carried. Members of the group would exchange information on available females and the whereabouts of husbands and other protectors. The young males accumulated an incredible fund of knowledge about the layout of promising houses and even on the habits of unmarried girls' parents; in some cases they might be known to copulate at a certain hour every night, thereby offering the ideal chance to seduce their offspring. Unmarried girls were usually harder to woo than women whose husbands were temporarily absent. The parents, when themselves not engaged in intercourse, were the main obstacle; some would bolt all doors and windows and force girls to sleep in inaccessible corners, even forbidding them to go out to the latrine at night.

Parents' attitudes to their daughters' sex life tended to be ambivalent and mercenary. While guarding against impecunious night raiders, at other times they would not only condone their daughters' sexual relations with a number of mates but even actively encourage such affairs and would even push them off onto Westerners if the potential rewards were sufficiently spectacular. The presence of a fishing vessel in any port of the Marquesas could lead to wholesale bartering of favors in exchange for ammunition, clothing, and tools, while a virgin might even be traded for an outboard motor or a sewing machine.

Daylight encounters in the bush and nocturnal raiding parties largely served as a substitute for customs similar to those found by Malinowski in the Trobriands. Previously such night crawling was unknown, and it was devised as the native answer to the missionary veto on former arrangements, particularly the bachelors' houses, abolished in the 1920s in the Marquesas.

In addition to furtive encounters by day and ingenious night raids, another form of teenage copulation survived. While many girls were now closely guarded by parents, a few were more blatantly promiscuous and would provide serial intercourse for a whole group of boys. Such groups approached the girl and made a direct request. The order of service would be agreed beforehand and all would then proceed to an isolated house or to a hiding place in the bush. The waiting males would sit around as each one took his turn to copulate, watching and joking. In some cases, while she was having intercourse with one of their companions, others would also indulge in sexual play with the girl. This form of fornication continued to be popular.

While they might laugh at the standard Western form of intercourse, Polynesians exceled more in the quantity than the quality of their own performance. Since the more decorous setting of the bachelors' houses had been replaced by furtive night raiding and hurried encounters in the bush, speed had become the essence of success and often a few hurried kisses were all that preceded the sexual act, which under such circumstances rarely took more than five minutes and often was over in two or three.

Variant postures were seldom tried; as one experienced raider put it: "The result is the same no matter how you do it."

Mahu

In former times homosexuality was fairly widespread, more as a supplement to the many other options than as a basic ingredient of Polynesian sex life. Homosexuals were never actively condemned, let alone punished. In some islands noble ladies were attended by males who were transvestites, insofar as the term can be applied to places where differences between male and female attire are minimal.

Homosexual acts were looked upon as a perfectly acceptable outlet in cases where the supply of females was inadequate; such activities probably have increased in recent years as a result of missionary campaigns against traditional forms of heterosexual intercourse. (In recorded cases, group homosexual acts actually took place on the private verandahs of missionaries who, unaware of what went on, would make the boys foregather under their own roof to keep them away from the girls.) In very small island communities cases may nowadays arise where few if any females are available to satisfy the unattached males. To quote a specific example: One valley, Ho'owme, on Nuku Hiva in the Marquesas, had in 1970 a population of thirty-five, including five adolescent boys and two unmarried girls, both jealously guarded by their parents. Deprived of other outlets, the five boys simply formed, for recreational purposes, a loose group that also served as a convenient camouflage for homosexual activities. To this end they would often spend the afternoon in a remote corner of the valley. Everybody knew about this, but the matter became a subject for joking more than censure. Other people would chide them, asking who had played the girl's part on any particular day. As an alternative, bestiality was at times practiced with chickens; since the birds always flapped their wings violently during the performance, it came to be known as the Nuku Hiva fan.

Homosexual practices were not merely the last resort for youths who could find no other partners; male transvestism is an old tradition that still survives. The first European to report this was British Lieutenant George Mortimer, in command of a ship that visited Tahiti in 1789; he tells how one of his mates persuaded the most seductive of the dancing girls to go with him on board the ship. He was utterly nonplussed when the ravishing damsel was stripped of her paraphernalia and turned out to be a dapper young boy. The Tahitians treated the incident as a huge joke.

Transvestism is a widespread institution in Polynesia, whether in Samoa, Tonga, or Tahiti. Today the typical transvestite, or mahu, assumes the feminine role from an early age and at puberty will start wearing adult women's clothes, including a brassiere. Mahus prefer to cook and sew and do other women's tasks; nowadays they are much in demand as maids. In Tahiti tradition has become prey to Western influences; several bars serve as centers where mahus can prostitute themselves to Western tourists—a practice liable to cause misunderstandings—and beauty contests are even organized for Miss Tane (Miss Male).

Oedipus in Oceania

The ban on incest—still a potent force—reached obsessive proportions in Polynesia, where it was even taboo for a man to utter certain sex-related words in front of his sister. The more usual restraints on intimacy between brother and sister were extended to more distant relations.

Among the ordinary people the prohibition on incest applied to blood relatives, and intercourse between a man and his wife's sisters, married or unmarried, was common and socially acceptable; the term in Tahiti for sister-in-law, *el vahine,* also meant "future, or possible wife." Since sexual relations were also permitted between a man and the wife of any name brother (someone with whom he had changed names), the range of permissible contacts within the family circle was wide. Although many societies have extended the incest ban beyond the basic family unit of parents and children, its scope varies greatly from one group to the next. Sometimes the ban applies only to secondary relatives, such as father's sister, mother's sister, sister's daughter, and brother's daughter. In addition, our own society and some others include first cousins. However, 72 percent of the 133 groups mentioned in this context in the Ford and Beach survey have more extensive prohibitions, embracing a far greater number of relatives.

The problem of incest, basic to human sexuality, is as old as anthropology, and on no other aspect of sexual behavior has so much ink been expended in the anthropological literature. This powerful taboo's origins, nonetheless, are still deeply controversial, and every new theory simply reflects the latest current trend. Scholars had already been arguing about the subject for many decades when Freud in 1913 presented it in a new light and startled post-Victorian society with his much-publicized Oedipus complex, and his theories about infant sexuality, which he advanced but which he had not been the first to formulate. His interest sprang from the number of his patients whose complexes were centered upon acts of incest, real or imagined. For Freud, the incest taboo served as the indispensable barrier to a child's physical passion for his mother, leading to murderous conflict between father and son.

The study of matrilineal societies that began not long after Freud produced his theory argued strongly against the validity of the Oedipus complex, since it could not be applied *in toto* to a group in which not the father but the mother's brother played the paternal role. Moreover, while Oceanian myths often relate to incest, they illustrate the sins of brother-sister relations, but there is a notable absence of any patricidal mother love or of any desire on the part of the son to supplant his father. In contrast, among the Etoro of New Guinea, we even find a permitted relationship between father and son verging on the incestuous; semen, delivered directly from penis to mouth, is considered indispensable for a boy's healthy growth. The father does not himself produce the tonic but is responsible for finding a suitable person who supplies the need and usually chooses a near relative.

Earlier students of the subject (in particular the great French anthropologist, Émile Durkheim) had viewed incest as the distant echo of a deep-seated phobia produced by early man's terror of the blind forces of nature, which he worshiped as gods who had decreed this ban for reasons best known to themselves and who would destroy any who defied it. In support of this notion, Sir James Frazer in *The Golden Bough* gave a whole series of examples of peoples who were convinced that if a member of their tribe committed incest, their crops would be blighted.

The incest taboo is now more commonly viewed as an extension of the widespread institution of exogamy, forbidding marriage between people of the same clan or even the same tribe. Claude Lévi-Strauss has written at length on the subject in *Elementary Structures of Kinship* and basically accepts this view. He scorns the idea, which writers are so loath to abandon, that the ban can be explained on eugenic grounds as a precaution against the dangers of inbreeding (a popular theory in recent years). The eminent scholar insists that answers to the riddle are elusive, since the rules themselves are seldom logical; for instance, some societies actually favor marriage between cross-cousins (the respective children of a brother and sister) while forbidding those between parallel cousins (descended from two brothers or two sisters).

Lévi-Strauss is equally unconvinced by psychiatric theories on the subject. In spite of any alleged incest repugnance, it exists today on quite a large scale, and the number of reported cases has greatly increased; moreover, for psychoanalysts, the more universal phenomenon is not so much repugnance toward incestuous relations but their active pursuit. Lévi-Strauss sees the taboo not as some mysterious and deep-seated phobia but more simply as the keystone to the rule of exogamy, or marrying out, as a means of preserving a minimum level of coexistence with one's neighbors. For Lévi-Strauss "the ban is less a rule which forbids marriage with mother, sister, or daughter, as one which obliges the giving of mother, sister, and daughter to another."

The attempts of anthropologists and psychiatrists to explain the mystery are not wholly convincing, and both tend to ignore certain practical aspects of the problem. The reaction against incest is extremely ancient and in some form may have predated man. Studies made in the 1970s, for instance, showed for the first time that incest exists among rhesus monkeys as well as among chimpanzees and gorillas; however, it is rare. The prohibition was certainly practiced by the Australian aborigines, among whom the term for incestuous relations was among the worst insults in their vocabulary.

On the purely practical level, all tribes without exception seek to set strict limits to sexual relations between relatives, including those between members of different generations, and to define the duties of one generation toward another. But no set of rules could conceivably cater to a situation in which a man might raise a family with his wife, or wives, and then, at the age, say, of forty, be free to start a whole series of new families by fornicating with his own daughters and producing offspring who would thereby become half sisters to their own aunts and for whom the man in question is both father and grandfather. Such conduct, as certain writers have not failed to point out, would make a mockery of the whole finely balanced order of kinship, typical of tribal society, to whose very fabric the incest taboo is therefore basic. The ban on incest, on a par with the sexual aspects of initiation rites, is a trait that underlies the human condition. Like genital mutilation, the taboo is to be seen less as a kind of "natural" instinct than as a balancing force, created by society to serve certain ends. In a field vital to the group's survival, it affirms the preeminence of social needs over private impulses (among which incest ranks as a potent force). It marks the victory of the collective over the purely individual; it stresses the group's demand that people cannot do as they please in matters of sex— an imperative that is basic to man's development as a social and sexual being.

CHAPTER FOUR

Eros Before Columbus

Common Customs

The first humans to set foot in the New World trekked from East Siberia to Alaska across the land bridge that then joined the two continents. This process probably began some fifty thousand to sixty thousand years ago and continued until about 10,000 B.C., when the sea level rose at the end of the fourth Ice Age, the Beringia landmass sank beneath the waves, and Asia and America came to be separated by a shallow sea.

Although scholars agree that America was peopled mainly in this way, doubts persist as to how far America before Columbus —and before the Vikings, who left certain traces in Newfoundland—received other visitors, whether from China, Africa, or even Europe. The topic, discussed ever since America was discovered, has produced heated arguments and still yields an annual harvest of books about the origins of the first Americans, each with its "new" theory, most of which were already advanced over a century ago. Evidence is scanty but hypotheses abound, and claims are made for such implausible candidates as Hebrews, Hittites, Abyssinians, and Greeks, not to mention the Australian aborigines. Regardless of their point of departure, the earliest remains of man found in the New World belong to the *Homo sapiens* species, whose history spans a mere fraction of the time since the first protohumans. Logically, therefore, sexual customs in the two hemispheres share many common traits. As we have already seen, throughout the Old World, whether in Africa, Asia, or Oceania, a regular pattern of tribal sex life tends to repeat itself, and it is hardly surprising that many of the same customs are found in America, where the arrival of man was relatively recent in terms of human evolution.

The reports of early Spanish and Portuguese conquistadors and clerics are rich in detail but laced with prejudice, since their authors were horrorstruck that the native Indians did not already behave like good Catholics and had sexual taboos different from those of Europe. These pioneers wrote at some length about the more primitive peoples in, say, the Caribbean islands or Brazil, but were more concerned with America's two higher civilizations, those of Mexico and Peru. Although these empires soon succumbed, tribal life in many places went on much as before for several centuries. This tribal existence, both in North and South America, was more objectively described by later European visitors, many of whom were Jesuit missionaries. The anthropologists came last but were lucky to encounter certain peoples whose customs had changed little since Columbus; a few still cling to the same way of life today.

The end of this chapter will touch upon America's higher civilizations—thereby anticipating parts of the following chapter, dealing with the emergence of the first great cultures of the Near East. First, however, a few traits of tribal sex life are worth stressing that are more in evidence among the American Indians than elsewhere.

Sexual customs already described in an Old World context and merely repeated in another setting need only a brief mention. Throughout the Americas, except among subjects of the Aztec and Inca empires, premarital promiscuity was not only tolerated but even encouraged. Ample accounts exist, for instance, of bachelors' houses or their equivalent in Brazil. On reaching the married state, polygamy was the rule for those males who could afford it, and monogamy, far from being a virtue, was merely the unenviable lot of those who could not pay for more wives, just as, say, in Polynesia or Australia.

In many parts of North America a practice existed that has often inaccurately been described as group marriage. For instance, in the Omaha tribe a man who married a woman could also wed her sisters, her aunts (her father's sisters), and her nieces (brother's daughters). A number of tribes followed the Omaha system; for instance, among the Crow Indians of Indiana a husband had rights over all the sisters of his wife, and the same custom was observed in distant Louisiana. If the system hardly amounts to group marriage, since only one male was involved, a nearer approach to this was made by the Tlingits of the West Coast of Canada, where a wife would, as in Australia, have auxiliary husbands, and a brother or other near relation of a husband could perform his duties to his wife in his absence.

Indians of North and South America generally shared the incest taboo of peoples of the Old World. Orgiastic rites, not unknown in the Old World, also accompanied certain festivities, including initiation ceremonies; they were particularly common among the Aleuts, and the Innuits, an Eskimo tribe; at certain of their feasts all inhibitions were cast to the winds in a frenzy of promiscuity.

Spain and Sodom

Although Christopher Columbus discovered America in 1492, Spaniards came face to face with its great civilizations only a generation later, following Cortes' expedition to Mexico in 1519 and Pizarro's occupation of Peru in 1532. Accordingly, the Spaniards' first impressions were derived not from the Aztec and Inca empires but from peoples whose culture was more comparable with that of, say, Polynesia, or black Africa. Although their accounts of the higher civilizations cover a broader range of topics, addiction to sodomy pervades their reports of the first tribes encountered in the Caribbean islands and on the mainland; the conquistadors had less to say about other aspects of their sex life, such as premarital and marital relations, and emphasized the vices more than the virtues of their new subjects.

In such accounts sodomy, or *sodomía*, applies not only to anal intercourse between two males but also to intercourse between male and female, using the female anus instead of the vagina. The word, of course, derives from Sodom, an ancient city in Palestine; for reasons which, as we shall later see, have no foundation in history, it gave its name to a particular form of pederasty. Spanish sources refer alternatively to sodomy as "the sin against nature," "the nefarious vice," or the "abominable sin." While probably aware that covert homosexuality existed in their own country, what appalled the Spaniards was its nonchalant public acclaim in the New World. In Spain itself it did not pay to be found out; laws against sodomy were ruthlessly applied, and even heterosexual anal intercourse was punishable by death.

Such outrageous conduct was first noticed on Columbus's second expedition. Diego Alvarez Chanca, the admiral's physician, in a letter written in 1494, describes the Caribs of the island of Guadeloupe: "To the boys made captive they cut them off the (virile) members and use them until they become men, and then when they wish to make a feast, they kill and eat them, for they say that the flesh of (uncastrated) boys is not good to eat. Of these boys, three came fleeing to us, all with their members cut off."

The first historian of the New World, Pietro Martire d'Anghiera (1457–1526), known in English as Peter Martyr, had more to say. His work was later translated into English in the reign of Queen Mary and describes events that took place in the Isthmus of Panama during the explorations of Vasco Nuñez de Balboa. He gives full vent to his indignation:

Unnatural Lechery.
Vaschus (Vasco Nuñez de Balboa) founde the house of this Kynge infected with the most abhominal and unnaturall lechery. For he founde the Kynges brother and many other younger men in womens apparell, smoth and effeminately

decked, which by the report of such as dwelte abowte hym, he abused with preposterous Venus. Of these aboute the number of fortie, he (Vasco Nuñez de Balboa) commanded to bee gyven for a pray to his dogges. . . .
Naturaul hatred of unnatural sinne.
When the people had harde of the sever punysshment which our men had executed uppon that fylthy Kynde of men, they resorted to them as it had byn to Hercules for refuge, by violence bryngyng with them al such as they knewe to bee infected with that pestilence, spettynge in theyr faces and cryinge owte to owre men to take revenge of them and rydde they owte of the worlde from amonge men as contagious beastes. This stinkynge abhomination hadde not yet entered amonge the people, but was exercised onely by the noble men and gentlemen.

Richard Eden, the translator, adds a marginal note of his own in italics: *"I wolde that all men were of this opinion,"* a rueful hint that a few members of the English Court were no strangers to these upper-class vices.

The presence of such transvestites was universal throughout Spanish America (as well as in North America) and in some of its remoter villages is not unknown today; for these passive sodomites the word *bardaje* was everywhere used, derived from the Arabic *barday,* meaning "captive young man." Among the earliest New World chronicles were those of Fernandez de Oviedo, whose "Natural History of the Incas" appeared in 1526; because his writings were the first to appear in the vernacular, they gained rapid acceptance in Europe. Like others, he picked on Indian vices more than virtues, in particular drug addiction, suicide, cannibalism, and above all, "unnatural" intercourse. To quote from his *General History of the Indians,* published in 1536:

> . . . In many parts of Tierra Firme the Indians are sodomites. Very common among the Indians in many parts is the nefarious sin against nature even in public. The Indians who are headmen or principal who sin in this way have youths with whom they use this accursed sin, and those consenting youths as soon as they fall into this guilt wear *naguas* (skirts) like women . . . and they wear strings of beads and bracelets and the other things used by women as adornment; and they do

not exercise in the use of weapons, nor do anything proper to men, but they occupy themselves in the usual chores of the house such as to sweep and wash and other things customary for women.

The same author castigates sodomy in the harshest terms, even when committed with a female partner:

> . . . The chief Behechio had thirty wives of his own, and not only for the use of copulation which married men usually have with their women, but for other bestial and nefarious sins; because the chief Goacanagarí had certain women with whom he copulated in the manner vipers do it. . . . However, much worse than snakes were those who did such things, because nature does not provide vipers with another manner of engendering, and they are forced to such action. . . . if this king of chief Goacanagarí carries that reputation, it is clear that he was not the only in that nefarious and filthy crime; because the common people (and even the whole kingdom) soon try to follow. . . .

Oviedo further insisted that in Hispaniola and other islands a favorite male adornment depicted a man mounted on another man. He found one of these trinkets in the port of Santa Marta in Colombia and smashed it in pieces. He does not indicate how he could tell whether the passive partner was a man or a woman, something that is seldom clear in the countless Peruvian illustrations of sodomy. Oviedo concurs with Peter Martyr and others in concluding that the custom was most prevalent among the upper classes and that a particular type of bardaje, males in female dress, was socially accepted. His conclusions, though disputed by certain writers of his time, such as Bishop Las Casas, have on the whole been confirmed by later and more objective reports, though his assertion that sodomy was the sole cause of syphilis may be more open to doubt.

Another early chronicler, Lopez de Gomara, wrote in the same vein: Not only did he find men dressed as women in Panama, but also in present-day Colombia and Venezuela. The Spaniards, faced with the unfailing presence of bardajes among peoples whose souls they sought to save, turned away in disgust. It never even came to their notice that in the eyes of their own people the bardaje was as much saint as sinner, often treated with the profoundest respect. If they could lay their hands on these transvestites, they simply threw them to the dogs. They were not concerned as to how boys became bardajes or what rites accompanied the change, details provided by later accounts.

The Peoples of the Plains

In contrast to Spanish America and Brazil, accounts of the sex life of the North American Indians mainly derive from eighteenth- and nineteenth-century writers, who were close observers of customs that in some cases survived into the twentieth century. Moreover, these observers were less obsessed with transsexuals and also .wrote on such subjects as marriage, divorce, and premarital intercourse.

Nevertheless, like the Spaniards, they never ceased to wonder at the ubiquitous bardajes—known by a variety of names—together with other forms of institutionalized homosexuality, which varied from tribe to tribe. Their surprise might have been less intense had they been more familiar with certain peoples of other continents. Most significant in this respect are descriptions of the precise equivalents of the bardajes among the Chukchis who inhabit the northeastern tip of Siberia that lies nearest to America. Accordingly, those who stayed behind in this cheerless waste shared the custom with those who crossed the land bridge into the New World; hence, if the early migrants (say, fifty thousand years ago) brought with them this practice, it might well date from the very dawn of the era of *Homo sapiens.* Just as in so many North American tribes, a Chukchi might in early youth be smitten in his dreams with the desire to become a female and would adopt the dress and pursuits of women; not uncommonly a Chukchi shaman would have both a bardaje wife and also a female spouse, with whom he had ordinary heterosexual coitus. A peculiar habit was the use by women of an artificial penis made of the large calf muscle of a reindeer. Among the Kamchatkas, of the Kamchatka Peninsula farther to the south, there were many male transvestites, dressed as females; some rose to be shamans and would perform a curious rite in which they pretended to give birth to children—another custom that, as we shall see, was widespread in the Americas.

Renowned American anthropologist A. L. Kroeber, who wrote sparingly on sex, nonetheless stressed that transsexual homosexuals, whom he calls perverts, had a recognized status among all North American tribes and this status often conferred privileges, such as the right of preparing the dead for burial or cremation. A German scholar, Adolf Tullman, gives a list of peoples who accepted the presence of some form of bardajes; the list is so long as to be almost a roll call of the tribes of North America. These bardajes everywhere had a different name; among the Zunis of the Las Vegas region they were called *la'-mana;* a report written in 1916 states that only three la'mana were still living, though a man who was then seventy years old remembered a time when there were still nine. Among the Crow Indians of Indiana they were called *bote,* meaning literally "not men, not women." Five bote survived until 1899; they cultivated female voices and gestures and lived in the women's quarters. Among the Navaho of New Mexico, bardajes were called *nadle;* they were held in great respect, were thought to bring good luck, and often were rich. In the original legendary battle between men and women, the men had won only because the nadle took their side and tipped the scales in their favor.

The institution was sanctified by countless myths. The first appearance of a Zuni male in female attire occurred when their god Chaakwena was captured by another tribe and was made to dress as a woman. The Sioux of Kansas had another colorful legend: The greatest warrior of his time returned from a victorious campaign; on his first night at home he dreamed that the Great Spirit had visited him and told him to give up war and become like a woman. The next morning he summoned his family and made known his decision to adopt this form of life, from which no one could dissuade him.

Mohave Morals

Among North American Indians whose sex life has been most closely studied are the Mohaves, living on both banks of the

Colorado River between Needles, California, and Parker, Arizona. Based on fieldwork in 1931–32, psychiatrist George Devereux described the mores of this group in his doctoral thesis and thereafter in a whole series of articles published in the 1950s and 1960s in psychiatric journals. His conclusions are based on the recollections of old people who remembered the customs of the past; his data concur in general with those of A. L. Kroeber's *Handbook of the Indians of California,* published in 1953.

The astonishing range of Mohave sexual options makes today's California teenagers seem almost hidebound by comparison. They are listed by Devereux in an article "The Psychic Disturbances of an Indian Tribe" published in 1961: "Mohave perversions include masturbation, mutual masturbation, fellatio, but not cunnilingus, anal intercourse, limited exhibitionism, limited voyeurism, group cohabitation, punitive mass rape, incest, male and female transvestitism and homosexuality, bestiality, and extreme obscenity of speech and gesture." In a much briefer list of peculiar traits not present, he includes sadism, masochism, and gerontophilia.

The easygoing Mohaves viewed sex as a source of pleasure, and the older people would press the young to enjoy themselves for as long as they could. Intercourse in general, sexual swear words, and obscene names were the subjects of endless ribald gossip and cheerful banter. Even bestiality was treated as a joke, and it was thought funny for a man to have intercourse in public with a donkey; even nowadays luckless calves and heifers are not immune from such advances.

All accounts agree that, while a form of marriage existed, the Mohaves were—and are—very promiscuous. Aphrodisiacs were regarded as superfluous, and even rape, except for mass rape, was a meaningless concept, since the women were so ready to oblige; for a man to press a drunken female into having intercourse did not rank as rape, since those who imbibed freely were supposed to be aware of what might be in store for them. Prostitution, except with white men, was unknown. A rare exception to this rule was a lesbian shaman Saboykwisa, who was notoriously anxious to provide a good living for her "wives" and prostituted herself for money, though she was already richer than most members of the tribe.

Women fornicated with whites solely to raise money in the days of the mining camps, but this has now virtually ceased. The usual price was twenty-five cents. In the era of the covered wagon, the whites often balked at this princely fee, and a man or a boy would be sent with the Mohave woman to enforce payment; admittedly she did not have to give much in return for her money, since by Mohave standards coitus was quickly over with whites, whom they despised for linking sexual favors with money or gifts.

The Mohaves favored suggestive names, about 20 percent of which were overtly sexual. The two sexes were invariably confused; a man might call himself "Charcoal Vagina" and the woman would retaliate by taking the name "Charcoal Testicles." "Copulates Incessantly" was the name of a very old and puritanical shaman, also known as "Whiskey Mouth," and a man might call himself "Twenty-five-cent Vagina" or "Got Pregnant in the West" as a slur on those women who went off and offered themselves to whites in Los Angeles. "Pound His Penis" implied homosexual tendencies, since supposedly transvestites would like to pound their genitals, making them go inside the body and look more like vulva. Other colorful names were "Vagina Full with Fleas" and "Rotten Rectum."

In such a permissive society, marriage was a loose arrangement that could be dissolved at will by either party. Only the great hunters and warriors of the past could afford more than one wife, and where there were several spouses, none of them was head wife. Jealousy was treated as a vice, and not much stress was laid on fidelity. The story is told of a husband who found his wife with another man. When his white employer asked him why he did not shoot her, he replied that she was not worth a cartridge.

In contrast to such easygoing ways, the attitude to illegitimate offspring was pitiless. Children known to have been born out of wedlock were buried alive, a treatment thought to return them to the womb of earth. To get rid of these unwanted creatures, abortion was practiced, either by the effective if brutal method of strangling the fetus in the womb, or by stamping repeatedly upon the mother's stomach. Certain other prohibitions were enforced, such as a ban on intercourse during funeral ceremonies. Orgies and group promiscuity, far from being ceremonial, as among many peoples, were merely provoked by drinking. Drunken women were abused seriatim by a quickly gathered group of males, who would sometimes even dispatch messengers to call for reinforcements.

On one such occasion a husband, though quite drunk, fought off other men who each in turn were submitting his wife to anal intercourse. He conceded that they had a perfect right to indulge in vaginal abuse but claimed that her rectum was his exclusive preserve. Mohave men did not like the smell of women, in particular of their genitalia, and this aversion seems to have led to a kind of anal fixation, of which the homosexual implications will be described later. The smell of the vagina was compared to that of fish, a taunt that annoyed the women, who even fought with men who teased them on this score. As a consequence, cunnilingus was unknown, though occasionally in group intercourse a man would be forced face downward onto a female's vagina, an act that supposedly was apt to cause blindness. Women, on the contrary, liked the smell of males, and fellatio was much practiced.

Mohave aversion to the true vagina led Devereux to write of a "vaginalization" of the anus among the Mohaves. He insists that the anal stage in their psycho-sexual development was basic to character formation. The stage began early in life, since parents took a lenient attitude to infantile anality; the psychiatrist even considers that the act of flinging mud at each other was also symbolic of anal-erotic practices, since the penis became associated with feces. The women as a whole, far from resenting such male predilections, regarded anal intercourse not merely as a means of birth control but also as a positive favor. Even young girls would submit to male partners in this way, before they had been deflowered; the rectum was thought to be larger than the vagina between the ages of ten and fourteen.

The proven capacity of Mohave males to achieve orgasm at a very tender age—according to most accounts when they were six years old—could hardly be satisfied by anal erotics, practiced either with females or with other males, which belonged more to a later stage in their development. Masturbation was frequent, notwithstanding certain reports that the wealth of other outlets made it superfluous. Like other Mohave customs, onanism was sanctioned by myth, and the god Matavilye himself recommended that girls should masturbate both themselves and each other; masturbation, often by older men, played an important role in the preparation of future female shamans. The god further ordained that both boys and girls should build small mounds of soft earth; the boys should thrust their members into such mounds, while the girls should rub their genitalia against them. Girls often also made use of bananas; one tribal informant recalled an unfortunate case when the banana broke in two, and the girl had to be taken to the hospital to have the second half removed from her vagina.

Mohaves shared with neighboring tribes the myth of Coyote the Trickster, who spent an entire day having intercourse with his father's nephew, his cousin in the male line. Coyote sought other pleasures, apart from those of incest with his own family. He was very proud of his huge penis and of its stupendous feats; he claimed he could sling it across the Colorado River and copulate with a woman standing on the opposite bank. Such were its dimensions that women with whom he had intercourse invariably died; if he saw "cocky" men swimming in the river, he would copulate anally with them until they also succumbed—he even killed his own daughter when he had intercourse with her while both swam in the river together.

In spite of the god's errant ways, incest taboos were a matter of fairly constant concern. Mohaves jokingly compared incest, in the form of relations with one's own daughter, to the behavior of a man who married a very young girl and then carried her around on his back and himself attended to most of the household chores. During coitus, a man was not supposed to kiss the woman's breast, because the act resembled sucking and thus by implication incest between mother and son. True incest, in spite of rules that also applied to cousins, was not unknown but often led to censure and remorse. In certain cases, an odd stratagem was used: If a boy wanted to marry his cousin, a horse would be killed and mourned for, as though it were the boy. The latter, having thus "died" and been "reborn," was no longer regarded as a relative of the girl and could marry her. Another strange belief was held: If an individual, with the help of a sorcerer, could use black magic to kill a loved one, sexual favors could properly be demanded of the soul of that person, even in cases where the taboos on incest would apply to the living.

Alyha

Among the Mohaves addicted to anal eroticism the *bardaje* tradition was strong, and more data on the accompanying *bardaje* ritual survive than for most other tribes that must have practiced similar rites. The Mohaves recognized only one kind of homosexual: the male transvestite taking on the woman's role in intercourse and known by the term *alyha,* and female transvestites playing the male part and called *hwames.* Their partners were not regarded as homosexuals. The Mohave creation myth blessed the transvestite state, adopted only after an elaborate ceremony. Transvestism had been foretold and approved by the god Matavilye; on his deathbed, when the people were all around him, he told them that some of their lives would be different and that some among them would turn into transvestites.

Nahwera, a very old singer, was said to be the last person alive to remember the initiation songs for alyhas and hwames. He and other informants, none of whom were themselves alyhas, told how, according to legend, "from the very beginning of the world it was meant that there should be homosexuals, just as it was ordained that there should be shamans. They were intended for that purpose. While their mothers are pregnant, they will have dreams forecasting the anatomic sex of their child . . . the dreams of their mothers will convey certain hints of the homosexual leanings of their future child." For several years after birth such tendencies would remain hidden, but they would come to the fore before puberty. If there is a desire in a child's heart to become a transvestite, it then begins to act different, casting away toys and even clothes appropriate to its sex. A boy thus affected will pick up dolls and toy with them just like a girl. He refuses to wear a breechclout and demands a skirt. He watches the womans' gambling game, called the Utah-game, as if he were under a spell. A girl in a parallel situation will spurn dolls and play with bows and arrows.

Devereux obtained three good versions of the transvestite initiation rites, accounts that differed only in matters of detail. When the child was about ten years old, its relatives would notice its strange ways and begin to plan the decisive step. In the case of a boy, they prepared in secret his female apparel, since the ceremony was supposed to take him by surprise. Word was sent to various settlements, inviting people to attend. The time and place were set by his parents, and if he acted as expected, he became an initiated homosexual. If not, the gathering scattered, to the relief of all concerned.

As part of the ritual, a singer drew a circle into which the boy was led by two women, usually his mother and maternal grandmother. If he was willing to remain standing in the center of the circle, it was almost certain that he would go through with the ceremony. He would then join with fervor in the prescribed singing and dancing, and at the end of the fourth song, he was proclaimed to be an alyha. The women then took him down to the Colorado River, and after a bath he received his skirt. The same procedure was followed for the female hwame, who then donned a breech clout. The songs themselves, when translated into English, are little more than a confused jumble of words; the gist of the first of them can be condensed into the sentence "This transvestite fellow is now happy as a bug because he got a skirt." In another version of the rite, two women would paint the boy's face white and after four days he was painted again, before he became an alyha.

New transvestites were henceforth obliged to duplicate with precision the behavior patterns of the opposite sex; this point was crucial, since they were duty-bound to make "normal" individuals of their anatomic sex feel toward them as though they truly belonged to their adopted sex. They also assumed a name befitting the opposite sex and would resent being called by their former names.

The alyha, once initiated, was considered ripe for marriage to another man, usually a fairly prominent member of the tribe.

But the match was not arranged as for ordinary girls, and suitors did not visit the house of his parents. Courting took place at gatherings attended by widows, divorcées, and other women. At dances even boys who had no intention of marrying an alyha flirted with them as if they were women. Once married, the alyhas made excellent wives and the hwames became industrious husbands. Thus the assurance of a well-kept home was an inducement to marry an alyha. Hwames, however, faced special problems. They might at times resort to violence and might pick up a hunting bow to attack the seducer of their wife. Nonetheless, being women in the physical sense, they were at a disadvantage if driven to violence to protect their spouses from insult or assault. A hwame's wife was often fair game, because no one feared her anatomically female husband; even the willingness of *hwames* to work hard was a poor consolation to their wives, who were apt to be teased mercilessly.

As part of their adopted role, transvestites not only behaved as members of the opposite sex but also claimed its physical traits. Alyhas were adamant that their penis was really a clitoris and their anus a vagina, and the hwames hotly resented any reference to their vulvae. Such resentment often led to mockery, but if anyone teased an alyha, all ladylike pretenses were cast aside, and he was apt to be mauled severely. Intercourse with an alyha wife was surrounded by an etiquette of its own. Kuwal, who had several alyha wives, had both rectal and oral intercourse with them but remarked that if you copulated rectally too often, the alyha would get hemorrhoids. A man could play with the alyha's penis when it was flaccid, but Kuwal stated he would never touch his wife's member when it was erect; he would not dare to do so for fear of being killed.

Alyha wives would scratch themselves with sticks between the legs to feign menstruation. They even indulged in sham pregnancies. When they decided to become "pregnant," they ceased to fake menstruation and followed the usual taboos even more strictly than real women. They publicly boasted of their condition and ignored the jeers provoked by this pretense. As time went by, they would stuff rags and bark under their skirts in increasing quantities to make their abdomen swell. Finally, they pretended to suffer from labor pains, went into the bush, and defecated like a woman sitting over a hole. They solemnly buried the feces as if they were a dead infant and then would go home, pretending that their child had been stillborn. After their return, they would wail pitifully for the imaginary child.

Notwithstanding a tendency to occasional violence, the alyhas were basically peaceable. They were not expected to take part in tribal raids, in which their only task was to help the women to prepare the welcome feast for the returning warriors. They even joined with the women in taunting those ordinary males who did not go to war.

Far from occupying an inferior role in society, the transvestites were not merely accepted, they were also credited with supernatural powers. Alyhas were believed to cure venereal diseases and to be especially lucky at gambling. Hwames often were powerful shamans. In this respect the Mohaves were not unique, and some other California tribes went even farther in honoring transvestites. Among the Yuroks, situated along the Klamath River in northern California, about one in a hundred of the men preferred the life and dress of a woman; these men were called *wergem*, and their adopted status was not merely a calling but also a career, since many came to be revered as shamans. Among the Yokuts of the San Joachin Valley, apart from those of the chief and the herald, only two other offices were held for life, and these were reserved for transvestites. One was the clown, *youdanchihiauta*, and the other a kind of joker, *yauelmani hibetits*, who wore a mask at sacred ceremonies, spoke indecently, and acted nonsensically. The Yokuts accorded their male transvestites one of the highest honors in a tribal society: They alone could handle corpses and prepare the dead for burial or cremation. Both at funerals and at annual mourning ceremonies, they conducted the singing and led the dancing.

The approach of the Mohaves and their neighbors was not lacking in common sense, since it served to relieve tensions by depriving modes of atypical behavior of the glamor of secrecy and the fear of retribution. They thereby created, in psychiatric terms, "an abscess of fixation" by localizing the anomaly in a small area of the body social. But aside from practical considerations, their versions of the institution of bardaje had a more profound significance, both social and religious, bound up with their view of the visible world as a kind of dream. They conceived of life as preordained by their shamans' dreams and visions; these, suitably interpreted in the light of Mohave mythology, laid down the exact course of future events. The shaman supposedly had his first dream in the prenatal stage; in later life he came to remember it and to receive its message anew. Nonshamans also could have dreams in the fetal stage that could change not only an embryo's character but also its sexual proclivities. The transvestite state was not, therefore, a mere concession to one of the facts of life. Already blessed by their creator god, it was a product of the conviction that a person's life was predestined by dreams.

The True Hermaphrodite

Accounts of the lives of the Mohave transexuals, and of the underlying mythology, reveal that while they bore their share of tribal chores, they were treated with respect and at times with awe. The same tendency was just as pronounced elsewhere: The eighteenth-century Illinois called their bardajes to council meetings and on matters of any import sought their advice. The Sioux gave an annual feast in their honor and regarded them as sacred beings. The belief that the androgynous, or third sex, is endowed with special powers was by no means confined to America. Among the ancient Scandinavians transsexuals became powerful sorcerers. Traces of the notion reappear in higher civilizations; the three great gods of India at times act as females or display organs that are part female; the ancient Greeks carved countless statutes of hermaphrodites, half man and half woman, and in Greek legend change of sex is not uncommon.

This strange aspect of human sexuality, the cult of the androgynous, is hard to explain. Psychiatrists may reveal man's bisexual nature but not its implications for religion. People often tend to suppose that in real life individuals do not exist who are truly half man and half woman and that such beings, honored in myths and legends, are figments of the imagination, comparable with that fabulous beast, the unicorn. Such suppositions are unfounded, since modern medicine recognizes a variety of human types, born neither wholly male nor wholly female, though such cases are fairly rare. A few such conditions deserve mention: One is called hypospadias. Its victims have incompletely formed male genitals but at puberty tend to grow female breasts. The development of the penis is never complete (as we have seen in connection with circumcision), and the skin does not wrap properly around the undersized organ. This condition can nowadays be remedied surgically. Nonetheless, sufferers from hypospadias can hardly be considered truly male, and sometimes doctors don't know whether to classify a hypospadial hermaphrodite infant as male or as female, since the penis sometimes is so small as to be more like a clitoris.

In contrast to the semimasculine hypospadiacs who develop female traits, certain individuals, perhaps the prototype of the legendary Amazons, are positively feminine in the chromosomal sense but their adrenal cortex does not function properly and releases a product that acts like androgen, the male sex hormone. In these individuals, known as adrenogenital females, the external genitals then become masculinized and in a few cases the process is carried so far as to produce a perfectly normal-looking penis and scrotum on persons who are essentially female, though, like the Amazons, they often developed a physique that was almost grotesquely masculine. Since 1950, however, it has been possible to control the androgenital tendency with cortisone.

In medical terminology, true hermaphrodites possess at birth both testicular and ovarian tissue. Such beings may have an ovary on one side of the body and a single testis on the other, or even one of each organ on both sides; in some cases their external genitalia look more like those of a male, and in others of a female. The internal organs also usually contain both male and female elements, the female elements on the side of the single ovary and the male on the side of the testis. These hermaphrodites usually grow up to conform to the way of life of the gender to which, somewhat arbitrarily, they were first assigned.

102

Certain other types of hermaphroditism exist, such as gynecomastia, when breasts grow spontaneously on an otherwise normal boy, due to a localized insensitivity to the androgen produced by his body. In yet another form, the external organs are completely masculine, but together with two testes, the internal organs include a uterus and fallopian tubes. The choice of sex for such individuals at birth is apt to cause problems unless full diagnostic tests are made. A tendency persists to assign babies with imperfect organs, such as those having what looks like either a large clitoris or an undersized penis, to the female sex. Consequently, statistics show that more hermaphrodites later request a change from living as a female to becoming a male, rather than the reverse.

This digression, serving to show that hermaphrodites, half man and half woman, do exist in real life, may help to explain the cult of the androgynous and the status of the transsexual in so many societies. Early religion was based on a terror of the unknown and instilled a fear, amounting to a fixation, of abnormal phenomena—say, an eclipse of the sun or the birth of an oddly formed being. Like dwarfs and certain other freaks, strange creatures with attributes of both sexes might easily become objects of veneration among primitive peoples, in whom they could inspire both love and fear. The reverence accorded by some tribes to male transsexuals was sanctified by myths; like so many others, these seem likely to have had some true-life origins, in the form of awesome beings who were real hermaphrodites, giving rise to traditions that conferred special status on ordinary transvestites.

Macho Mothers

The curious custom known as *couvade* shows that at times even American Indian heterosexual males were not averse to playing a female role. In many regions of America, at the birth of a child the father would take to his bed and behave exactly as though he and not his wife was the chief sufferer. Couvade was not unknown in the Old World. Poet and scientist Apollonius of Rhodes, in his *Argonautica,* describes the equivalent of couvade in 200 B.C. among Scythians living on the eastern shores of the Black Sea. Marco Polo found a modified form in Turkestan, and it was also practiced by the Dravidians of southern India, where it has long since died out; it is absent in Africa and in Oceania. Couvade was, however, far more universal in pre-Columbian America, where it also survived much longer, and well-documented reports bear witness to its existence throughout the length and breadth of the Americas, from northwestern Canada down to Patagonia in the extreme South. Many such accounts were written by missionaries in the seventeenth and eighteenth centuries, though even today it is not altogether extinct in the Amazon jungle.

In the most typical cases, the husband remains in his hammock and pretends to be lying-in, simulating the groans and contortions of labor pains and sometimes even putting on his wife's clothes. While in bed, he is pampered and fed with dainties as he nurses the newborn infant; in some instances (as, for instance, among certain tribes of Brazil) he receives congratulations and even gifts from friends and relations; in others he is shut up in solitary confinement.

On many Caribbean islands the unfortunate mother would be promptly sent back to work while the father reclined in his hammock, as though he were sick, and followed a rigorous course of dieting. The other women of the house would respectfully attend the husband and compliment him on the safe delivery of the infant, while the poor mother went about her household chores and received no special favors. Among the Jivaros of Ecuador the woman's fate was even harsher: She had to undergo the pangs of childbirth outside the home, exposed to the elements, while her husband reclined indoors, coddling himself and dieting for some days. In Guyana, on the other hand, the wife and husband would receive the same treatment: Neither could bathe, work, or eat anything except a watery gruel of cassava meal; in conformity with another quaint taboo, the husband must not scratch himself with his fingernails but instead could use a specially provided splinter from a palm tree.

Stories of fathers who actually weaned their children are less well attested, though in the Echo Médicale des Cevennes for 1901, a Dr. E. Mazel describes a man who could make a stream of milk flow from his breast by applying pressure. In 1798 Dr. Juan Castelar told before the Medical Faculty of Madrid the story of a wife who had given birth to twins but could produce little milk; however, by dint of simulated sucking by the children, the breast of her husband, a peasant named Lozano, reportedly began to secrete milk.

The origins of couvade, like other customs such as circumcision and the incest taboo, remain a mystery. Many anthropologists think it was a product of the matriarchal system at the moment when fathers first began to assert their rights to parenthood (in places such as the Trobiand Islands, where the father's role was incidental, there was no couvade). At a time when the biological role of the father was not recognized, his surest claim to be recognized as a parent was to act the part of a second or substitute mother. By simulating childbirth, the father makes himself inseparable from the child over which he would otherwise have few rights.

Such views of couvade are not lacking in logic, but perhaps are oversimplified. Psychiatrists are increasingly aware of a not uncommon wish on the part of boys to bear children; some find among their male patients as a whole an intense and persistent envy of the female ability to reproduce. As we have seen, male envy of females is less often discussed in psychoanalytic writing than the reverse. For psychiatrists, a very human characteristic is a feeling of insecurity and a dissatisfaction of both boys and girls with their own sexual condition. Such feelings seem to have been especially marked among the American Indians and are evident both in the homosexual institution bardaje and in the heterosexual rite couvade.

The Ascetic Aztecs

Higher civilization first began to appear in Mexico and Peru in about 1500 B.C. From coastal Peru, the Moche erotic pottery tells much about sex life in the early centuries of the Christian era; however, little comparable evidence from that era exists for

Mexico. In contrast, copious data show that not only the Incas of Peru but also their contemporaries the Aztecs, who ruled much of Mexico in the last century before the Conquest, were far from sharing the easygoing attitudes to sex of, say, the Mohaves or the Caribs.

In this respect, Incas and Aztecs may be compared with the early empires of the Old World; as we shall see in the next chapter, they opposed intercourse out of wedlock and subjected the love life of their subjects to much closer control than any tribal chiefdom. But the New World empires differed from those of the Old in that such systems of control, while they were strictly applied to the citizens of their own capitals, Tenochtitlán and Cuzco, and to neighboring cities, were more loosely observed in most conquered regions, where sexual behavior is more akin to that of Indian tribal life; for instance, the Spaniards complained of the presence of bardajes in Aztec-controlled lands but found none in the capital. Accordingly, instead of referring to the empires of the New World in later chapters, which deal with those of the Old, I prefer to anticipate events and to consider briefly at this stage their code of sexual behavior, observed more in their capital cities than in the vast expanses of America as a whole. The customs of the centers of New World civilization are hard to treat separately from those of outlying places, since they are intermingled in the accounts of the conquistadors, who in their sweeping advance encountered a medley of diverse peoples.

The Aztecs conquered vast tracts of present-day Mexico but left the peoples of this empire largely to their own devices under the aegis of their former rulers, on condition that they paid tribute. Hernán Cortés and his exiguous force spent some months on the Caribbean coast before pressing inland toward the heart of the empire. Among the coastal peoples the Spaniards were appalled by their addicton to those very "vices" so typical of tribal Indians already found by Columbus, in particular the presence of bardajes. Such accounts harp on sodomy, referring to anal intercourse both between two males and between male and female. Cortés himself made the earliest reference to this Indian predilection in his first letter to Emperor

Charles V. Cortés reports that he had been informed on good authority that the people of the region were all sodomites and practiced this "abominable sin."

Bernal Díaz del Castillo, whose account of the Conquest, recorded many years later, is spellbinding but not always accurate, writes more specifically of the subjects of the famous fat chief of the coastal town of Zempoala, where Cortés stayed for some time; he tells how among the chief's subjects there were boys dressed as girls and states that when the chief presented his Spanish guests with girls, they had to be innocent of the sin of sodomy. The passage is silent about Spanish ways of checking the girls' freedom from this taint, nor does he reveal whether the ruler ever resorted to the obvious ruse of passing off bardajes on his guests as girls.

Fray Juan de Torquemada, in writing of Guatemala, which shared the same Middle American culture, tells a story of how in the dim past the devil had appeared to the natives and convinced them that homosexual sodomy was no sin; following this visitation, fathers would give boys to their sons as wives (transvestism has not altogether vanished today from the remoter parts of Guatemala). Torquemada, however, at least conceded that the Old World was scarcely better than the New and reminds his readers that Emperor Hadrian caused his lover to be worshiped as a god, that the Greek philosophers each had their boyfriend *(mozo)*, and that even the French were not immune from such vices.

Another of Cortés' soldiers, known as the "anonymous conqueror," relates that in Pánuco, in the North of the present-day state of Veracruz, the people were not only sodomites but also had a cult of the human phallus. However, unlike in Peru, few archaeological pieces in Mexico bear witness to a phallic cult in earlier times. Those that exist come more from the Colima region on the Pacific Coast than from the Caribbean littoral.

Whatever might have happened farther afield, on the people of their capital of Tenochtitlán and on those of nearby cities, the Aztecs imposed rules that were ostensibly puritanical and aimed to enforce the sanctity of family life. Polygamy was permitted, but only to the nobles. Fray Bernardino de Sahagún, whose twelve volumes form a compendium of every conceivable aspect of Aztec civilization, quotes a whole series of standard homilies used to define civic virtues, as applied to both ruler and ruled. One such homily is a formal address prescribing a form of words recommended for a father in addressing his son when telling him the facts of life, in terms that might have appealed to middle-class parents in nineteenth-century England. The father should impress the need for temperance in all things on his offspring, who must be cautioned not to throw himself at women like a dog; the gods had designated one woman for the use of each man. Any form of premarital sex is cursed as likely to cause immediate sickness, and in the longer run to produce premature wrinkles. Those who indulge in sexual relations before marriage will find that they are later unable to satisfy their wives; they will be like a maguey cactus that still appears to flourish but that has already lost its juice (out of the juice of the maguey was made the sacred beverage, pulque); finding that her husband has impaired his virility in previous adventures, a wife will then be driven to seek other lovers.

Had no alternative options been available to the boy, such imprecations would have been pointless. However, the existence of prostitution and even of pederasty is confirmed at length by Sahagún in another volume. In one passage he describes the "public women" who sell their bodies from early youth and who are totally shameless:

> Of the public women. The whore is a public woman and is like this: she goes about selling her body, starting since young and does not leave it when old, she goes drunk and loose, she is beautiful and polished, and under this without shame; and gives herself to any man, and sells her body, because she is very lewd, dirty and without shame, talkative and very vicious in the carnal act. . . . She has the habit of calling the people; to make gestures, to turn an eye on men, to talk winking the eye, to call with her hand, to move the eye in an arch, to go laughing for everyone, to pick up the one she likes best, and to be wanted she deceives the young men, or youths, and she wants to be well paid, and she goes procuring these for those and selling other women.

According to Sahagún, Aztec laws against adultery were draconian; women who were unfaithful and had bastard children are described as traitresses. One of his illustrations depicts the stoning of an adulterous couple. Another portrays a hermaphrodite female, on whom he also comments; in the English translation of the sonorous but repetitive phrases of the Nahuatl language the passage reads as follows: "The hermaphrodite is a detestable woman, a woman who has a penis, a virile arrow, testes; who takes female companions, female friends; who provides herself with young women, who has young women. She has man's body, man's build, man's speech. She goes about like a man. She is bearded, she has fine body hairs, she has course body hairs . . . she never desires a husband. She hates, detests men exceedingly; she scandalizes."

Sahagún blasts the male counterpart of such beings in strident tones: "The sodomite is an effeminate—a defilement, a corruption, a filth; a taster of filth, revolting, perverse, full of affliction. He merits laughter, ridicule, mockery; he is detestable, nauseating. Disgusting, he makes one acutely sick. Womanish, playing the part of a woman, he merits being committed to the flames, burned, consumed by fire."

The account suggests that the ascetic Aztec, unlike most American Indians, disapproved of such people, but also that he nonetheless tolerated their presence as a necessary evil, to a degree unthinkable in Spain. The pious friar, himself scandalized by these aberrant ways, even credits the Aztecs with a belief that those young children were especially blessed who died before they could witness such enormities and that they would go straight to the presence of god, a sentiment reflecting Catholic doctrine more than native religion.

Peruvian Perversions

In contrast to Mexico, ample data on aspects of Peruvian sex life survive from an era long before the Spanish Conquest. The Moche civilization, which flourished on the northern part of the Peruvian coastline during the first seven centuries of our era, is renowned for the genius of its potters. These Moche vessels, of which thousands exist today, are so lifelike as to form a kind of literature in clay, rich in descriptive detail of the people's temples, houses, animals, boats, weapons, clothes, and even their infirmities. Many pots are molded to portray couples copulating in an obviously ritual context. In the millennium before the Moche period, erotic scenes are much less frequent and the gods usually are presented as sexless or hermaphrodite, though from 400 B.C. onward, ceramic art was already beginning to depict erotic behavior.

In the Moche pottery a bizarre range of activities is shown, mainly between men and women but occasionally involving two males; notable, however, by its absence is "normal" or face-to-face intercourse between male and female. Because this art abounds in other variants, such as fellatio and particularly anal intercourse, it was until recent times regarded as degenerate and perverse, though many pieces could even then be viewed with special permission in the Larco Hoyle Museum in Lima. Peruvian scholar A. Poznansky ruefully observed in 1925 that in Moche ceramics, "not one single way of abnormally performing the *libido sexualis* was absent"; as a consequence, he described them as "horrifying." Clay models of bestiality provoked even greater rage, and the ratio of pieces devoted to that subject were simply ignored. The greatest of all Peruvian archaeologists, Julio Tello, admitted that in the early part of the century, in a misguided attempt to obliterate such a stain on the nation's reputation, many had been destroyed; Tello confesses that its frequent portrayal in Moche art implied a widespread habit of zooerasty with llamas; few such pieces survive.

Not only the more standard forms of coitus but also orthodox love caresses are equally absent, unless one includes a few scenes in which a female embraces a skeleton. About 22 percent of the Moche pieces represent genital handling and caressing, and in almost every case the woman touches or masturbates the erect male organ; in no instance is self-masturbation portrayed. In all, eight coital positions have been identified, including variants in which the passive partner either lies on one side with the active partner behind, lies face downward, kneels, stands, or sits. Coitus, even between man and woman, is nearly always anal. In one curious scene, a man sodomizes a girl who lies on her face between her two parents and pretends to be asleep. Invariably, the features of the male or active partner in coitus are impassive, revealing not the faintest hint of enjoyment; the faces of men masturbated by women are grim rather than gleeful. In numerous specimens devoted to oral contact, mainly fellatio performed by women on men, the expressions are equally blank. A special category of jar is made to contain water. The spout takes the form of an erect penis, from which the water is drunk, as if performing an act of fellatio.

Rafael Larco Hoyle, who amassed the largest collection of these pieces, agreed that in 95 percent of all cases, heterosexual intercourse took place anally. Nonetheless, their collector, in defense of his country's honor, hotly denied that any Moche pots depicted homosexual intercourse, notwithstanding the endless accounts by Spaniards of such practices in sixteenth-century Peru. A large number of jars showing anal coitus admittedly indicate that the passive partner is female, in some cases because the vulva can be seen, in others by the feminine coiffure or by some particular garment; clothing and coiffure are, however, most unreliable guides in a region later reported as infested with males dressed as females. Not until 1974, when material in the Peruvian National Museum of Anthropology was reexamined, was a piece discovered that plainly concerns sodomy between two males, both of whose genitals can be seen. Another curious pot shows a true hermaphrodite equipped with both penis and vulva, into which he vainly tries to insert the penis, situated below. In another case a hermaphrodite, also possessing both penis and vulva, is about to amputate the penis with a knife.

Two more overtly homosexual pieces are briefly described by Peruvian archaeologist Federico Kaufmann Doig in his book on sex life in ancient Peru. However, no one had dealt in any detail with the homoerotic aspect of Moche art until anthropologist Manuel Arboleda read a paper on the subject at the forty-third Congress of Americanists in Vancouver in 1979. Using a large sample of seven hundred specimens, he drew attention to several, in addition to others already identified, that were clearly homosexual scenes. In one of these one cannot see the genitals of the passive partner, but he wears a catskin headdress and a serpent bell, two adornments that, as Arboleda showed, are exclusive to males, whether in an erotic or a nonerotic context; other scholars have been misled into thinking that the passive partner was female on the sole grounds of a typically feminine hair style. A combination of male and female dress and coiffure may derive from a long tradition of intercourse with *bardajes,* whose accouterments in later times were certainly not always wholly female. Arboleda also throws more light on some of the strangest ceramic scenes of copulation between two skeletal figures, or between one skeleton and one flesh-covered being. These skeletal figures, known as *carcanchas,* are a pervasive element in early Peruvian religious art, and their presence in such acts underlines the symbolic content of Moche erotica in the guise of a message that in the world of the dead a form of life continued; the skeletal carcanchas, since they are at times shown in contact with ordinary beings, did not suffer their presence to be ignored in the world of the living.

Certain pots even show a kind of orgy between a group of skeletal individuals; in others, carcanchas masturbate in couples. One such fleshless figure holds a living baby during the act, while another plays the flute. One unique specimen portrays a kind of erotic ballet in the world of the dead; four dancing skeletons look upward to a fifth masturbating figure at the moment in which he ejaculates. A few of these scenes are homoerotic; in one of them a nude male carcancha lies behind a fully clothed individual; the testicles of the former are visible, while the headdress and bodily adornment of the latter are typically male. Another scene involves two carcanchas, both of whom wear male breechclouts though their genitals cannot be seen.

The religious background to this Moche art is confirmed by scenes that depict two deities in acts of anal intercourse. The tradition survived into later times, and a vessel from the Moche region but belonging to the Chimu culture, contemporary with the Inca, shows a huge bird, a common religious emblem, having anal intercourse with a human being; in another piece from this period, a man copulates with an agglomeration of potatoes in the form of a woman, clearly a symbolic fertility rite, since the potato was the main element in the native diet.

The Incas

Like the Aztecs, the Incas of Peru had puritanical leanings not shared by all the subjects of their empire. The laws against incest were particularly severe: For intercourse with his daughter, a man would be flung over a precipice; the crime, but apparently not the punishment, was even more hideous if she was a virgin and consented to the act. If a woman fornicated with her son, both were to be killed in the same way. If a man had intercourse with the sister of his father or mother, the couple were both to be hanged or stoned, a penalty even applied to relations between cousins in the second degree. Sodomy was equally proscribed, and sodomites were to be dragged through the streets, hanged, and then burned with all their clothes.

By a peculiar paradox, the Inca rulers' implacable ban on incest among their subjects did not apply to themselves. According to chronicler Fray Juan de Torquemada, "There was a universal law in all the Kingdoms of Peru subject to the Inca kings, that nobody should marry his sister, cousin, aunt, or niece . . . but as who makes the law has the power to annul it, these lords and kings among themselves tolerate this and married as they pleased." The friar explains that the custom of royal incest probably was a survival from the time when the Inca tribe was a matriarchy and property passed in the female line. Moreover, as in ancient Egypt, the custom would have ensured that both parents of a new ruler were truly of royal blood.

Spanish lamentations about sodomy in the Inca Empire are even louder than their complaints about Mexico. Cieza de León (1520–54) was the first Spaniard to give an objective report on the subject, based on personal observation. He went to America when he was fifteen years old, played an important part in the subjection of the New World, and in 1541 wrote his *History of Peru.* His references to sodomy are numerous but reasonably balanced. For instance, in the region of the present-day city of Cali in Colombia, he denies that sodomy existed there, though he observed that the local nobles married their own nieces. However, farther down the coast, at Puerto Viejo in Ecuador, there were women in abundance, including many of great beauty; but their charms were lost on their menfolk, who flagrantly sodomized each other and even boasted of such acts.

> Farther inland, the situation was, if anything, worse: The devil has introduced this vice [sodomy] under a kind of cloak of sanctity, and in each important temple or house of worship they have a man or two, or more, depending on the idol, who go dressed in women's attire from the time they are children, and speak like them, and in manner, dress, and everything else imitate women. With these, almost like a rite and ceremony, on feast [days] and holidays, they have carnal, foul intercourse, especially the chiefs and headmen. I know this because I have punished two, one of them of the Indians of the highlands, who was in a temple, which they call *huaca*, for this purpose, in the province of the Conchucos, near the city of Huánuco, the other in the province of Chinca, where the Indians are subjects of his Majesty. And when I spoke to them of the evil they were doing, and upbraided them for the repulsiveness of the sin, they answered me that it was not their fault because from childhood they have been put there by the caciques to serve them in this cursed and abominable vice, and to act as priests and guard the temples of their idols. So what I deduced from this was that the devil held such sway in this land that, not satisfied with making them fall into so great sin, he made them believe that this vice was a kind of holiness and religion, to hold more power over them.

The Incas at times sought to stamp out sodomy among their subjects on the coast, but Cieza makes it clear that they met with scant success. The Spaniards were so scandalized by what they found that instructions for use in confessing Indian converts, approved by the Provisional Council in Lima in 1583, contained the following:

> Question 21. Have you committed the nefarious sin with another person?
> Question 22. Have you committed bestiality with some animal? (To women these questions must be adapted to their

persons. And none of the above questions may be asked except that expected to be done by the person under confession. In Quechua and Aymara language we must adapt in this commandment the words pertaining to male and to female) . . .

Special sermons circulated to impress upon the Indians the awful fate that awaited adulterers and, more particularly, sodomites, put matters very plainly:

Sermon XXIIII. Of the Sixth Commandment. In which it is taught how much adultery angers God and how he punishes it, and also how fornication with an unmarried woman, even on a single occasion is a deadly sin, and of the other manners of lewdness because of which God punishes the Indian nation . . . God punishes also this sin with diseases; what do you think is the *Bubas* malady but punishment for this sin? . . . Above all these sins is the sin we call nefarious and sodomy, which is for the man to sin with man, or with woman not in the natural way, and even above all these, to sin with beasts, such as ewes, bitches, or mares, which is the greatest abomination. If there is anyone among you who commits sodomy sinning with another man, or with a boy, or with a beast, let it be known that because of that fire brimstone fell from heaven and burnt the fine cities of Sodom and Gomorrah and left them in ashes. Let it be known that they carry the death penalty under the just laws of our Spanish kings. Let it be known that because of this the Holy Scriptures say that God destroys kingdoms and nations. Let it be known that the reason why God has allowed that you the Indians should be so afflicted and vexed by other nations is because of this vice (sodomy) that your ancestors had, and many among you still practice.

CHAPTER FIVE

Sex and Civilization

From Tribe to State

The higher civilizations of the world, whether in Egypt, China, or Mexico, were created by peoples who until then had followed a tribal way of life. The previous three chapters have dealt mainly with the sexual habits of a few of those societies that had never risen above that state; similar practices survived in many others, but accounts often are meager. Over countless millennia these peoples developed well-integrated patterns of sex life that are now vanishing; many now belong to Third World nations that outwardly conform to "Western" moral codes that the West itself now tends to set aside.

The factors that led to the birth of the first civilizations in Western and in Far Eastern Asia are complex and controversial and lie beyond the scope of this book. The passage from fiefs ruled by petty chiefs to states subject to great kings is not easy to trace, and no consensus exists among scholars as to how this happened. These higher civilizations originated in places where

117

people were living in settled villages and whose farming skills already yielded a surplus over daily needs, indispensable for the creation of a true state; they made pottery and wove textiles; they built for themselves simple homes and larger public buildings. Tribal chiefdoms, from which the world's first states emerged, were hardly exact replicas of those found thousands of years later by Renaissance Europeans, say, in West Africa or Brazil; nonetheless, their culture was in some ways comparable. Such practices as temple prostitution and large harems were inventions of higher civilization, but many other customs observed in the first true states, such as those of Mesopotamia, were a legacy from their tribal forebears, whose mores thus provide a point of departure for studying the sex life of the world's major cultures, including our own.

Marriage is one aspect of tribal life that inevitably reappears in all advanced societies and that merely defined the rules more precisely. Marriage, or pairing in some form, was already subject to strict regulation, and in certain chiefdoms one finds incipient polygamy. Even embryo harems existed, whose occupants had to work for their masters and were not yet condemned to a life of indolent luxury.

In some cases, what were taken by missionaries for native customs had been brought by Europeans. Before they came, prostitution hardly existed in black Africa, where girls were astonished when first offered beads or an old skirt for copulating with white strangers; no one had previously sought rewards for such an agreeable and commonplace act. Once established, harlotry then became rampant; in Uganda mothers would give to their newborn daughters the name Mlaya (Swahili for whore) in the hopes that they would one day join this lucrative profession. When they write of prostitution in the Third World, anthropologists are mainly describing customs introduced by their own ancestors.

Tribal society was generous not only in its concessions to human promiscuity in the form of teenage bachelors' houses but thereafter offered extramarital sexual options, such as the sharing of Pirauru wives among the primitive Australians; wife-lending in Polynesia and elsewhere; serial intercourse for married women when they gave sexual tuition to young boys. These outlets were seldom available to the wives of chiefs, who wanted their women to be intact.

Notwithstanding such relaxations, marriage was invariably subject to strict control, designed to protect the family unit. The exceptions, or safety valves, such as wife-lending, merely proved the rule; almost everywhere plain adultery was taboo and punishable by death. When people married, they entered an entirely new condition and renounced the freedom to do as they wished.

Clear-cut rules to protect the married state were thus a feature common to tribes and to higher civilizations. In contrast, the latter set severe limits on the freedom of youth, as part of the male cult of the virgin bride. Teenage permissiveness among tribal peoples is so widespread that only in exceptional cases was the bride expected to be a virgin. For instance, in the fairly complex Zulu society, girls who offered their favors before marriage were pegged to an anthill to be devoured. However, such restraints in nineteenth-century Africa may have derived from civilized Egypt; in many parts of the continent, such as the Bissagos Islands off Angola, boys and girls were not merely encouraged but even compelled to sleep together. The question of what was done with unwanted babies produced by adolescent sex remains—as we have seen—an enigma.

The whole sexual panorama altered dramatically when advanced societies outlawed premarital free love; it has only become once more acceptable in the West in the past two decades, a curious instance of the readoption of an abandoned tribal custom.

Since each type of society seems to develop a sexual code that serves its particular needs, the question remains to be asked: What led so many tribes to condone and even promote fornication among their young? The stress on female virginity at a higher cultural level fulfills obvious purposes, but bachelors' house lovemaking surely also, consciously or unconsciously, served some social ends that are harder to define. Certain drawbacks of the system are evident: not only the risk of producing surplus offspring (no longer a problem today) but also loss of parental control over adolescents, whose efforts, undistracted by the pursuit of Eros, were needed by the family for hunting, farming, and hut building.

Advanced societies demanded greater efforts from their people to provide not only necessities for themselves but also luxuries for their kings; they offered them in exchange variety and entertainment, in the form, for instance, of lavish and elaborate ceremonies. Tribal life tends to be dull and, as can be seen today, youthful boredom leads to aggression. But what better antidote to aggression than the thrills of sexual adventure as an outlet for the exuberance of youth? This was surely more realistic than the reverse notion of the missionaries in Polynesia, who encouraged soccer as an antidote to lust.

Mandatory coitus for the young could serve a dual purpose: to reduce aggressive tendencies in general, and in a more particular sense, to defuse adolescent sensuality that, if unassuaged, might later undermine the married state. Higher civilizations were better equipped to codify the rules of marriage and to impose them on couples who, denied the pleasures of youthful free love, were more vulnerable to the lure of promiscuity. The tribal solution was simpler: to ensure that by the time the young were wed they were already sated by years of continuous copulation. Sex in excess can become monotonous, and for the tribal married couple, intercourse, already *déjà vu,* offered few surprises. Early freedom would thus help to stabilize marriage by reducing the urge, defused by years of promiscuity, to seek new partners.

Apart from the basic problem of relations between male and female, both before and after marriage, the previous three chapters stressed certain practices or taboos fundamental to human sexuality. Three such persistent elements survived among the world's great cultures: circumcision or genital mutilation; fear of incest; a propensity, open or latent, to be attracted by one's own sex. Each culture, whether primitive or advanced, had to formulate its own response to these factors.

Sexual mutilation will recur in later chapters in connection with the odd survival of clitoridectomy (usually called female circumcision) in so many states of modern Africa. Male circumcision has posed fewer problems, except among the Australian aboriginals, whose bizarre variant caused excruciating pain and imposed lasting disability. Clitoridectomy, which also causes anguish, viewed as a way of stressing the contrast between male and female in male-dominated Muslim society, helps to reinforce this domination. Male circumcision enhances masculinity in the form of a more eye-catching virile member; it has certain connections with phallicism, the cult of the erect penis, which is almost as widespread as the incest taboo.

This taboo, like circumcision, is bound up with religion, due to the lurking fear that even private acts of incest would bring down the gods' wrath upon the whole community. This obsession often is described as instinctive, but in a previous chapter the ban on incest was viewed less as an innate phobia than as a creation of human society to serve practical ends. The mere urge to reproduce, present in the simplest organisms, may be innate, but beyond this point of departure, sexual conduct in a given society depends less on primeval urges than on how people have been taught to behave.

On the other hand, homosexual tendencies in one form or another seem to be part of our biological heritage, not altogether absent in animals, though favored by a limited if so far undetermined proportion of the human species. Wherever a realistic approach is made, unmanageable problems scarcely arise, since no property rights are involved. On the contrary, in many tribes the presence of a third sex was duly recognized; neither addicted to hunting and warfare nor constricted by child-rearing, they were useful to society; transvestites were the object of respect more than derision and at times inspired veneration. Sexual systems developed over the ages accordingly took full account of certain basic human needs.

But while these simpler societies applied a certain logic to their sex life, blending permissiveness with propriety, success in this field did not solve every social problem; their life was no idyll and always had its somber side. Not only was petty warfare endemic, but also its main purpose often was the capture of victims for sacrifice to the gods. Nonetheless, discounting euphoric tales of the noble savage, many tribes impressed the first white visitors as well-balanced entities before they had been slaughtered by invaders, poisoned by rum runners, and castigated by missionaries, whose alien morality was a force hardly less disruptive than arms or alcohol.

The Rise of the State

The rise of the first states and empires did not occur simultaneously all over the world; by 3000 B.C. those of Egypt and Mesopotamia were already taking shape, but at the other end of Asia, China made no comparable advance until after 2000 B.C. The change occurred later in the New World, and the first civilizations of Mexico and Peru date from about 1500 B.C. In Egypt, Mesopotamia, and China, there arose what are now often called "hydraulic states"; the term implies that tribes were transformed into kingdoms mainly by the need for planning, in order to harness the waters of the Nile, of the Euphrates and Tigris, or of the Yellow River; such planning involved a closer control over peoples' lives and brought into being true states, capable of building elaborate irrigation systems, needed for a growing population that no longer could be fed by simpler forms of agriculture.

While the embryo state controlled more people than a single tribe, mere numbers counted less than administration; unlike the monolithic Egyptian kingdom, Mesopotamia, the land between the Tigris and the Euphrates, consisted of a cluster of city-states, each possessing tens rather than hundreds of thousands of citizens.

Once new methods of social control were devised, they were not solely used for damming rivers or for raising armies. Authoritarian rule led to the creation of a bureaucracy, greatly aided in the Old World by the invention of written records; it served to enforce the dictates of a resplendent ruler, whose subjects (for instance, in Mexico and much of the Far East) were forbidden on pain of death to look him in the eye and whose grandeur was sustained by an entourage of nobles, court ladies, and eunuchs, supported by a cohort of scribes who faithfully recorded his subjects' deeds—and also their misdeeds.

High on the list of priorities for regulation and control was sex life. The well-being of a great kingdom depended not only on improving water supplies to provide fertile crops; the king also required that his subjects themselves be fertile and multiply, for the power of his realm and the pomp of his court depended on manpower. Regulation of the relationship between the sexes was a legacy from tribal society, in which fertility cults were universal. But with the advent of civilization, sex life, including that of the ruler himself, became a prime target for much tighter control. Rules were devised to encourage or forbid certain practices; ostensibly decreed by the gods, their true purpose was the creation of a stable and prolific society.

A single volume cannot cover the sexual customs of the whole world. Instead specific examples will be chosen, with special emphasis on those, such as in China and India, that illustrate outstanding traits of sex in civilized society. Although the age-long struggle of Western man against the dictates of the world's most sex-negative creed is not our main theme, a single chapter will cover Christians, Jews, and Moslems, whose religions have common roots, though in their attitudes to sex they stand poles apart. The second part of the present chapter treats the pioneer civilizations of Egypt and Mesopotamia, whose documents and works of art offer rich data on the subject, even if they are less explicit than the sex manuals later produced in China and India and by Islam.

Every civilization has a definable personality, and in each case sexual customs are integral to that personality. Many such customs, observed until recent times, have now been abandoned, while others survive in adulterated form; whether alive or dead, they retain a certain relevance in a world in which all cultures tend to merge into a common whole. For partly fortuitous reasons, Western civilization has spread its tentacles more widely than any precursor, and its impact, both psychological and material, has been devastating. But obviously the sex life of an all-embracing culture of the future should not be just an outmoded echo of our own inherited system, derived from Christianity, but also must take into account the mores of other cultures.

The sex life of the two earliest civilizations and of all those that followed—as we shall see—had certain common features distinct from tribal mores. The outstanding trait is the growing dominance of man over woman. In tribal societies, in spite of local differences, woman, as the prime producer not only of children but also of food, had well-defined rights. But while Egyptian woman retained a certain status, in contemporary Mesopotamia she became little more than a household chattel; if in China her position was at least dignified, man was her absolute lord and master, and only in the last reign of the last dynasty was the country ruled by an empress dowager.

Symbolic of this reduced status was the harem, of which early forms are already found in Mesopotamia. Harems were to become a status symbol of so many empires of the non-Western world, culminating in the hordes of females secluded from society at the behest of a single human being, such as the Turkish sultan. The custom was widely copied by the nobility, who would purloin for their pleasures the pick of the prettiest women. The standing of the wives of ordinary citizens in such societies was also reduced to a point where (for instance, in ancient Greece) they served as mere housekeepers to men whose sexual interests lay elsewhere, or where (as in some Arab countries today) the man still rides his donkey, while the woman walks behind.

The domination of male over female, acquired by him as a form of property, made it imperative that brides and even secondary wives should be virgins, though in many places the husband found the actual task of defloration distasteful and delegated it to others, including priests. Whereas the bachelors' house, that sanctuary of premarital free love, survived in tribal societies, higher civilizations generally took the opposite view and banned premarital outlets for girls, leaving male adolescents with the brothel as their only option. This obsession with bridal virginity is integral to the process of male supremacy. Once a wife came to be regarded as little more than another possession, the purchaser naturally demanded an object that was at least untarnished; an Arab sheik today would no more think of taking a nonvirgin wife than of buying a used Cadillac.

As recently as 1934, English anthropologist J. D. Unwin expressed the problem in reverse and made of bridal virginity the precondition of civilization rather than its outcome. In his study of eighty tribal societies, on the lines of the Ford and Beach research on two hundred groups, attitudes to premarital coitus are stressed more than any other quality. Unwin sets out to demonstrate that those tribes who had advanced to a point where they built temples to their gods (defined as deistic) were precisely those that banned adolescent lovemaking and insisted that brides should be intact. As examples, he cites the Fijians, and the Bagandans of Uganda. According to his elaborate charts, the Fijians were among the few groups in Oceania who both built temples and demanded virgin wives. The Tahitians posed a problem for Unwin, since they also built temples, and he vainly tried to demonstrate that stories of their sexual promiscuity were mere fables.

Having made key issues of premarital continence, and avoidance of such practices as wife-lending among married couples, he used sexual abstinence as a yardstick for measuring the energy and creative potential of a given group, declaring that societies that allowed premarital relations (defined as zoistic) would lack vital energy and thus would never create a true civilzation (though his more abstemious Fijians and Bagandans have achieved little in that respect). For Unwin, moreover, any attempt to create a store of cultural energy by limiting postnuptial opportunities for sex was useless unless premarital options had first been reduced to a minimum. Once this was done, then postnuptial sexual activities—or rather the lack of them—were the decisive factors, and for a society to attain vitality, even these outlets had to be severly curtailed! Thus culture is presented as the product of continence.

According to the same author, a truly rationalistic approach to life, man's highest achievement, could be achieved only by societies, such as Western Christianity, that imposed monogamy. Other civilizations that permitted polygamy or even indulged in modified monogamy could not attain that state of grace. Sexual repression released a store of pent-up forces, leading to a situation where "the society begins to distinguish between the slovenly or elegant, between the vague and the exact." Such notions, expressed a mere half century ago, now appear trivial, and it may seem ludicrous to imply that polygamous Chinese culture was slovenly. However, Unwin's views deserve mention, since the question of whether human creativity is favored more by sexual satisfaction than by repression is relevant, and we shall return to it.

While male supremacy led to an obsession with bridal virginity, this in its turn created prostitution, which became another common feature of civilized states, though rare in tribal society. Prostitution and the cult of virginity went hand in hand, for if girls led cloistered lives, young males, together with married men seeking fresh partners, had no other recourse but the rented favors of women excluded from the normal system of marriage. Prostitution, as we have seen, had no place in societies where young women could be had for nothing; the claim to be the world's oldest profession is therefore nebulous, since for millennia women had worked as weavers, potters, farmers, and furriers before the demand for harlots arose.

In higher civilizations, with certain exceptions, prostitution was tolerated and often encouraged as a harmless outlet for the young and a safeguard to the married state. Inevitably a clearcut hierarchy developed among those who sold their favors for money, to cater for different grades of clients. While common whores were plentiful in brothels and on the streets, the existence of a deluxe class of women, trained to give pleasure to the elite, became a hallmark of civilization. Usually known as courtesans and at times by their Greek name, *hetairai,* their charms were spiritual as well as physical; to entice the more fastidious client, they learned to play musical instruments, to recite verse, and even to converse on learned topics. The Japanese geishas are a rare example of their survival in the modern world, in somewhat altered form.

Together with the cult of virginity and the resulting spread of prostitution, a third tendency followed the rise of civilization: Tribal tolerance of homosexuals was modified though not necessarily abandoned. In a kingdom ruled by a supreme monarch, all human conduct had to conform to a general pattern, subject to the control of his bureaucrats; homosexuals, as nonconformists to this pattern, a society within a society, were apt to be seen as a challenge to the established order and thereby become suspect; seldom, however, outside the non-Christian world, did such suspicion lead to active persecution, though the first laws to keep them in check were passed in Mesopotamia four thousand years ago. Moreover, certain civilizations that outwardly condemned male homosexual practices in effect encouraged them. In such societies, as among the gibbons, a few *macho* males monopolized the pick of the females. The remainder were then faced with a shortage of women, a situation that had already confronted the primitive Australians for different reasons. These deprived males were left with few options but homosexual acts or relations with harlots. The stress on prenuptial virginity restricted the supply of such female partners and also increased their cost. If prostitution went hand in hand with civilization, prostitution was a luxury that many men could seldom afford; they thus had fewer inhibitions in adopting other practices, which in many instances were regarded as not sinful. Some women faced parallel problems, since the inmates of the harems were condemned to a chaste existence, only rarely interrupted by a night with their master, and for them also lesbian practices were the only alternative outlets.

But if in specific respects the treatment of sex in higher civilizations was novel, in others age-old customs were upheld. The ban on incest was not only retained but even reinforced, with special exceptions that merely proved the rule, such as the dynasties of Egypt and Peru. Some but not all civilizations clung to some form of circumcision or genital mutilation.

Phallicism, the cult of the erect penis, is another legacy of primitive society to civilization and may be seen as the dramatic symbol of man's cogent pleas to his gods to provide plentiful crops and fertile women. Priapic figures are found from earliest times, wherever man has attempted to mold the human body; the oversized organ represents the powers that govern both childbirth and farming. Phallic fetishes have always been popular among the more backward tribes of Africa, while at the opposite end of the cultural spectrum, phallicism became a major factor in the religions of ancient Greece and Japan; in India the cult was carried to extreme lengths. Even Christian Europe was not immune, and Church legislation in the Middle Ages imposed a penance of bread and water for three successive Lents on anyone who performed incantations to the phallus.

The Land Between the Rivers

Egypt was long regarded as the cradle of civilization, but the first decisive steps are now known to have been taken in Mesopotamia. The impressive ruins of Uruk date from 3200 B.C., and 3000 B.C. marks the invention of written tablets that offer copious and priceless data on the Mesopotamian way of life. To treat the birth of the first civilizations as "sudden" is an overdramatization; their development, though certainly spectacular, is now seen as a more gradual process. But when compared to millions of years that separate the first human hunters from the first farmers, the change was nonetheless rapid.

In Mesopotamia each city-state had its own king, the god's elect, backed by a literate bureaucracy, centered upon the god's great temple. Since the population of a state was fairly small, rules, once formulated, were easy to enforce. Orderly and prolific marriages were all-important to a region whose kingdoms were often at war, for which manpower was a vital asset also needed to build the king's palaces and temples.

The civilization of Sumer, the first of Mesopotamia, lasted until the twentieth century B.C. and consisted of city-states. The Sumerian family was a closely knit unit, based on a limited form of monogamy, whereby each man had one wife, though by law and custom he could also acquire concubines if he could afford them. Marriage was formalized in a way hitherto undreamed of, and from earliest times it was governed by a written document —a binding deed in which the husband laid down before witnesses the rights and duties of his spouse, the sum he would pay if he divorced her, and the penalties she on her side would suffer if she was unfaithful. Before this deed was executed, it had also to be agreed to by the parents of the future wife. The change from simpler forms of union was radical. Couples were now told in writing what they might and what they might not do. A very ancient practice, mentioned in the famous epic of Gilgamesh, the Babylonian Noah, had been the right of the king, rather than the future husband, to deflower the bride. If any other man violated a betrothed virgin, the penalty was death; if he had a wife, she might be given to the girl's father as a prostitute.

Long after the decline of Sumer, Hammurabi (1792–1750 B.C.) united Mesopotamia into a powerful empire based in Babylon. In legal matters Babylon was the forerunner of Rome; Hammurabi was one of the world's great lawgivers, and his code governed in the most specific terms the relations between man and wife. No less than 64 of the 252 articles of the code contain family law. Many of these were concerned with money; the bride was normally chosen by the young man's father, and marriage among the well-to-do required the provision of a large dowry payable in cash. In Sumerian times gifts of the girl's family had been made in the form of cattle, sheep, and even lesser items such as dates, cakes, and butter, a survival of the custom of marriage by purchase.

In Sumer also, perhaps as a vestige of the tribal practice of premarital sex, ordinary couples, but not the children of the nobles, had been allowed to live together for a probationary period of about a year before getting married. Hammurabi's code no longer allows for any form of premarital intercourse.

In Mesopotamia, by a gradual but relentless process, women were totally subjected to men, notwithstanding any safeguards in the marriage contract. Even in early times men were given certain absolute rights over their wives; like any other form of merchandise, they could even be delivered to a creditor as security for repayment of a loan. The practice was approved by Hammurabi's legal code, which merely limited the period of a wife's servitude to a creditor to a maximum of three years.

A spouse's duty was to produce children and, according to the earliest known Sumerian legislation, a thousand years before Hammurabi, a woman who refused to perform her conjugal duties was to be thrown into the water and drowned; wives could also be divorced without having committed any fault. As a gesture of magnanimity, a husband who divorced his wife could keep her on in his house as a slave if the judge agreed. Adultery on the part of a wife, regarded as a trespass on the husband's property, was punishable by death if she was caught *in flagrante* (a custom retained by Muslim law). The husband's control over his family was absolute, and the children, as well as the wife, could be handed over to creditors. Hammurabi's limitation to three years tended to be disregarded; a story survives from the New Babylonian Empire (605–539 B.C.) of an individual who had to serve his father's creditor for ten years. With the passage of time the subjection of women was further intensified. By the eleventh century B.C., under the Assyrian Empire, a married woman, in anticipation of Mohammed's rule, was forbidden to go out into the street unless she covered her features with a veil, though this was forbidden to concubines and prostitutes.

Another symptom of the growing servitude of women in Assyria was the institution of the king's harem, which already flourished in Mesopotamia. This marked the beginning of the custom of cloistering a whole concourse of women whose sole purpose in life was the occasional chance to share the bed of a sex-sated potentate.

Nonetheless, in spite of the growing domination of man over woman, in Mesopotamia she still retained certain rights, of which she was deprived by later cultures. Her dowry remained her property till death, when it went to her children; it could not be seized to pay her husband's debts. She was also allowed to buy possessions without the spouse's permission; if he was absent, she ran his estate. Moreover, if the husband was able to afford concubines, it was often the wife herself who selected these from among her personal slaves.

The rise of civilization in the Near East presents a strange paradox: Woman was degraded, but she was also deified. While individual women were increasingly subjected to man, the cult of fertility, in the person of a great mother goddess, became a passion. Only later, as an extension of the policy of male supremacy, was the same principle also applied to the pantheon, and some kind of sun god, such as Ra in Egypt, usurped the rank until then occupied by the great mother (the notion that the sun is masculine and the earth feminine is fairly universal and applied even in the New World).

Life in these first kingdoms was based on farming, and the economy depended on the yearly harvest. Hence, while the Sumerian kings of Uruk and Lagash also worshiped a male sun god, the highest honors were paid to the goddess of fertility, originally known as Innana. A very early inscription in the Temple of Uruk states that the king owes his authority to Innana, the shepherdess of his people; because she, like Isis in Egypt, symbolized fertility, she was both the universal mother and the goddess of love, personified by the female deity rather than by a male eros, who was her subordinate lover. For nearly three thousand years after the rise of Sumer, Mesopotamians adored a mother goddess, under various names, who was enamored of a beautiful youth, an earlier version of the Greek Adonis, sometimes also described as her son. Innana's lover was called Dummuz. For part of the year she would enjoy his favors, but for the remaining months he descended into the underworld amid wild scenes of popular lamentation. His disappearance and eventual return to the arms of the goddess symbolized the withering of vegetation and its revival in the spring.

A thousand years later, when Babylon had succeeded Sumer, Innana was replaced by a new mother goddess, Ishtar; her cult spread with astonishing rapidity but, unlike Innana, she officially ranked below the sky god, Marduk, who, as creator of the world, was also king of the gods; though not an erotic deity, he stood for the new spirit of male supremacy. Ishtar, on the other hand, was essentially a goddess of love; each year the onset of winter marked the loss of her lover, Tammuz; on his descent into the nether regions, the women of the land gave vent to their despair by an unbridled display of grief, tearing their hair and performing wild dances. Tammuz's return the following spring was marked by even more frenetic rites. The king himself led the way; fortified by a potent aphrodisiac, he would tear off his clothes in front of his assembled people and make passionate love to a high priestess as representative of the goddess, whose grief now gave way to joy. The celebration of the reunion of the divine pair then degenerated into an orgy, in which women gained momentary freedom from their fetters.

Mesopotamia was the home of temple prostitution, another institution that was to flourish throughout the civilized world and that reached a pitch of intensity in India, where it still exists in muted form today. Symbolized by the king's union with the high priestess, it appeared in remote antiquity in Sumer and was part of Mesopotamia's cultural legacy to Greece. Two types of temple prostitution have to be distinguished: In the first, the woman offers herself once only to the god; in the second, she dedicates her life to a shrine as a sacred harlot. The most vivid account of the first category, which had not changed greatly over several millennia, is given by Greek historian Herodotus of the scene in a Babylonian temple dedicated to Mylitta, another name for the mother goddess. Every woman of the kingdom once in her lifetime was bound to do homage to the deity by offering the use of her body. No exemption was granted to the highest in the land, who drove to the temple in sumptuous covered carriages, followed by a throng of attendants. Once within the sacred precinct the women, rich and poor alike, sat in serried rows, leaving open passages along which male visitors could make a tour of inspection before taking their pick. The man would throw a silver coin into the lap of the votary he chose in the name of the goddess, and she then followed him into the inner recesses of the temple, where niches existed for the purpose. After this single experience, the woman's sex life would be confined to relations with her husband. The silver coins went to the upkeep of the temple.

To the Western mind, the association of worship with venal intercourse may seem both blasphemous and obscene. But in the ancient world, sex in such a context was for both man and woman a sacrament, symbolic of union with the goddess herself. Intercourse thus performed was a kind of communion, a pious act and an integral part of the state religion. From the man's point of view, the main concern was not the payment of money or the satisfaction of lust but the desire for intimate contact with the divine.

Such a once-and-for-all offering of her body was not necessarily a form of sexual deflowering for the woman, since it seems that there was no fixed age at which the gesture had to be made. Nonetheless, a wise female would complete the performance while she was still in the first bloom of youth; beautiful girls attracted their man in a matter of hours, while those who were older or uglier might have to remain on the premises for months on end before being chosen.

132

While all women had to offer themselves once in the temple, many other girls, often of good family, were dedicated for life to the second form of prostitution and lived in the temple, offering their favors to all comers. Far from any shame being attached, those chosen were held in the highest esteem as servants of the goddess Ishtar. Parents would deliver a daughter to the temple at a very tender age. Like the courtesans of other cultures, they were taught not only the arts of love but also dancing and singing.

Temple prostitution, both a public institution and a source of temple revenue throughout Mesopotamia, was the forerunner of other forms of harlotry; and the fact that the women were regarded as "holy" does not alter the more down-to-earth aspects of their calling. Different classes of such prostitutes were early established, and in the Sumerian sanctuary of Uruk there were three categories, of which the lowest, called the Marimate, had an evil reputation.

Temples often housed male as well as female prostitutes, and consecrated sodomites, mentioned on occasion in the Old Testament and cursed by its prophets, also originated in Mesopotamia. For instance, males were available in the temple of Ishtar at Erech and other places; they were described in texts as "men whose manhood Ishtar has changed into womanhood." Neither male nor female prostitutes were wholly confined to the temples, and according to a passage in the Gilgamesh epic: "Daily a feast is celebrated in this town where boys may be had for pleasure and girls may also be admired." Boys as well as girls were maintained as extra sleeping partners in the houses of the rich. However, Babylonia could claim the distinction of passing the first laws against homosexuality, though their effect seems to have been limited. A rather ambiguous passage in Hammurabi's code made such acts a punishable offense. The penalty was drastic: public castration in the marketplace.

From Cheops to Cleopatra

In ancient Egypt, the birth of civilization brought about similar changes in sexual customs: consolidation of the married state, a cult of prenuptial chastity; a reticence toward overt homosexuality. In Egypt also the stress on bridal virginity led to the rise of prostitution, both secular and religious.

Among the civilizations of the Near East, the state at the beginning was centered upon the temple, and temple prostitution therefore serves as a good example of how sexual practices could be made to serve politicoreligious institutions. At the time of the first dynasties of Egypt, contemporary with those of Sumer, the great mother was worshiped with equal fervor. But while Mesopotamians were content with one mother goddess, the Egyptians had three: Hathor, Nut, and Isis. Hathor, as the giant cow who had risen out of the primeval flood, was the mother of all creation. The sun was thought to burst forth every morning out of her great bosom, whither it returned in the evening. She was also the goddess of the west, associated, as in many lands, with death. Hathor thus presided over the beginning and the end of life. Her bosom was both the night and the earth, which gave birth to all plants and living things. Hathor was also goddess of dates, which played a key role in the Egyptian economy. The summit of the date palm was the place where the sun was born and whence he first rose into the sky.

Behind Hathor stood the mysterious Nut, the mother of all mothers since the beginning of the world; from the esoteric rites of this goddess men were excluded. While Hathor nourished the sun in her bosom during the night, Nut bore him on her back during the day. In Egypt the conventional roles of male earth and female sky deities, present, say, in China or Mexico, are thus reversed; the sky goddess Nut is the spouse of the earth god Geb, usually depicted as lying underneath her in scenes of intercourse.

Isis, as the patron of agriculture and who had first taught man how to till the soil, was the third and leading member of this divine matriarchy. Isis was spouse and sister of Osiris, who had given Egypt its laws. According to the central legend of Egyptian mythology, he was murdered and dismembered by Seth; Isis recovered his scattered limbs and restored them to life. Thereafter Osiris ruled over the kingdom of the dead, forever cherished by a people obsessed with the afterlife. It was of Horus, their son, that the reigning pharaoh was the living incarnation. Hence Isis in Egypt became the eternal mother who had given birth to the god-king.

If the pharaoh held the power, the queen mother thus was the source of that power and stood behind the throne. As the mother of the god, Isis inspired unique affection and piety. In statues she often is represented as suckling the infant Horus. A special festival was held in her honor in December to celebrate the rebirth of the sun, and the scene would be reenacted in which she nursed her holy child, Horus, in a stable.

The relations between man and woman in early Egypt, whether in the pharaoh's family or among his subjects, mirrored those of their gods. At the beginning, therefore, man, far from dominating the scene, was as much the servant as the master of the established matriarchy; woman, represented by Isis, was the mother of god and of everything else, the creative principle behind all things. On very ancient vases, women are often painted as bigger than men.

Basic to such concepts was the failure to associate the sexual act with childbirth; woman alone was the procreator of future generations, and man's part in this process was incidental. Only when man's role in procreation was recognized was he able to challenge this female supremacy. On the divine plane, this challenge led to the emergence as king of the gods of Ammon Ra, who then took the place of the female Hathor as the great sun deity. The procreative roles of man and woman were then reversed; and in later times the man's semen was held to be the true begetter of offspring, which the woman simply nurtured in her body. Greek historian Diodorus Siculus maintained that the latter-day Egyptians regarded the father as solely responsible for conceiving children.

But if Egypt, originally a matriarchy, developed a trend toward male domination, its success was partial, and woman clung to certain vestiges of her former primacy; she never became her husband's personal property, as in Mesopotamia and elsewhere. In some respects male supremacy came to be asserted; rules governing divorce favored the husband, who could set aside his wife more or less at will; equally, laws on adultery weighed more heavily on the woman, who could be burned at the stake for infidelity. Monogamy was diluted by provisions whereby the pharaoh and his nobles could have concubines as well as wives. But the wife retained her former rights on property, which continued to be inherited through the female line.

The failure of Egyptian man to become the absolute master is reflected in the royal family, behind which loomed the image of Isis, the great mother, who delegated her power to the earthly queen mother. Babylon only had one legendary woman ruler, the Semiramis of the Hanging Gardens; but even after the male Ra had become king of the gods, three great queens—Hatshepsut, Nefertiti, and Cleopatra—were to become famous rulers of Egypt.

Hatshepsut (1505–1483 B.C.) fully assumed the role of Isis. One of her inscriptions reads: "I am Isis, the queen of the whole land, I am the sister and spouse of Osiris, the mother of the king Horus." While Nefertiti was mainly distinguished for her beauty, Cleopatra, possessed of Nefertiti's glamor and Hatshepsut's strength, both ruled the kingdom and conquered the heart of Caesar.

Moreover, apart from these famous figures, during the disturbed times around the middle of the second millennium B.C., the wives of other pharaohs also came to dominate their husbands, who were then relegated to the rank of mere prince-consorts. The balance was later restored by an antifeminist movement in the army, and the name of the great Hatshepsut was erased from all public buildings. But the women proved the victors in the end. In the eighth century B.C. a woman became high priestess of the temple of Ammon Ra in Thebes, whose oracles had to be consulted before any fateful decision was taken; the Temple of Ammon, immersed in high politics, then became a center of female influence during the next two-hundred-years, until Egypt was conquered by Persia.

The custom of royal incest was a crucial factor in the power struggle between the male and female principal. A king's spouse who was at the same time his sister and who therefore was both reigning queen and daughter of former kings, was well placed to pose as the pharaoh's equal, to share and at times to monopolize her husband's power. Royal incest in Egypt derived from the divine pair Isis and Osiris, but religion was not its only basis. Incest among the gods is central to the mythology of many other peoples but without giving birth, as in Egypt, to political institutions; any tribe that traces its origins back to a single pair of ancestors presupposes incest between their children, or between parents and children, as the only way to continue the line. Moreover, incest was seldom if ever practiced by the earlier pharaohs who built the pyramids. Only centuries later did brother-sister marriages become a custom, and in some dynasties the heir to the throne, to be recognized as ruler, was obliged to marry his sister. The tradition then died out again but was revived from time to time; this last occurred under Alexander the Great's successors, the Ptolemies from whom Cleopatra descended; she herself seized power from a weakling husband-brother.

A more rational cause for royal incest derives from the Egyptian laws of inheritance. Since property passed on a man's death to the wife and her relations, a pharaoh who wished to keep together the family heritage, often amounting to most of the country, and to prevent it from falling into the wrong hands, was therefore obliged to marry his sister. If in the pharaoh's case the practice also served to preserve the purity of the royal blood, the laws of property were decisive for the nobility, who copied the fashion set by their rulers of brother-sister marriages; once people became convinced that such marriages were no sin, the pecuniary advantages were obvious. In Egyptian love poetry, couples address one another as "brother" and "sister" in conversations that are openly erotic, and this often was, in fact, their true relationship.

Royal incest was not confined to Egypt and spread to other parts of Africa. For example, the Azanda of East Africa insisted that their chiefs enter into sexual partnerships with their own daughters.

The cult of the phallus, deep-rooted in ancient Egypt, can also be traced back to the divine couple Isis and Osiris. After Isis had recovered the scattered remains of the murdered Osiris, in the place where each limb was found she caused an appropriate statue to be erected and worshiped forever after. The only parts still missing were Osiris' genitals, which Seth had thrown in to the Nile, where they were eaten by fish. The lost member was replaced by a wooden substitute, the original of the countless wooden phalli found in tombs. The purpose of these funeral offerings was to restore the man's virile force in the next world.

Images of Osiris' phallus were also worshiped in temples. In later statues, he was usually endowed with an outsize organ, and the special figures of the god designed to be carried in processions often had a threefold phallus. In other processions, Osiris' giant member would be born in an urn. Comparable practices survive in Indian temples today. Shiva, the leading Hindu deity, is often depicted with an erect phallus; alternatively, a large carving of Shiva's phallus will be carried in processions.

In Egyptian art, the penis is always of impressive dimensions, unlike the rather puny members depicted by Greeks and Romans, though they were also ardent votaries of phallic cults. In Egyptian religious ceremonies, women wore huge phalli that could be moved upward and downward by attached strings. The Turin papyrus, in its illustrations of coital positions, always endows the man with a large penis. In later times, an immense golden phallus over a hundred feet high was reportedly carried in an annual procession in Alexandria. Many temple reliefs show not only Osiris but also other gods with erect phalli, and a phallic deity, Khem, precursor of the Greek Priapus, was widely worshiped as the god who furthered the continuance of the human race.

The early spread both of the cult of phallicism and the practice of circumcision confirms the notion, previously mentioned, that the two had common origins, even though in India phallicism later flourished as never before, while circumcision was absent, as also among the Greeks and Romans (who actually tried to discourage the practice when they conquered Egypt). For the Egyptians an impressive penis was a divine attribute that also became a human status symbol, as illustrated in the Turin papyrus; phallicism therefore went hand in hand with an operation that enhanced the virile aspect of the individual member. It is unknown how widely circumcision was practiced, but it cannot have been confined to the elite, since several of the earliest tombs *(mastabas)* contain pictures of circumcised workmen. Many frescoes and reliefs show nude circumcised men, and one text refers to a group circumcision of 120 males together, as a kind of survival from tribal initiaton rites. Two portrayals of the process itself exist; the operator kneels to the task, which is performed with a flint instrument.

Female circumcision (or rather, excision), later to become a scourge of Moslem Africa, also seems to have been practiced in Egypt, since Strabo, the first-century B.C. geographer, states on two different occasions that the Jews followed the Egyptian custom of circumcising girls. However, Egyptian texts and illustrations do not mention the matter, and mummies offer no conclusive evidence.

On the other hand, texts often refer to sexual variants such as masturbation, anal intercourse, and even bestiality. Masturbation is mentioned in several of the pyramid texts of the third millennium B.C. To quote one of these: "Atun became as one who masturbates in Heliopolis. He put his phallus in his hand to excite desire. The son and daughter were born, the brother and the sister, Shu and Tefnet." From this it appears that the male seed was at that time already thought to be the decisive factor in generation, at least among the gods. Written two thousand years later, a fourth-century B.C. papyrus is more explicit: "I was the one who copulated with my fist, I masturbated my hand. Then I spewed with my own mouth. I spat out what was Shu and sputtered out what was Tefnet."

Bestiality probably was related to the custom of depicting the gods themselves with human bodies and animal heads. Animal-human contacts appear on tombs, and Herodotus writes of intercourse between Egyptian women and goats. Similar practices have continued to find favor in the Nile Valley; reports from the long period of Turkish rule tell of goatherds who anointed their penises with honey as an enticement to suckling kids and of other males who sought satisfaction with female crocodiles, rendered helpless when rolled over on their backs.

References to homosexuality occur in ancient texts but are few in number. A passage in the *Book of the Dead* states: "I have

not done that which the gods abominate. I have not defamed a
slave to his superior—I have not had sexual relations with a boy.
I have not defiled myself." But this passing reference cannot be
taken to imply any general condemnation; a curious ordinance
prohibited homosexual intercourse in Memphis but not elsewhere. If homosexual acts were at times frowned upon, this was
perhaps because they did not serve to produce more subjects for
the pharaoh. The gods themselves suffered from no such inhibitions. The great legendary struggle between Seth and Horus
was tinged with a strange element of homosexual romance; Seth
expressed his admiration for the buttocks of Horus, who told
this to his mother: "The majesty of Horus said to his mother Isis
. . . 'Seth desires to have intercourse with me. . . .' " Isis advised
caution, saying that Seth was too strong and violent for Horus.
He should instead place his fingers between his buttocks and
catch the semen ejaculated by Seth "without letting the sun see
it." After this peculiar act had been duly performed, Isis, as a
kind of counter measure, fed Horus's semen to Seth on a lettuce;
this led to the birth, from the forehead of Seth, of the moon god
Thoth, sometimes called "the son of two lords."

Texts suggest that anal intercourse between males was a privilege shared by gods and pharaohs. King Pepe II, the last ruler
of the Old Kingdom, was enamored of one of his generals, and
the heretical Akhnaton (1372–1354 B.C.) seems eventually to
have abandoned Queen Nefertiti for the embraces of his son-in-
law. Transsexual traits were present in the great Queen Hatshepsut, who wore men's clothes and often is represented with
a beard.

Anal penetration, an indignity that Horus was at such pains to
avoid, was regarded as a sign of submission, an attitude that was
to survive in Egypt and other parts of the Turkish Empire. A
coffin text includes the statement: "Ra has no power over me,
for I copulate between his buttocks." Ra thus becomes power-
less as the passive partner in a sexual act.

Further evidence suggests that the Egyptians, like the Moche
of Peru, were fascinated by anal eroticism involving both sexes.
Not only is anal intercourse between man and woman portrayed
in various tomb pictures, one of the illustrations of the Turin

papyrus, which deals with the amorous adventures of Ramses III (1195–1164 B.C.), shows the elderly pharaoh advancing on his partner from the rear, while she crouches on all fours. Egypt is not known to have produced sex manuals, but this document nonetheless provides a fund of information on the subject. One scene depicts Ramses in a state of utter prostration, being carried away to rest by his partner, aided by a small girl, while another infant upholds his huge but limp phallus. The two little girls appear in another drawing in which Ramses' partner bends over a miniature chariot; they are accompanied by a neat and tiny figure with erect phallus, whose part in the act has been hotly debated by scholars.

Ramses III showed concern for the sexual activities of his subjects as well as his own. An inscription of this pharaoh, addressed to the god Ammon, states: "I have carried them (the war captives) away; the males to fill thy storehouse; their women to be subjects of the temples." Other inscriptions leave no room for doubt that such women were temple harlots who were all regarded as Ammon's wives. The principle, as much a fertility rite as a form of sexual satisfaction, is the same as in Mesopotamia, but the practice seems to have developed later in Egypt. Prostitution of a more secular kind was freely available from the earliest times. Herodotus not only accuses a later pharaoh of selling his daughter to a brothel but even makes the farfetched assertion that the pharaoh, Cheops, builder of the Great Pyramid, defrayed part of the gigantic cost by installing his own daughter in a common whorehouse, where she sold her body to all comers.

CHAPTER SIX

The Classic World

The Beautiful and the Good

In England's more exclusive schools for boys, studies, until World War II, were centered upon ancient Greek and Latin. Greece was revered both as the spiritual heir of Egypt and Babylon and as the parent of our own civilization; pupils were taught not only to translate the Greek classics but also to write their own. At more advanced levels they learned to compose iambic verse, following precise rules of the classical playwrights. However, by a curious form of discrimination, in girls' schools Latin but no Greek was taught.

The boys' schools were all-male establishments, and the pupils lived in total isolation from the opposite sex, to an extent unthinkable in ancient Greece. But woe betide any boys who, after a day spent poring over the classics, thought to experiment with certain Greek customs and were caught in the act; summary expulsion followed, and those affected were marked for life.

The study of Greek in English schools was intensified in the nineteenth century, at the very time when homosexuality came to be viewed with increasing repugance if not terror. But somehow the curriculum drew a veil of silence over those homosexual relationships, lauded by lyric poets and lampooned by comic playwrights. To devise such a curriculum was a triumph of ingenuity, since the homoerotic element was so fundamental to Hellenic culture that the German Hans Licht, in his work on sex life in ancient Greece, states that without this basic ingredient, its civilization might have followed quite different patterns.

Nonetheless, the teaching in English public schools could rely on the support of European scholars of the time, who turned a blind eye to this aspect of Greek culture and dismissed all friendship, amounting to love, between men and boys as mere camaraderie; they brushed under the carpet unmistakable references to physical contact in the texts and presented the Greek masters as blameless intellectuals who might flirt with abstract theories but never with their pupils. One may cite the work of a great German scholar, L. Schmidt: In his two weighty tomes on Ancient Greece, published in 1882, pederasty receives one casual mention.

Previous generations had fewer illusions. The French novelist Stendhal, who wrote early in the nineteenth century, in his *De l'Amour* left his readers in no doubt that the Greeks indulged in "perverse" forms of love. Modern scholars generally agree with Stendhal, and few would pretend that friendships between Greek males were solely "platonic." Irrefutable proof to the contrary is graven on hundreds of vases; some depict homosexual contacts, while others bear inscriptions in which men declare their passion for boys.

It would, however, be quite wrong to go to the opposite extreme and to pretend that all Greek men were hardened pederasts. Males were expected as a matter of course to marry; society therefore encouraged a man, at different stages in his career, to form relationships both with women and with adolescents of his own sex. While it was thought desirable for a boy to have an older male lover, when he reached manhood he would then marry. After this mainly heterosexual stage—when he was, say, forty years old—he would in turn seek a boy lover. This formalized man-boy relationship was a mainstay of the city-state; through his attachment to an older man, the Greek youth acquired not only an education in the arts but also training for war.

144

Sex was integral to the Greeks' sensuous view of life. They were imbued with a love of beauty for its own sake, and for them the naked human body represented its purest form. Beauty was inseparable from virtue, and the ideal of "the beautiful and the good" formalized this link. The training of the mind thus went hand in hand with that of the body, exemplified in the Hellenic Games; they were held as early as 720 B.C., and runners always appeared in the nude. Far from regarding the exposed penis as something shameful, to be hidden from view, it would arouse pious awe as the instrument of propagation. In this cult of the naked body, particularly that of the young male, Greek culture was a departure from that of the ancient Near East, from which it inherited so much, as did also the Jews of the Old Testament; but the two peoples drew very different conclusions, as we shall see, from the same traditions.

Second only to the Hellenic love of beauty was the quest for pleasure; the Greeks sought a cheerful enjoyment of life, including love in its many forms. A certain cult of the androgynous blurred the distinctions between such forms. Physical differences between the two sexes seldom were stressed; the adjective *kalos,* meaning "beautiful," was applied to men just as much as to women and was therefore the equivalent of both handsome *and* beautiful in our language. Masculine and feminine figures painted on vases are almost identical in form and even have the same facial contours. The Greek Eros was therefore, as we shall see, basically bisexual.

The Greek Woman

The more intriguing aspect of Greek mores, the socially approved homosexuality, accordingly forms part of a general pattern and should not be viewed in isolation from Greek attitudes toward women.

Just as all Greek males cannot be defined as active homosexuals, it would be just as inaccurate to regard all women as mere chattels, purchased to keep house for men who were only interested in each other. The position of women in the Hellenic world is hard to assess by modern standards. In the first place, their status varied greatly from place to place; in some cities they were kept under lock and key and forced to lead a life of oriental seclusion, while in Lydia it was taken for granted that unmarried girls should go out and pay for their clothes and even their marriage dowry by prostitution.

Greek history offers many examples of men's love for women as well as for boys. At the height of the classic age, Pericles, who saved Athens from the Persians, does not seem to have been attracted to his own sex, and he loved no one but Aspasia. The central drama of the heroic age, the Trojan War, began when Paris abducted not a boyfriend, but the all-too-feminine Helen.

The pressures on a male to marry and to lead for a time an ostensibly heterosexual life were more compelling than those that prompted him to seek boy lovers. Exclusive homosexuals were an object of ridicule; hardened bachelors in Sparta faced all kinds of petty persecution. For instance, the magistrates would compel them to strip naked in the depth of winter and march around the main square of the town singing a ditty that mocked their celibate status. If in Athens celibacy was not officially prohibited (Plato never married), the obligation to have at least one son impelled young men to seek a wife. The Greeks vied with the Chinese in recognizing a solemn duty to engender male heirs to conduct their father's funeral rites and to continue his line.

Women, moreover, disposed of certain escape valves from the restraints placed upon them. In parts of Greece, a special festival in honor of Dionysus took place, in which women and girls alone took part. At night, dressed in goatskins and with disheveled hair, they would climb to the summit of the nearest mountain; frenzied with wine (which they otherwise seldom drank), they performed wild dances that ended in orgies.

Nonetheless, such outlets were limited in scope, and a woman's principal role was to bear sons. Her place was in the home and she was not free to walk alone in the streets. A wife did not go out to dinner with her husband and was excluded from eating with him when he entertained male visitors. Wives had no part to play in social life; their conversation was trivial, since they had no chance of obtaining a decent education and knew nothing but what they learned from their mother, limited to domestic tasks such as spinning and weaving wool, together with a little music and dancing. Such ignorance left a spiritual void between husband and wife. Even Pericles, so true to Aspasia, maintained that the best women were those of whom men spoke the least.

Accordingly, though we think of the Greeks as our spiritual mentors, in their attitude to women they were more akin to the Babylonians than to ourselves. A woman, for instance, had no claim to fidelity on the part of the husband; quite apart from boys, a married man could have as many female concubines as he could afford, and sensual pleasure thus was dissociated from marital duties. Xenophon, leader of the famous expedition to Persia in 399 B.C., quotes Socrates as saying: "Surely you do not suppose that lust provokes men to beget children, when the streets are full of people who will satisfy the appetite, as also are the brothels. No, it is clear that we select for wives the women who will bear us the best children and that we marry them to raise a family." Such attitudes were time-honored, and the poet Hesiod, who lived four hundred years earlier, toward the end of the eighth century B.C., put the matter even more bluntly when he wrote: "Get yourself first of all a house, a woman, and a working ox. Buy the woman, don't marry her. Then you can make her follow the plow if necessary." Typical of the Greek view of women is the widely held belief that most females, if they had the choice, would have been born males.

The situation of wives nonetheless offers a one-sided view of the woman's plight in Greece. In addition to those who played the part of spouse and housekeeper, another class existed, for whom sex was a business. Among such women, class distinctions were sharp; at the summit of the profession stood the courtesans, known as *hetairai.* They were held in higher esteem than wives and were far better educated; well versed in Classical literature, they even attended lectures on learned topics. Like the Japanese geishas and unlike ordinary Greek wives, they set out to amuse their patrons by their sparkling conversation. They are often mentioned in literature, and in several Greek comedies hetairai play the role of heroine. The famous hetaira Phryne is an example of the respect they commanded. She presented a magnificent figure of Eros to the town of Thespiae; its inhabitants returned the compliment by commissioning the great sculptor Praxiteles to execute a gilded statue of Phryne, which was set up in the main square between those of King Archiadamus and King Philippus. The hetairai were noted for their knowledge of male foibles and for their skill in turning them into ready cash. Regular catechisms were devised for teaching such skills, first propagated by word of mouth but later set down in writing, though no such manuals survive. A poem of Propertius, however, exists in which a procuress lectures a girl on how to extort as much money as possible from her client. Above all, she must inspire jealousy, by acting as if she had other lovers.

Among the many practices inherited from Mesopotamia was the presence in temples of religious prostitutes, who also ranked as hetairai. The largest band belonged to the temple of Aphrodite Porne at Corinth (*porne* was the term commonly used to describe women who offered their body for money). According to the geographer Strabo, the temple of Aphrodite was so rich that it was able to maintain more than a thousand hetairai. In Greek literature Corinth is famed for its debauchery; for the sake of these women, dedicated both to the goddess and to sex, many strangers visited the city, and this thriving tourist trade provided much of its wealth. Temples in other places also housed prostitutes; in certain cases victors at the Olympic Games would donate girls to the shrine of a deity.

Remote in status from the hetairai were the inmates of countless brothels, many situated in harbor districts of towns on the sea. The girls would display themselves outside the establishment, sparsely clothed and with bare breasts. The city would fix reasonable prices, payable in advance; the owner paid a value-added tax, based on the receipts of the girls. A special class of officials was charged with brothel supervision and taxation.

Brothel whores were the lowest form of harlot. At an intermediate level, between them and the hetairai stood the countless girls who, usually as a part-time occupation, walked the streets in harbor districts. Their methods of picking up customers were not unlike those of today. As an added refinement, one girl, whose shoe has been preserved, had engraved upside down on its sole the words "follow me" so clients could follow her foot-prints.

Paiderasteia

It might be argued that the Greek male was so amply supplied with female partners that even if he had positively shunned boys, he would hardly have been sex-starved. Pederasty, however, was as old as Greek civilization itself. Some would-be apologists have insisted that it was alien to the spirit of the Homeric heroes and was introduced by the Dorian invasion in the eleventh century B.C.; others even suggest that it thrived in Classical Greece from the fifth century onward only and therefore was an early symptom of Greek decadence.

Nothing could be farther from the truth, since such tendencies are apparent at the outset; they then showed a remarkable staying power, since they were as strong as ever in the Hellenistic period that followed the death of Alexander the Great in 323 B.C. Indeed, by that time art forms that depict the homoerotic had become more blatant; whereas Eros was formerly portrayed as a handsome young athlete, in the fourth century B.C. he becomes an effeminate child.

Passion between persons of the same sex was not even invented by the heroes, since the tradition goes back to the gods. When Zeus carried off the handsome young Trojan Ganymede to be his lover in heaven, he boasted openly of his intention to sleep with him. Apollo loved Hyacinth. Though Orpheus adored Eurydice, after he had failed to rescue his beloved from the underworld he renounced all love of woman; he did not, however, remain celibate, but turned instead to boys.

Socrates thought that the story of Achilles and Patroclus in Homer's *Iliad* lacked any erotic element. This denial, concerning heroes who lived almost a thousand years before Alexander, hardly tallies with Achilles' insane grief at the death of his friend and with his decision to stay in Troy and avenge Patroclus, even though he knew that in so doing he doomed himself to an early death.

Several centuries after Achilles but well before the classical age that reached its apogee in the fifth century, evidence of homoerotic passion becomes more tangible. Graffiti inscribed on rocks on the island of Thera (now known as Santorini) in the eighth and ninth centuries B.C. are dedicated exclusively to boys, since the compliments paid, such as "good" and "beautiful," are in the masculine gender. A seventh-century inscription from Thera is even more explicit; it reads: "Invoking the Delphic Apollo, I, Crimon, here copulated with a boy, son of Bathydes." From the sixth century onward countless vase inscriptions survive that proclaim the beauty of a boy, who is often named; this custom is not, however, mentioned by any writer. These vase dedications are not graffiti, since they were painted on the vessel before firing and were therefore treated by the painter as part of his design, as ordered by the client.

The classical comedies refer more frequently to the love of women. But in early lyric poetry, homosexual affairs occupied a major place. Theogonis of Megara lived and wrote in the sixth century; only fragments of his work have come down to us, but of these some 158 lines are devoted to his favorite, Cyrnus. Homoerotic lyrics were no fleeting fashion; of the thirty idylls of the poet Theocritus (310–245 B.C.), no fewer than eight are exclusively devoted to youths.

Inscriptions dedicated to girls are much rarer in paintings; generally vases portray boys and youths and pay much more attention to detail than when depicting girls; even the most erotic females, such as the legendary sirens, often have a boyish look. Some vessels not merely illustrate beautiful youths but also show actual scenes of copulation; these mostly date from 570 to 470 B.C., the great age of erotic vase painting. In most instances, the boy and his older suitor are portrayed facing each other; the latter bends his knees and thrusts his penis between the boy's thighs; anal copulation is shown only in rarer paintings of two males of more or less the same age. In contrast, various writers refer to sodomy but never to intercrural copulation, as shown on vases.

In addition to those that depict intercourse, a much larger number of vases portray more decorous scenes in which men merely court boys, with varying degrees of success. The intention is nonetheless obvious; for instance, one vase first shows a scene of this kind, followed by another in which the same pair copulate. However, such a happy ending was not to be taken for granted, since a favorite theme is a youth who scorns an older man's advances. Taken in isolation, such scenes might seem to lack any erotic intent were it not for certain telltale details. Often the boy is offered a cockerel or a hare, identical to those at times held by the younger partner in illustrations of homosexual intercourse. Sometimes a small figure of Eros flies above or between the two male figures.

While poets and vase painters amply record such homosexual affairs, they say little about how they were conducted. Whereas the English "pederasty" always has a sexual connotation, the original Greek word *paiderasteia,* meaning "love of boys," does not itself imply physical contact. Nonetheless, according to Greek custom, every man of a certain class sought to win the affection of some boy, to whom he not only acted as guardian and friend, but of whom he usually also became the lover in a physical sense. This was, however, only one element in a much broader relationship between adult man and adolescent boy that involved a common existence, leading to the gradual initiation of the younger into the social activities of the older, centered upon the club, the gymnasium, and the banquet.

We are not told what the older man's wife thought about such arrangements; the boy's family, on the other hand, presented no problem. The mother had little to say in the matter, since from the age of seven a boy would have been removed from her care. The father took a curiously limited interest in the education of his sons and was only too happy to hand over the task to another adult; possibly the boy's father had by this time found his own lover, whose upbringing was of more concern to him than that of his own offspring.

In such relationships conventions were formal. For instance, in Crete, the suitor would first declare his ardor to the family of the beloved. If they consented, he would carry the boy off to a mountain retreat, where they would spend an idyllic two months together. When this honeymoon was over, they returned to the city, where the youth was solemnly feted; his patron lover gave him a suit of armor and other gifts, and the boy then became his shield-bearer. Others were not as generous as the Cretans, and sometimes the lad had to be content with a little bird, or a ball to play with. In a certain sense gifts were a reward for services rendered, since by a curious convention the younger partner was in theory supposed to derive no bodily satisfaction from sexual contact with the older. To admit to physical pleasure would be to act like a woman, and boys who appeared to do so were despised.

These friendships had their moments of crisis, and many tales are recorded of quarrels and even brawls, usually ending in a tender reconciliation. When two or more men coveted the same youth, jealousies became intense. The biographer Plutarch, in his life of Themistocles, relates how the hostility between the Athenian statesman and the equally renowned Aristides arose from their mutual passion for the handsome Stesilaos of Ceos. A youth might also be jealous of his lover; when Alcibiades arrived at Agathon's dinner party, as described in Plato's *Symposium,* he gave open vent to his dismay when he found that Socrates was sharing a couch with the host, regarded as a great beauty. Love between males could lead to suicide. Melas, a beautiful Athenian boy, looked with scorn on an alien suitor, Timagoras, and bade him jump off the Acropolis if he wanted to prove his devotion. Timagoras took him at his word; Melas, filled with remorse, then took the leap himself.

Since the lover was expected to give presents to the beloved, the distinction between homosexual eros and downright prostitution was at times blurred. In Greek comedy in particular, romance and whoring were reduced to the same bodily act, whose motivation was mercenary. Moreover, since prisoners of war from other city-states were apt to be sold to brothels, some of their inmates were just as well bred and at times better educated than the clients.

Among those who started life in this way was Phaido of Elis, who later held the famous dialogue with Socrates about the immortality of the soul; a lad of good family, he was captured when still very young in a conflict between Elis and Sparta. The Spartans sold him to Athens, where he was bought by a brothel owner. Socrates met him on a visit to the establishment; with the help of a rich friend he was purchased from the owner and freed.

Homosexual prostitution of a purely commercial kind was efficiently organized. Surviving accounts ring with customers' lamentations over the cupidity of boys greedy for cash. One who sold his body to men for money was called a *pornos* (masculine equivalent of *porne*). Some establishments in harbor districts conveniently housed both boys and girls, while others offered males only. Boys were available not only on the premises; they could also be rented from such houses for a given period, and surviving texts describe such contracts and name the sums paid. A number of free-lance or peripatetic youths also solicited patrons in the streets; they would follow a client to his house or submit to his caresses at night in some deserted spot. In total contrast to those taken as lovers by warriors, they tried with the help of cosmetics to look effeminate.

Apart from war captives, most other male prostitutes in Athens were also outsiders. This was mainly due to a curious law whereby an Athenian citizen who had ever sold his body for money was forbidden, under pain of death, from holding public office or even from expressing his opinion in the Assembly or Council. Sir Kenneth Dover, in his book *Greek Homosexuality*, describes at length a prosecution under this law. In 346 B.C. the orator Demosthenes, together with a certain Timarchos, made a lawsuit against the envoys who had signed a peace treaty with Philip of Macedon, on the grounds that the terms were unfavorable to Athens. The envoys, however, were able to make a countercharge against Timarchos and won their case; the basis of the charge was that the defendant, who had certainly been active in the Assembly and had also held public office, had been a male whore in his youth. It is not known when or why this law excluding former prostitutes from politics was passed.

Although straight male prostitution of this kind obviously was not peculiar to Greece, the socially approved man-boy relationship is more original and offers a good example of how natural urges, suitably channeled, can become a bulwark of the ruling institution, in Greece the city-state. War between cities, or confederations of cities, was endemic, and one is apt to forget that the elite were first and foremost warriors, obliged by frequent emergencies to abandon their philosophy and their farms and obey the call to arms. And basic to *paiderasteia* was the need to show valor in war. If the older suitor lacked courage, the romance would founder. His beloved also was judged by his bravery; according to a fifth-century inscription found on a stone in Athens, "Lysitheos declares that he loves Mikion more than all the other boys in the city, for he is courageous."

Paiderasteia thus reinforced the city's war potential, and at times it even came to be regarded as a violation of duty if a man did not draw to himself a suitable youth to be trained in the arts of peace and war; a boy's reputation also would suffer if he was not honored with a friendship of this kind. The older partner was expected to offer an example of physical courage to his beloved, and the younger partner likewise had to show himself worthy of his lover as soon as he was old enough to serve; in certain cases he would withhold physical favors until the lover had proved his worth in the field.

Plato, writing in the fourth century B.C., after Athens had ceased to be a major power, illustrates the point when he states in his *Symposium* that an army composed of pairs of lovers, inspiring one another to perform acts of heroism, would be unbeatable. "I for my part am at a loss to say what greater blessing a man can have in earliest youth than an honorable lover, or a lover than an honorable favorite . . . so that if we could somehow contrive to have a city or an army composed of lovers and their favorites, they could not be better citizens of their country than by refraining from all that is base in a mutual rivalry for honor, and such men as these, when fighting side by side, one might almost consider able to make even a little band victorious over all the world."

This ideal was actually realized in the fourth century B.C. in the elite fighting corps of Thebes, known as the Sacred Band; formed in 378 B.C., it consisted of three hundred men, grouped in pairs of lovers. With the aid of this force, venerated throughout the Greek world, Thebes achieved a brief hegemony after the period of Spartan rule that followed her defeat of Athens in 404 B.C.

For Plato this form of love provided not only training for war but also education in a higher sense. The adulation of the younger partner for the elder was regarded as a stimulus to study. By an irony of history, Plato's teaching gave birth to the term "platonic" love. The philosopher admittedly drew a distinction between "sacred love," based on spiritual harmony, and "profane love," which aimed only at physical satisfaction. Later schools, such as the Stoics, carried this notion a stage farther and even went so far as to praise sexual abstinence. This sex-negative undercurrent in Greek thought culminated much later in the neo-Platonists, who, as we shall see, influenced Christian teaching. Classical Greeks had other views, and Plato himself makes it perfectly clear in the *Symposium* that more was involved in his "sacred love" than a desire to improve the mind: "Everything that the lovers do for the boys they cherish, the prayers and entreaties with which they support their suit, the oaths they swear, the nights they spend on the doorstep of the beloved one, and the slavery they endure for his sake, which no real slave would put up with." Such bonds of love serve in two works of Plato, *Symposium* and *Phaedrus,* as the starting point for his whole metaphysical theory, based on the response of the older male to the younger, who is the quintessence of beauty, both of the body and the soul.

Lesbos

While their husbands courted boy lovers, it would have been surprising if the women were never tempted to seek consolation with each other. The term "lesbian" derives from the birthplace of the poetess Sappho, the island of Lesbos. Her active life covered the first quarter of the sixth century B.C., before the great age of Athens. The surviving fragments of her poems overflow with terms of endearment for her own sex, though uncertainties persist as to how far they imply carnal desire; some scholars have insisted on her innocence in that respect. But she is known to have gathered around her a circle of young girls, and for these she expresses such passion in her verse as to cast doubt on any denials of sexual implications.

Her contemporaries probably took the carnal element for granted, since the Greeks did not regard lesbianism as a vice and were more interested in Sappho's personality than in any sexual predilections, which barely deserved comment (classical literature contains only a single reference to female homosexuality). Sappho accordingly was made the heroine of no less than six plays, but in all these she has male lovers, and more direct associations with lesbianism stem from commentators of later times. However, the historian Plutarch states that female homosexuality was widespread, at least in Sparta. Lesbians were also called tribads (from the Greek verb meaning "to rub"). A famous tribad, Philaenis of Leucadia, even wrote a manual on sexual postures for women.

The legendary Amazons, or female warriors, who were held to possess certain manly qualities, are portrayed more as hermaphrodites than as lesbians; they were clad like men, and reputedly burned off their breasts in order not to be hampered when bending the bow or hurling the javelin. The Amazons used the heavy arms of the heroes, were excellent horsewomen, and even fought from war chariots. No description implies a reversal of the sexual impulse, and they were never described as inclined to love of any kind. In plastic art they are a favorite motif, but without any clear sexual identity.

Priapus

The average Greek had plentiful sexual options, both male and female; if neither was available, onanism was an acceptable substitute, as attested to by various authors. Plastic artists were fond of depicting such scenes; for instance, a cup in the Royal Museum of Brussels shows a garlanded youth performing the act. Female self-abuse figures less often in literature, but this is simply because writers were more interested in men than in women. Probably, since alternatives were fewer, women had more recourse to masturbation than men did. Examples even survive of the "self-satisfiers" the women used. The wealthy commercial city of Miletus specialized in the manufacture of these devices.

The third-century poet Herondas relates how two girls talked without embarrassment about this instrument, known as an *olisbos.* One of them, Coritto, has acquired an olisbos, and her friend Metro is most anxious to borrow it and also asks for the name of the maker in order to buy her own. Coritto describes in detail how to find the master worker, and Metro goes off to get one of the devices for herself.

Orgies served as another variant on intercourse between two partners. Orgiastic ceremonies, a common feature of religions of the ancient Near East, often involved self-mutilation. Already in the seventh century B.C., the Greeks had borrowed the cult of the Babylonian Tammuz, by then known as Adonis, who was killed by a boar and despairingly mourned by Aphrodite until his annual rebirth. Hetairai not only served Aphrodite, great mother and goddess of love, as temple prostitutes; they also played a leading role in the worship of another mother goddess, Rhea, often called Cybele, whose lover was Attis. Her priests and worshipers would roam over forest and mountain carrying blazing torches and uttering savage cries. In their frenzy they would at times even castrate themselves. Cybele's beloved partner Attis reportedly gelded himself, and after he became a eunuch wore female garb. He subsequently died, and at the annual festival of the great mother, to mark the grief of Cybele for her lover's death, devotees slashed themselves with knives designed for the purpose and decorated with precious stones.

Cybele's priests were known as *galli.* After self-mutilation at the feast of the mother goddess, they would dash their severed members against the image of the deity; like Attis, they thereafter dressed as women. The apparent purpose behind the practice was to make the priests resemble their goddess as closely as possible. Though eunuchs had already fulfilled a whole range of functions in Mesopotamia, the notion of the eunuch as priest developed only later, as an aspect of the worship of Cybele and Artemis, the great goddess of Ephesus. Artemis in Ephesus was served by both female virgins and by eunuchs; by the act of mutilation, the latter also achieved a state of chastity, bereft of sexual organs that contrasted with those of the goddess.

THE RAMPANT GOD

The Greeks inherited from the Near East the cult of the phallus, personified by the god Priapus, the companion of the orgiastic Dionysus, whose son he is sometimes called. This cult was important in Athens, which obliged its colonies to send to Athens huge phalli as a form of tribute, to be used in the festival of the Dionysia at the end of the wine harvest. The comic playwright Aristophanes describes a family on its way to the ceremony. In front went the oldest daughter, carrying a giant phallus, painted red; after her came the master of the house, singing an erotic song to celebrate the feast. As the merrymaking reached its climax, men cast off any inhibitions caused by the presence of their families; frenzied with wine, they indulged in open lovemaking with hetairai and with handsome youths. Vases have been found on the Acropolis showing young maidens at this feast dancing wildly and brandishing huge phalli.

The symbol of Priapus was the erect penis, engraved on many coins minted in his honor. In a favorite portrayal, the god stands upright and raises his dress in front to serve as a basket for fruit and flowers. Sometimes the fruit is absent and he merely raises his garb to show his outsized penis. Since the sexual impulse had engendered the human race, he was a key figure in the pantheon; he was identified at times with the sun god Helios and with the cosmos; one carving of his symbol, the phallus, bears the inscription "the savior of the world."

Though often linked to Dionysus, Priapus had his own sanctuaries in many cities. As champion of fertility, he fostered the growth of the crops; in addition, he was thought to ward off thieves and birds. Rough wooden figures of a naked Priapus, painted red and with large erect member, were commonly to be seen in fields and gardens; such images carried a bundle of reeds on their head, which would rattle in the wind and scare away the birds.

As guardian of the crops, Priapus was a benignant deity. The phallic symbol offered special protection against the evil eye, which supposedly became so bewitched by its aspect that it ignored other victims. A huge penis would be painted wherever the evil eye was most feared, and phallic images have been found both in public places and private dwellings, on household implements, and even on dresses and ornaments. Certain phalli were designed so that they could be carried by a handle, while others had claws and wings. The winged penis was found in Pompeii, and replicas are even sold to tourists today.

Androgynous attitudes in Greece led to a curious link between Priapus, the supermale, and the girlish Hermaphroditus; portrayals of the two deities reveal traits in common, such as the way they lift up their dress. Priapus sometimes has the breasts of a woman, so that it is not always clear whether Priapus or Hermaphroditus is intended.

Hermaphroditus

Greek institutionalized homosexuality has no exact equivalent elsewhere, though certain parallels exist, for instance, among the samurai, the military elite of Japan. In contrast, other Greek practices, such as orgiastic festivals, temple prostitution and phallicism, were common to many cultures. A question therefore remains: Why did this institution thrive in Greece rather than elsewhere?

This question is hard to answer today, for however much one may insist that Western civilization derives from Greece, it also inherited from the Old and New Testaments an implacable ban on homosexuality that implied drawing a sharp dividing line between the sexes. As a result, the Judeo-Christian and Greek points of view are diametrically opposed, and even in the more liberal climate of today, a residue of such feelings remains.

In Greece, as we have seen, androgynous, or bisexual, attitudes narrowed the gap between heterosexual and homosexual love. While other peoples stressed the masculinity of man and the femininity of woman, the Greeks minimized them; in the idealized hermaphrodite, they disappeared altogether.

In Greek art sexual characteristics are understated. The corpulent women of the Near East, with their dangling breasts and spreading hips, were not to Greek taste. Whether the inscription names a figure as Hermes or Aphrodite, the body is boyishly slim and the arms girlishly fine. Statues of gods and humans are not purposefully desexualized, as in the Middle Ages; any distinction between the sexes is simply reduced to a minimum.

This cult of the androgynous is also reflected in Greek religion. The cult was based on an ancient tradition, since it was commonly believed that humanity began with three sexes; the first had two male organs, the second two female organs, while the third was androgyne, having one of each. In Amathis, on the island of Cyprus, as part of a religious rite, a youth was obliged once a year to lie in childbed and to imitate a woman in the pangs of labor, thus recalling the institution of couvade, so widespread among more primitive peoples. The Greeks were much given to transvestite ceremonies, and even men of heterosexual habits would appear in women's clothes at religious festivals. The hermaphrodite god Aphroditus was represented as bearded in certain statues, with male sex organs, but had the bodily form and wore the dress of a woman.

Such usages were inspired by the legend of Hermaphroditus, a dazzlingly beautiful boy who at the age of fifteen was loved by Salmacis, nymph of the spring of that name. Against his will he was enticed by Salmacis down into the water and forced to copulate; the gods granted her desire for eternal union with her lover by joining them into a single two-sexed being. The god Hermes and the goddess Aphrodite then decreed that every man who henceforth bathed in the spring would emerge semivir (half man, half woman) and be effeminate in character.

Far from being a latter-day fashion, hermaphrodite gods existed in early times, and their cult was widespread. Hermaphroditus himself often appears in plastic and pictorial art, and rooms in private houses, baths, and gymnasia were adorned with his statues and pictures. Beautiful sleeping figures of Hermaphroditus survive; sometimes also he is shown copulating with Pan or with a satyr. Another hermaphrodite deity was Leucippus; he had origianlly been a girl, but at his mother's bidding he was changed by the god Leto into a young man. Sex change also occurs in Greek mythology—a famous case was the soothsayer Tiresias; born a boy, he was changed into a woman and then back into a man. Even the heroic Achilles was believed by later Greeks to have lived part of his life as a girl.

The hermaphrodite state was thus in Greece an ideal rather than an abasement, a notion inherited in part from previous civilizations. The Syrian Baal is sometimes represented as two-sexed, and bearded images of the great Egyptian goddess Isis have also been found. Even the androgynous nature of the Hebrew Yahweh is made clear in the Book of Genesis: "In that day God created man . . . male and female created he them, and blessed them and called their name Adam." Thus at the beginning Adam was both male and female, and it was only after God had taken away part of Adam's body that Eve, the female, was created as a separate entity.

A range of intermediate types of humans, with characteristics of both sexes, does exist in real life, as we have seen. In tribal societies they were often venerated, but in higher civilizations the concept more than the person was idealized and raised to the status of a cult. In Hindu mythology, Shiva and Parvati originated as the two halves of one androgynous god, Virag. The great Brahma was also hermaphroditic and usually stands upon a lotus, symbolic of that state; early statues represent Shiva with his right side male and his left side female. Chinese legends pay tribute to transsexual beings, and the annals of the Liu Sung dynasty report a case in the third century A.D. of a hermaphrodite who was capable of having intercourse either as a man or as a woman and was given to excesses in both roles.

But if the notion of an intermediate sex is widespread, it is especially prominent in Greece. To understand the Greek attitude to sex, it has continually to be borne in mind that the dividing line between the two sexes was narrow and easily crossed, and distinctions that were obvious to other peoples were to them meaningless. To quote again Sir Kenneth Dover: "So long as we think of the world as divided into homosexuals and heterosexuals, and regard the commission of a homosexual act, or even the entertainings of a homosexual desire, as an irrevocable step across a frontier which divides the normal, healthy, sane, natural and good from the abnormal, insane, unnatural and evil, we shall not get very far in understanding Greek attitudes to homosexuality."

The Greeks actually took pride in this feature of their culture and were not at all ashamed to regard themselves as mentors of other peoples. Xenophon makes King Cyrus of Persia ask: "Is it your intention to teach Greek customs to that young man lying next to you since he is so handsome?"

Other societies have shown respect for the effeminate male—or semivir—but such tendencies stop far short of the Greek system of formalized homosexuality as the quintessence of the good and the beautiful. The function of the man-boy relationship as a bulwark of the military establishment is basic; ideally suited to the small and select armies of Greek city-states, it would have had no place in the mass forces of ancient empires, such as their Persian adversaries. But warring city-states have existed elsewhere, and if in Greece institutionalized homosexuality assumed such importance, this was surely due to a combination of factors, as an answer to both Greek intellectual and military needs.

To the heirs of an age-long tradition of female inferiority, to which they added their own ideal of bodily grace and mental agility combined, a purely heterosexual society had obvious limitations. The Greek male sought not only physical but also intellectual gifts that few women could acquire. While the spiritual element in the relationship is obvious, the Greeks themselves perhaps tended in decorous vase paintings to understate the sexual aspect of the system; possibly, however, any conventional restraints on homosexual acts that existed in theory did not prevent the two partners from seeking in practice from their relationship the fullest physical as well as spiritual fulfillment.

As the Romans Do

The very word for sex derives from the Latin *sexus,* and Roma written in reverse spells "amor." However, the Romans made few innovations in this field. They mainly followed in the footsteps of the Greeks, with a certain shift of emphasis: Where the Greeks idealized the love of boys, most Romans favored women.

Rome's success story begins with a sexual assault, the rape of the Sabine women. The first king, Romulus, invited his neighbors, the Sabines, to a banquet. They brought their women and children to the feast, in the midst of which the hosts drove out the male guests and fell upon their wives. The war that followed started badly for the Romans. By an odd turn of fortune, however, the situation was saved by the Sabine women, who apparently bore no grudge against the rapists; the women threw themselves between the combatants and persuaded them to make peace and to form a single nation.

The rule of the Tarquinian Dynasty, founded by Romulus, ended in another story of sexual violence, the rape of Lucretia. The assault on the Sabines is the reverse of the more typical national legend, since it does little credit to the Roman males, though it exalts the status of their women. The rape of Lucretia, equally inglorious, merely offers a lesson that it is better not to quarrel over women, since it brought down the dynasty that fought so doughtily over her.

The Roman poets extolled their lovers, whether male or female, in passionate verse. For instance, Catullus, whose affairs were ardent and unhappy, wrote poems addressed to members of his own sex until at the age of twenty-six he met his great love, Lesbia. In the case of Tibullus, a number of whose elegies have been preserved, it is difficult to determine at what stages in his life he adored Delia and when he loved the capricious boy Marathus.

Rome, like Athens, also had its women-haters. Certain Romans, such as the philosopher Seneca, would rail against the female sex and say that it was fatuous to marry and have children; Cicero, after separating from his first wife, Terentia, said that he would never marry again, for he could not cope with a wife and with philosophy at the same time. However, the status of women was far higher than in Greece, and from about the end of the Second Punic War in 201 B.C. a process of emancipation began, and women ceased to be household chattels. By imperial times the process had run its full course; this newfound freedom was not always put to very good use, and Rome was to be rocked by the scandals of its libidinous matrons.

By this time the nature of marriage had changed—the woman was expected to give her husband not merely offspring but also pleasure; should she fail to do so, he was entitled to seek it elsewhere. This was not difficult, since a man could have as many sexual partners, male or female, as he could afford. Prostitution of every kind thrived and was never disguised as a form of religion, since no prostitutes were connected with the temples. The great moralists, such as Cato, Cicero, and Seneca, were unwavering in their praise of prostitution as a positive safeguard to wedlock, since it kept men from stealing other peoples' wives and breaking up their marriages.

Rome was so much larger and so much richer than Athens, and sexual satisfaction was available on a correspondingly lavish scale. Every Roman city had its quota of brothels, which bore the Latin name *lupanar,* literally meaning "she-wolf's den." In addition to the common whorehouses, there were luxury establishments for the rich. One of these, the House of the Vettii, has survived intact, preserved by the volcanic ash that smothered Pompeii in A.D. 79. Pompeii was only a small town, and far grander establishments surely existed in the capital. Both the frescoes of the reception rooms in the House of the Vettii and those of the tiny cells designed for lovemaking leave nothing to the imagination, and the many erotic scenes are painted by skilled hands.

Quite apart from brothels themselves, both in Rome and in provincial cities girls were available for the same purposes in other convenient locations. Innkeepers and even owners of bakeries and cookshops might provide females to entice their customers. These, like the brothel girls, were invariably slaves. Many others walked the streets; they were known by a variety of names, and one category was called *bustuariae,* or gravewatchers, because they plied their trade in cemeteries and supplemented this source of income by working as professional mourners.

A curious feature of Roman brothels was the use of finely minted tokens or coins, many of which have survived. Suppose a customer wanted a particular girl—the occupant, say, of Cubicle 7, he would first pay at the cash desk, where he would receive a metal token entitling him to the use of Cubicle 7 and its occupant.

Both in public baths and in brothels, boys as well as girls were in plentiful supply. The host at a banquet might be expected to offer his guests a choice of fine-looking male and female slaves; for such prize exhibits, of every color, race, and age, a high price had to be paid in the slave market.

Rome at quite an early stage began to suffer from a population problem, due to the failure of freeborn citizens to produce enough offspring. Emperor Augustus enacted a series of laws on public morals whose aim was to compel men between the ages of twenty-five and sixty to marry and father children; one of these laws even made homosexual intercourse a punishable offense. Augustus' legislation seems to have had little effect, and Rome remained a highly sex-oriented, if unprolific, society. Thus Venus as goddess of love was worshiped with even greater devotion than her Greek counterpart, Aphrodite. Her cult was all-embracing; she was at the same time the guardian of honorable marriage, the goddess of harlots, and in a more general way, the mother of the nation. In this role of great mother, Venus came to be identified with Rome herself; the Temple of Venus and Rome, with its golden roof, was among the chief landmarks of the city.

The great shrine of Venus Venticurdia in Rome was served not by harlots but by vestal virgins. They were vowed to celibacy on pain of death, and in 114 B.C. three of them were condemned to die for yielding to the advances of Roman knights. A more gruesome fate awaited other vestal virgins who broke their vows of chastity. They were first beaten with rods and then, as though already dead, were led into a subterranean vault and buried alive.

Paradoxically, the vestal virgins worshiped the phallus as a god; this symbol was universal in Rome, and a miniature version was even hung around children's necks to ward off bad luck. In addition to the cult of Priapus, which spread to Rome, another god of fertility, Liber, of local origin, was also feted in ceremonies in which a huge wooden phallus was carried on a cart about the fields and through the city. Like the dionysia, the Roman bacchanalia were the scenes of wild orgies, in which women played a major part. Shocked by the debauchery that accompanied these festivals, the Senate in 186 B.C. tried to end them by law.

Under the empire, permissiveness was no longer confined to

orgiastic rites at set intervals. In marked contrast to Augustus, certain of his successors themselves set the pace. Tiberius, Augustus' stepson, had spent the last six years of his life in Capri, where he reportedly indulged in a life of debauchery with adolescents of both sexes. Although such stories run counter to what is known of Tiberius during his active career, the tales that surround his successor, Caligula, are less easy to dismiss. He is said to have worn women's clothes in public, appearing as Venus but sporting a golden beard. Besides abusing freeborn boys and seducing married women, including brides on their wedding day, he went so far as to debauch a vestal virgin, Rubia.

The emancipation of women reached a point where even the most scandalous conduct on the part of emperors was outmatched by that of their wives and daughters. Among the most notorious was Julia, the daughter of Augustus. In youth she was famed both for beauty and intellect. She was first married to Agrippa, Augustus' leading general. Her infidelities were notorious; asked why, in spite of her varied love life, all her children looked like her husband, she replied cynically that she never gave herself to a lover until she knew that she was pregnant by her own spouse. When Agrippa died at the age of fifty-one, worn out by a life of service to his master, Julia was married off to Tiberius, the emperor's stepson, who was thereby forced to end a happy marriage for reasons of state. He became so disgusted with Julia's wanton behavior that he retired to Rhodes and gave up the company of women altogether. After this separation from Tiberius, Julia threw all caution to the winds. In her nightly revels in the city streets a favorite site for her embraces was the Forum itself, beside the rostrum from which her father had promulgated his law against adultery. As an adulteress now turned whore, she would offer favors to unknown lovers. When he heard about Julia's conduct, Augustus was so outraged that he informed the Senate of her misdeeds, and as a result she was banished to Pandateria, a tiny island off the Campanian coast, where she was guarded like a dangerous prisoner.

Even more infamous was Messalina, married at the age of fifteen to the fifty-year-old Claudius (A.D. 41–54). She was responsible for the death of many blameless victims whom

Claudius executed at her behest and who were innocent of any crime, for Messalina was not only man-mad but also a murderess. Her central interest was sexual adventure. The man who satisfied her—no easy feat—became her protégé; any who refused her forfeited his life, denounced to the emperor as a conspirator.

Roman society followed the example of its rulers, and the divorce rate spiraled. Seneca remarked that some women counted the years, not by the names of the consuls elected for that period, but by their successive marriages. The poet and moralist Juvenal wrote of women who had as many as eight husbands in five years and who were once more divorced even before the green boughs that had adorned the gate of their house to greet a new spouse were faded.

Among the Roman elite, the emancipation of women attained proportions hitherto unknown, scarcely to be repeated for nearly two thousand years. Far removed from their previous lot as household chattels, the leading matrons deceived their husbands, defied their wishes, and often ended by divorcing them. In Rome, therefore, we find a society where originally sexual relations were based on the universal rules of the ancient Near East. But Roman sex life then took a very different turn; when the city acquired immense power and wealth, such rules were cast aside, particularly by its licentious matrons. The reaction to such excesses was gradual, but when it came it was dramatic; nearly three centuries after the time of Julia and Messalina, Christianity triumphed, and the Church fathers were free to impose their sex-negative fetters upon the pagan world.

CHAPTER SEVEN

The People
of the Book

The Old Testament

For Christianity alone, among world religions, sex was little but a necessary evil. As a grudging concession to human frailty, the early fathers spoke of marriage as at best an escape from worse sins; St. Paul, in principle against a man so much as touching a woman, in practice conceded that it might be better to marry than to face the fires of hell. For St. Augustine all coitus was repellant.

The mores of those many non-Western peoples, both primitive and advanced, for whom sex was not a curse but a blessing, are our main theme. Their sex-positive precepts may still surprise us, because they are so alien to our own traditions, whether Christian or Jewish. Yet it may be easier for Westerners to grasp the force of such precepts if they are conscious of how their own Judeo-Christian dogma came to the opposite conclusions, making of sex an ugly word, brushed firmly under the mat as unmentionable in polite society. The rules of most other cultures stand in total contrast to the attempt, sustained for almost two millennia, to fly in the face of human nature and to ignore that man is just as inclined to copy the more casual mating habits of the chimpanzee as those of the monogamous gorilla. The origins of this attempt long predate Jesus and stem partly from the Old Testament, which served as a basis both for Christianity and Islam; as we shall also see in this chapter, Mohammed drew different conclusions from the same text.

The shore of the eastern Mediterranean derived its culture from both ancient Egypt and Mesopotamia; from each of these, Christianity, also born on that shore, borrowed much. Throughout the whole Near East the mother goddess was adored, regardless of whether she was called Isis, Astarte, Ishtar, or Aphrodite; everywhere her role was the same, as a sensual deity symbolizing fertility in all its forms. Inevitably she had her spouse or lover, whether Dummuzi, Tammuz, Adonis, or Attis, who died—or disappeared into the bowels of the earth—each autumn and returned in the spring to his bereaved mistress.

Among the most fervent devotees of this cult were the Phoenicians, who lived in present-day Syria and Lebanon. Byblos, on the coast of the Lebanon, was a melting pot of many cultures, and vestiges of all are still visible. Here the mother goddess was called Aphrodite and her lover was Adonis, whose annual demise still moved Greeks and Romans to frenzied grief. As an added refinement to earlier legends, Adonis died annually when gored by a wild boar, and from his blood a scarlet anemone was said to have sprung. Roman eyewitnesses describe a form of ritual prostitution still practiced in Byblos on the day that marked Adonis' return from the underworld; the women had to offer themselves to all comers as part of the rites to ensure a good harvest.

The Canaanites, from whom the Hebrews wrested part of Palestine, were the Phoenicians' close neighbors and kinsmen and play an important part in the Old Testament. Once they had settled there, the pastoral Israelites became farmers; heedless of their own elders, they then began to worship the fertility deities of the Canaanites, whose particular version of the mother goddess was called Ashera, or Astarte.

170

Ashera as queen of heaven gained a large following in Jerusalem itself, and the prophet Jeremiah fulminated against "the women who wept for Ashera at the gates of Jerusalem." The worship of Jehovah, the embryo monotheism the Hebrews brought to Palestine, thus came under constant pressure from Middle Eastern beliefs. The spearhead of their attack was the cult of the mother goddess, and its seductions are a constant cause for lament in the Old Testament. A gruesome by-product of this cult was the practice of human sacrifice to Baal, or Moloch, sometimes described as Ashera's husband. Children were "passed through the fire" in honor of Baal, a practice castigated by the prophets.

Another local custom copied by Israel was temple harlotry. Certain females, such as the daughters of Moab, had in early times performed the sex act in honor of the deity, but Moses punished them by hanging. Nonetheless, under Canaanite influence prostitutes, both male and female, were attached to the temples, for the use of visitors and pilgrims. The Book of Samuel, for instance, tells how Eli's sons lay with "the women that assembled at the door of the tabernacle."

There were two biblical terms for prostitute: *zonah* for the profane and *q'deshah* for the sacred. The two were at times confused, as in the Judah-Tamar episode, where no clear-cut distinction is made between them. The Book of Genesis relates that Judah saw a veiled woman whom he took for a zonah; on a strictly business basis it was agreed that "he shall come into her," and would pay for her favors with a kid. But when his friend Hirah was sent to pay the harlot, he first could not locate her; later when she is found, she is called a q'deshah. Such incidents occur throughout the Old Testament, and harlots "who lie under the oaks on the hilltop" are mentioned in one of the last books, Hosea. These, plying their trade beyond the vicinity of any temple, were clearly zonahs.

Male prostitutes were denounced by the elders at an early stage and in the Book of Deuteronomy are even called "dogs." Those attached to temples were known collectively as *q'deshoth*, literally meaning "holy" or "consecrated." The term is rendered into English by the less complimentary "sodomite."

The Hebrews not only at times copied Canaanite forms of worship, including copulation with temple prostitutes; in addition, relations between man and wife conformed to the Mesopotamian pattern. The Old Testament attitude to marriage implicitly followed the code of Hammurabi; patriarchal control remained absolute, and the head of the family had undisputed rights of disposal over women and children. The ban on adultery contained in Moses' Ten Commandments was strictly enforced. Women offenders were drowned, as in Babylon, but false accusations also were punishable by death. Celibacy was not expressly forbidden but was treated as unnatural. If an elder brother died without issue, the younger brother was legally bound to marry the widow. Equally, if his first wife was barren, a man could officially marry a second wife; in addition, the keeping of concubines was a fairly common practice among the earlier Old Testament rulers and leaders.

Premarital sex was kept to a minimum by the simple device of early marriage, usually at the age of fifteen for males and even younger for girls. The principal aim was to make sure that every eligible person was married off; no one should be left without a mate of the opposite sex. The Song of Songs and the Book of Proverbs are fairly lenient toward coitus between unmarried males and females, on the strict proviso that penetration took place; the later Talmud texts are even more adamant that in intercourse among spouses, the semen must be deposited in the vagina. Failure to respect this rule was the sole offense of the hapless Onan, whose name has ever since been coupled with masturbation. Onan was compelled by law to marry his brother's widow, Tamar. He did not wish to do so, and when he duly had intercourse with her, he let his seed spill on the ground, thus failing to inseminate Tamar and thereby maintain his brother's line.

The Book of Kings is full of reminders of the flouting by its monarchs of ancient taboos. In this, the Old Testament rulers were merely the precursors of those countless Christian kings who were slow to practice what their prelates preached. Heathen permissiveness had reached its climax at about the time of the split between the two kingdoms of Israel and Judah in A.D. 926.

From this point onward, innate puritanism began to recover lost ground; prostitutes, whether sacred or profane (equally translated into English as "harlots"), came under heavy fire. Not only were ordinary whores proscribed, but also the laws of Deuteronomy laid down that "there shall be no female sacred prostitute (q'deshah) and no male sacred prostitute *(q'adesh)* of the sons of Israel." It is difficult to fix the date for this outright rejection of sacred prostitution. Throughout the Book of Kings, which carries the history of Judah and Israel down to the end of the monarchy in the sixth century B.C., the paradox is stressed: the de facto existence of a custom that for the latter-day narrator of the book is an abomination. Sex-negative attitudes gathered force, and by the seventh century B.C. the great prophets were fulminating against prostitution of all kinds, both sacred and profane. Among their most impassioned tirades are those directed against the consecrated temple sodomites. Though commonplace among their neighbors, they excited the wrath of these Hebrew prophets and could scarcely have attracted such abuse had they not also been popular in Israel.

Legislation against such "vices" was at first ineffective. Already King Asa, grandson of Solomon, tried to put away the male sacred prostitutes from the land. His son, Jehoshaphat, tried again and was no more successful, since they clearly survived until the Babylonian exile in 586 B.C. Three centuries of royal decrees backed by the prophets' invectives, failed to purge the temples of their presence.

The wrath of the prophets was directed not upon homosexuality as such but against the temple prostitutes to whom the term "sodomite" came to be applied. But the Old Testament itself contains not a hint that the people of Sodom and Gomorrah behaved as ancient Greeks, and there is no reason to suppose that the sexual habits of these two cities differed from those of the rest of Israel.

Sodom was reportedly guilty of the sins of pride, haughtiness, and of "doing abominable things." After the Lord had already decided to destroy the city, he sent a deputation of angels, who were invited to stay in Lot's house in that place, where a number of male citizens gathered, so that they might "know" them. The

Hebrew word for "to know" also has a sexual connotation. But aside from other problems posed by the courting of such asexual beings, it must be open to question whether copulation with an angel—if anatomically feasible—would be a homosexual act. The story as told in the Book of Genesis perhaps implies, but hardly states, that the men who sought to "know" the angels were homosexuals, though further suspicions on that score are admittedly raised by their offhand rejection of Lot's offer of his two daughters as a substitute for the angels. Whatever the besetting sin of Sodom, sodomy seems to have been practiced by all and sundry. Abraham, after a session of hard bargaining, extracted a promise from the Lord (already resolved on the city's destruction) that if even ten righteous people could be found there, the city would be spared. It is rather hard to believe that the people of Sodom could not have mustered even as few as ten confirmed heterosexuals and thereby escaped their awful fate. In the Koran version of the story, the men of Sodom are portrayed as more bisexual.

Lechery in Sodom—apart from the incident of the angels—is first mentioned in Jewish noncanonical writings from 200 B.C. onward, and in these it is merely condemned for general laxity. Only subsequent crusaders against homosexuality poured scorn upon the city as the birthplace of sodomy and as the symbol of the sin that was the cause of its downfall. This hatred of postexile Judaism for pederasty, centuries before the time of Christ, seems to have arisen because for Palestinian Jews, ever since Alexander the Great's incursion into their land, the Greek culture and Greek sexual customs were seen as threats to their own heritage. This reaction drew strength from their conviction that semen is precious, to be deposited solely in the female vagina and in no other place. A comparable stigma attached to masturbation, another waste of seed, named after the unfortunate Onan.

This latter-day revulsion against pagan practices was not aimed only at pederasts and onanists. Animal contacts attracted the moralists' censure; to avoid any possible temptation, Talmudic writers went as far as to forbid widows to keep pet dogs. In addition, the Jewish moral revival in the last centuries B.C.

174

gave rise to another strange obsession, eagerly adopted by the Christian Church: the ban on nudity. This ban not only reflects a general reaction against Greek practices but more particularly a veiled but intense fear of homosexuality.

Ascetic Antecedents

The sex-negative quality of Christianity is self-evident. However, the reverse proposition is less often stressed, that Christianity did not invent asceticism but that circumstances forced its teachers to espouse this cause to win converts.

St. Paul transformed a localized cult into a world religion. To achieve his purpose, he borrowed as much from Greek as from Hebrew traditions. As we have seen, the Jewish moral revival after the Babylonian exile had an austere, or sex-negative side, reflecting the resolve to resolidify Hebrew life after this demoralizing experience. Paradoxically, though this was ostensibly a reaction against Greek mores, ascetic forces also were gaining strength in Greece itself, and these forces had an even more profound effect on Christian teaching.

In the pleasure-loving society of Greece, hedonism had always been tinged with asceticism. Orpheus started life as a companion of the orgiastic Dionysus. Orpheus finally lost his struggle to recover Eurydice from the underworld; one version implies that he then became a homosexual, but according to another, in a fit of sour grapes toward womankind, he gave up all forms of sex. This version of the legend gave birth to the Orphic mysteries: For the initiate, the body was a foul prison in which the pure soul was incarcerated; immortality was the prize for renouncing the sins of the flesh. Orphism became popular and this latent dualism, the distinction between the higher and lower, the struggle between the soul and the body, was to become a powerful force in latter-day Greek thought. Hence in this sex-positive civilization, the tendency was never absent, though few classical Greeks took much account of such notions, which were at variance with their ideal of the beautiful and the good, and their cult of both body and mind. But the full effects of this latent countercult, in which the flesh became not the ally but the adversary of the spirit, came to be felt very much later.

At an early stage, this orphic doctrine was taken up by the followers of the semimythical mathematician Pythagoras; from Pythagoras it passed to Plato, who pointed to the dual contrast of idea and matter, sanctifying the soul and denigrating the body. But whatever the appeal in theory of this dogma, it did not tempt Plato's own circle into abandoning the joys of profane as well as sacred love.

In the following century, certain philosophers went farther than Plato. The Epicureans, a name now used to describe a gourmet, were in their own day more concerned with denouncing the pleasures of the bed than with praising those of the table. According to Epicurus himself, "sexual intercourse never benefited any man." The Cynics, of whom the most famous was Diogenes, took the same view. Diogenes lived in a tub; ensconced in such an implausible setting for lovemaking, he successfully shunned the temptations of the flesh. Another sect, the Stoics, did not condemn sex altogether but insisted that intercourse was permissible only if its object was to procreate children—a point that became basic to Christian teaching.

This antisex undercurrent in Greek thought gained added strength in the three centuries that divided the death of Alexander the Great from the birth of Jesus; its effect on St. Paul, the Greek renegade, was profound. It then gathered momentum under the Roman Empire. The third century A.D. marked the rise of neo-Platonism; its chief protagonist, Plotinus, went far beyond Plato in seeking mystical ecstasy by disciplining the body and by denigrating sex. Porphyry, pupil and biographer of Plotinus, condemned any kind of pleasure as sinful, including horse racing and dancing, but above all, intercourse.

Jesus and St. Paul

In its birthplace Christianity first imbibed the more austere spirit of postexile Judaism and then thrived in a broader setting, in regions where not Judaism but this latter-day Greek strain of asceticism was a potent force.

Jesus himself is presented in the gospels as asexual and throughout the ages has been portrayed by artists with a willowy body and loose blond tresses that make the Greek Hermaphroditus seem positively *macho.* Jesus spared few words for sex and was adroit in parrying questions on that topic; we do not know whether he was unconcerned or whether his interest went unrecorded. On one occasion Jesus angered the Pharisees by speaking against divorce, traditionally accepted; in St. Matthew's gospel he says that for a man to put away his wife is a form of adultery and that if the wife seeks a new husband, she is also guilty. His comments on the matter nonetheless included a broad escape clause (rejected by the Roman Church), since he allowed divorce "in cases of fornication." In another context he cited Moses, who had tolerated divorce "because of the hardness of your hearts." In the instance of the woman taken in adultery he merely said, "Let him among you who is without sin cast the first stone." In other words, for Jesus the real sin is hypocrisy.

When asked whether it was better not to marry, Jesus gave the surprising answer that celibacy was only for eunuchs, some of whom were made "for the kingdom of heaven's sake." The people of Palestine were no strangers to castration as a religious rite, at a time when the cult of Cybele was thriving as never before. Origen, a schoolmaster of Alexandria, who lived some two centuries after the Crucifixion, took Jesus at his word and actually castrated himself to become immune from the sins of the flesh.

References to sexual conduct in the New Testament are so ambiguous as to make interpretation hard. Jesus makes no distinction between thought and action when he states that lust is just as evil as adultery: "Everyone who looketh upon a woman to lust after her hath committed adultery already with her in his heart," an unsure guideline for those more concerned with rules of behavior than with passing fancy. These few casual remarks served as the foundation stones for the most restrictive code of sexual conduct in human history, complete with the most explicit catalogue of prohibitions, not always enforceable in practice.

The trend had begun with St. Paul, the hellenized Jew who

adapted both the life story and doctrine of Jesus to the current trends of the classic world. The apostle went far beyond even Jewish asceticism by taking a negative view of marriage. Not surprisingly, his most stringent asides were reserved for that sink of pagan iniquity, Corinth. He did not impose celibacy but merely described it as superior: "It is well for a man not to touch a woman." St. Paul, perhaps soured by his own unsuccessful wooing of the high priest's daughter, was imbued with an anti-womanism inherited both from Hellenism and Judaism. If one had to have a wife, she should be seen and not heard: "Let women learn in silence with all subjection." Whereas the Greeks treated women more as harmless chattels, for the Hebrews they could be positively wicked, and in the Old Testament the woman is traditionally the temptress and the harlot; Delilah caused Sampson's downfall, and Potiphar's wife tried to seduce Joseph. While for Paul the ideal course was to avoid contact with women, he grudgingly accepted marriage, and only marriage, as a sexual outlet for those who could not resist the temptations of the flesh: "Let every man have his own wife . . . for it is better to marry than to burn."

Whereas the generally sex-negative attitude of Christianity, as preached by Paul and his successors, thus has both Greek and Judaic roots, his hostility to homosexuality is more anti-Greek. Paul referred to "men committing shameless acts with men," and he made his attitude even clearer in his Epistle to the Romans: "And likewise also the men, leaving the natural use of women, burned in their lust, one toward another." However, only after his time did Sodom come to be equated with pederasty; Philo Judaeus and Josephus, who died in A.D. 96, the two Jewish writers most active at the time, first bestowed on Sodom this dubious distinction. Philo writes: "Not only in their mad lust for women did they (the people of Sodom) violate the marriages of their neighbors, but also men mounted males without respect for the sin against nature which the active partner share with the passive." Josephus, in accusing the Sodomites of raping the angels, calls the latter "young men." However, Christian antipathy toward pederasty is also in part a legacy of Persian Zoroastrianism, which influenced Judaism and was fanatically antihomosexual. The Persians knew the Greeks all too well, and this revulsion arose from a hatred of their customs. According to Zoroaster, the fiends and demons had been created by acts of unnatural intercourse by the Prince of Darkness. Anyone who committed a homosexual act was thereby thought of as a devil and ceased to be a member of the human race.

In previous chapters it was implied that each culture gets the sex life that it deserves, or more specifically, that serves its established aims and institutions, as far as they can be defined. But what had the Rome of Constantine done to deserve the imposition of such an antihumanist, or even antihuman, brand of asceticism? Far from being a passing fashion, it showed great staying power and was to reach a new climax thirteen hundred years later in the teaching of John Calvin. Unlike Islam, whose rise led to the creation of a new empire, Christianity thrived at a time when the fabric of the ancient world was disintegrating, a decline that it did not cause but from which it was able to profit.

The aim of Paul and his successors was to preach a creed that would win men's hearts as the outright enemy of the current laxity and decadence. Asceticism was forged into a major weapon in their armory between the time when the gospels were written and their formal triumph two centuries later. Christians were not the only ones to employ this weapon, for Christianity, far from developing in a vacuum, found itself in a world in which it competed with other self-denying creeds, as part of a reaction to the debauchery and inhumanity of latter-day Rome.

In addition to neo-Platonism, already mentioned, Gnosticism was an important rival; central to its thought was the time-honored concept of dualism—the existence of two worlds, one evil and material, the other good and spiritual. The Gnostics claimed to possess a saving *gnosis* or "knowledge" secretly revealed to their forebears; their spirits were imprisoned in their bodies, and the key to salvation was to free the body from this bondage. The doctrine implied a complete denial of the flesh and a grimly ascetic life. Some Christians were also Gnostics, though the latter insisted that Jesus had not been born of woman but had descended from heaven fully formed. To solve the dilemma, the Christians conjured up the doctrine of the Immaculate Conception, whereby Jesus was born of Mary but not as a result of any vile sexual act.

Gnostic influences thus strengthened the forces of puritanism in the Christian Church. Nonetheless, it could perhaps have stopped short of extremes of intolerance had it not been threatened on another flank by Manichaeanism, based on the teachings of the prophet Mani, who had lived in southern Babylonia, where he was crucified in A.D. 277. Following the Zoroastrian cosmology, Mani saw the world as divided between the forces of light and those of darkness. As an antisex ascetic, Mani far outdid Christians or even Gnostics: he taught that Adam and Eve were created as the result of a union between the son and daughter of the Prince of Darkness. This act, like any other form of procreation, was in itself evil, a doctrine that could lead only to the extinction of humanity, if carried to its logical conclusion.

Manichaeanism had a deep effect on Christian teaching, because St. Augustine (354–430 A.D.), who set the final seal on the antisexual bias of the Church, was himself a Manichaean for eleven years; he had also studied the neo-Platonist Plotinus. After his original faith had weakened, he first took a temporary mistress and then abandoned her to become a Christian. Augustine was much more vehement than Paul in his praise of celibacy and virginity and in his castigation of coitus as repugnant; every child was conceived by an act of sin on the part of his parents, and venereal disease had been created by God to punish lechers. As an utmost concession, Augustine refrained from total condemnation of marriage (which he called "a medicine for immorality"), since it transformed coitus from an act of pure lust to a painful duty; thereby, if used exclusively for procreation, it lost part of its vileness; any intercourse by the unmarried was anathema. This qualified acceptance is summed up by a statement of St. Jerome: "I praise marriage and wedlock, but I do so because they produce virgins for me." Coming from any other source but this most rabid of ascetics, such a declaration might be open to more than one interpretation.

While all sex not for procreation was thereby cursed by the Church fathers as deviant, the most diabolical sin was sodomy.

For instance, St. John Chrysostom was a rabid opponent of pederasty; but unlike most other crusaders in the cause, he insisted that tribadism by females was even more disgraceful, since women should have deeper feelings of shame.

Accordingly, the Church fathers of the era of St. Augustine consolidated the sex-negative character of Christianity. In the classical world before Rome became an empire, arguments had been advanced as to the evils of intercourse, but no one paid undue attention. Jesus himself expressed no outright opposition to the Old Testament tradition whereby a woman should sleep only with her husband, while for men other alternatives were not formally banned. The Church fathers changed all this by decreeing that if marital intercourse might be an inescapable evil—though celibacy and virginity were much more virtuous—other options were totally taboo, and sex was on no account to be treated as enjoyable. Nonetheless, early Christians taught that if sex was vile, marriage must be based on mutual love and understanding; arranged betrothals of the old kind were proscribed. This attitude could produce disconcerting results; when St. Agnes, a Roman girl born in A.D. 304 and true to such principles, refused the hand of a young man chosen by her family, they promptly consigned her to a brothel. Her first customer was struck blind, but St. Agnes restored his sight. She was canonized long before science had discovered that one virulent form of VD can cause blindness.

Thus the first four centuries of our era, from Paul to Augustine, witnessed a sexual revolution quite as radical as that which has occurred—in the reverse direction—in the 1960s and 1970s. As a result, European civilization adopted a code that defied all previous human experience, whether among the primitive Australians or the sophisticated Egyptians.

The Perennial Struggle

Emperor Constantine first adopted Christianity in A.D. 312, persuaded by his triumph in the Battle of the Milvian Bridge of the power of the Cross as a kind of magic charm. But the old gods died hard, and over a century passed before they were driven underground and the new post classic era really began in about A.D. 500, when the last Roman emperor of the West, Romulus Augustus, had been deposed. A Dark Age followed, after which, in the Middle Ages, Church control over mind and body was so absolute as to make the totalitarian tyrannies of our century seem almost tolerant. To question a mere syllable of Church dogma was to court death; sponsors of outlandish proposals that the world was round or that wine and wafers were not physically changed into flesh and blood in the Mass faced torture and immolation.

During the Middle ages asceticism began to wither and the troubadours even idealized courtly love. The essence of this cult was a vow of utter devotion to the services and to the praises of a high-born lady; she was the wife of someone else, often of the devotee's own feudal lord, and any thoughts of physical consummation would have been shameful. In Don Quijote's adoration for the peerless lady Dulcinea, in reality a village wench, Cervantes made a mockery of the religion of courtly love, which outlived even the Middle Ages. The cult is a bizarre compromise whereby St. Paul's denigration of woman was transformed into a form of adoration, but immune from the ultimate sin of consummation; to a Turk such attitudes would have seemed outrageous and in China they would have been utterly ridiculous. A much more blatant negation of Church doctrine was already practiced by those very Crusaders who sailed for the East under the banner of their sex-negative religion. A horde of harlots often would follow in their wake, and the French contingent that set forth in A.D. 1190 on the Third Crusade took fifteen hundred whores with them, though the grandest nobles ordered their sons to take their own sleeping companions, to avoid contagion from the common prostitutes.

The crusading harlots were a mere drop in the bucket among the total numbers by then dedicated to that calling. To quote only a few examples, by the thirteenth century, in most larger towns in England and France, brothels were a flourishing investment; King Henry II of England in 1161 invoked the aid of his bishops to draft strict laws for their control. At that time, the see of Winchester derived part of its income from sixteen bawdy houses in Southwark alone, mostly disguised as vapor baths, or "stews." In the fourteenth century, the Southwark stews became the property of the lord mayor of London, who packed them with Flemish whores. In 1260, King Alfonso X of Spain passed a law to govern the conduct of the ponces who controlled thousands of his kingdom's harlots. In deference to St. Augustine's dictum that fornication was vile, medieval rulers generally banned brothels from the vicinity of consecrated ground and banished them to special quarters, as happened for different reasons in nineteenth-century Tokyo.

From the fifteenth-century onward, the Renaissance nobility paid little more than lip service to Christian taboos, and the forces of asceticism were in full retreat. If the Pope's own paramours—but not always their children—were kept in the background, that scion of the Catholic kings, King Philip III of Spain (1598–1621), was an inveterate womanizer, though far outstripped by the "most Catholic" kings of France, where royal mistresses were more openly flaunted. This was the age of that proverbial violator of the marriage bed, Don Juan, whose fame the centuries have not eroded.

At times the prelates of the Church preached defiance of its precepts. An Italian Renaissance bishop, Alessandro Piccolonini, wrote in about 1540 a treatise called *Good Form for Women* in which he pleaded that a young woman, as soon as she had settled down with her husband, should carefully choose another lover. Europe then began to develop its own erotic literature, of which a vibrant example was the sonnets of Giulio Aretino, published in Venice in the 1550s, accompanied by woodcut illustrations. The Roman Church, like Islam, alternated between spells of asceticism and laxity, and the sonnets with their lewd woodcuts appeared at the precise moment when the Council of Trent, bent on banning pictures that might provoke lust, ordered that draperies should be added to Michelangelo's nudes in the Sistine Chapel in Rome.

Certainly cynicism was far from universal, and for the average couple, even among the well-to-do, Christian sexual precepts had not lost all meaning. Kings and prelates, regardless of their own proclivities, never ceased to abjure their subjects to lead chaste lives, and most of them probably did so, or suffered the pangs of Christian conscience if they strayed from the path of conjugal fidelity.

A renewed emphasis on Christian monogamy, typified by the grim austerity of Calvinist Geneva and the bland hypocrisy of Victorian England, hardly ranks as a mere wave of asceticism of the old kind after a period of laxity; it really forms part of another story. This revival of the sex-negative side of Christianity was less a return to the distant past than the preface to a new chapter in human history governed by different motives and far removed from the origins of the faith. By virtue of the Protestant work ethic, fervently preached in nineteenth-century England, hard work and an "ethical" family life were worshiped as golden calves. But the link was remote between the work ethic and the celibate desert fathers of the early Church or the Stylobates, who sat for a lifetime on a column. The new asceticism scarcely derived from the old and, as we shall see in greater detail, sprang more from the needs of the early industrial revolution for a workforce that was both prolific and pliant.

Respect for Christian sexual dogmas has declined dramatically at the beginning of what is often called the postindustrial era; in contrast, their formulation had been slow, starting with the prophets who rallied the Jews amid the laxity of Babylon and ending with others who railed against the lechery of Rome a millennium later. Even these bare comments on the struggle of European man against his sex-negative heritage, lasting nearly two thousand years, suffice to show that the drawbacks of an attempt to fly in the face of human reality are obvious; foremost of all is the creation of a climate of hypocrisy (the very sin that Jesus most condemned) and of a gulf between what people profess and what they do. Such furtiveness was alien, say, to ancient China, where sex was officially blessed and openly performed. Moreover, no one can ever quantify the mental anguish inflicted upon Christian believers throughout the centuries, an anguish beyond the comprehension of other people; accepting in their minds divine truths that every fiber in their body impelled them to ignore, they were forever haunted by fear of the fires of hell and thereby even suffered the torments of the damned during their life on earth.

In a belated attempt to take the sting out of the austere dictates of the Church, often blamed for its present loss of support, new "Christian" sex manuals have been written that advocate a more frank and open enjoyment of sex in the bedrooms of the born-again. "Fun Marriage Forums" are even held for evangelical couples in several cities of the United States. Tim and Beverly LaHaye in their book *The Act of Marriage* justify sexual foreplay between Christian spouses by citing the Book of Proverbs: "Her breasts satisfy thee at all times." They maintain that Christians who live by the word of God generally experience a higher degree of sexual enjoyment than non-Christians. But St. Paul and St. Augustine never sponsored Fun Marriage Forums, and their very creation surely marks the demise more than the renewal of traditional Christian teaching on sex.

With Allah's Permission

Few precepts of the Koran derive from ancient Arabia, where people worshiped a galaxy of deities, including three goddesses, based on the familiar pattern of the Near East. Mohammed's teaching owed much to the Old Testament, and he sometimes drew the same conclusions from that source as did Jesus. For instance, Mohammed foretold a universal resurrection, and even his doctrine of holy war recalls the Christian ideal of dying for one's faith. While Aaron, David, Solomon, Elijah, and Job figure in the Koran, many of the great prophets from later times are more conspicuous by their absence. Mohammed went so far as to call Islam "The religion of Abraham," who had supposedly founded the most sacred Ka'ba in Mecca. Mohammed's attitude to Jesus himself is ambivalent, though the Virgin Mary is the only woman to be mentioned in the Koran. Situated somewhere between the death of his first wife, Kadijah, and the Hejira, or flight to Medina, in 621, the Koran tells of his miraculous airborne safari from Mecca to the Temple of Jerusalem where, formally welcomed by the Angel Gabriel, he then met Moses, Abraham, and Jesus, together with Adam, described as the greatest of the prophets. Most of his attention was focused upon Jesus, whose claim to be the son of God and redeemer of humanity he dismissed as blasphemous; paradoxically, however, though for Mohammed Jesus was not divine, his miracles were authentic.

Therefore, in spite of their long enmity, much of Christianity and Islam derive from common sources. The Old Testament links the two faiths to Judaism, and for Muslims adherents of all three religions are known as the People of the Book. The teaching of Jesus and Mohammed, however, diverge radically on sex, since the latter's prospectus for paradise (from which unbelievers were of course banned), was a kind of garden, offering an eternity of copulation with cohorts of *houris,* whose virginity was miraculously renewed as fast as the faithful could relieve them of it. The blessed in this paradise reclined endlessly on couches set with jewels while perpetually youthful boys regaled them with wine, forbidden to Muslims on earth. *Houri* (Arabic *hur*) means "white one" or "bright eyes." *Houris* occur in several passages in the Koran; later Islamic texts gave more details and described them as so transparent that the marrow of their bones was visible through seventy silk garments. This view of a houri-filled paradise forms a stark contrast to the Christian heaven, with its promise of otiose bliss in the company of innocent angels. But if, in the hereafter, Muslims, unlike Christians, were offered free love without restraint, relations between male and female in this world were so highly regulated in Islam that the oft-repeated notion of it as a sex-positive religion is open to question.

Mohammed, born in about A.D. 568, was both ruler and conqueror, unlike the founders of other world religions. By A.D. 700 the domains of his followers stretched to India in the east and across North Africa as far as Ceuta (opposite Gibraltar) in the west. Among the most important factors in the Prophet's life was his marriage to Khadijah, a rich, forty-year-old woman he married when he was twenty-five. His devotion was unbounded and her influence immense; he had no other wife until she died. The effect of her loss on Islamic sex teaching was profound, since only thereafter, when almost fifty years old, Mohammed turned to polygamy and embarked on a new and hyperactive love life. Following the Hejira in 1621, he launched his career of conquest, and every victory was marked by a new marriage until his quota of wives began to grow as fast as his empire. In strict rotation he slept each night with a different spouse; he tried to divide his time equally between them and to treat them all with equal favor, a principle basic to Muslim doctrine. After Khadijah, his favorite wife by far was Aisha; when he married her she was a mere child and brought her dolls to the nuptial couch. Mohammed's late-developed sexuality brought him into conflict with his own Koranic law, already formulated, and that treated a man's marriage with the wife of his son as incestuous; the Prophet became so smitten with Zainab, his own cousin and wife of his adopted son Zaid, that eventually Zainab consented to a divorce so that Mohammed might marry her.

Basic to the treatment of sex in Muslim law is the persuasion that the Koran is not merely inspired by God but is the recorded word of God himself, for whom Mohammed served as the single mouthpiece, or prophet, and secretary. Hence, the Prophet is the perfect man, beyond blame for what, in others, might be transgressions. Had Khadijah lived longer, Muslim attitudes to sex might have been very different. But because the Prophet at a ripe age contracted a string of polygamous marriages, the same conduct had to be right and proper for his followers; he made this very clear when he declared: "I have married various women; whoever deviates from the path that I have traced is no follower of mine." However, it was not polygamy but marriage that was mandatory for both man and woman; polygamy is expressly permitted (but not enforced) by the Koran, on condition that a man give equal treatment to all his wives. Their number is not limited to four, a figure that derives from a later tradition.

Since in Islam Church and state were one, Church teaching on sex had the force of state law. Unlike Jesus, Mohammed himself, drawing from his own vast experience, was specific on sexual matters; he was in some ways a reformer, since he decreed that every married woman acquired a legal personality, which had not been the case in ancient Arabia. Some of his legislation was ostensibly designed to protect the female, and the Prophet himself had to protect and rescue his own wife Aisha, who became an object of scandal when she was accused of a liaison with a young soldier. Nonetheless, Mohammed regarded woman as an

187

inferior creature, her husband's vassal, for Allah had so willed it; the husband retained the children if they were divorced. Some theologians even proposed that women could not enter heaven, presented as an all-male society, except for the houris. The presence of ordinary wives in this erotic paradise involved obvious anomalies.

Koranic law laid an implacable curse on adultery, or more properly on *zinah,* the equivalent of fornication. It was a capital offense for a man to have coitus with any woman who was not his wife or his own slave-concubine. Paradoxically, intercourse with an underage girl did not amount to *zinah* and was a less heinous offense.

Attitudes to extramarital sex are as anomalous in Islam as in Christendom. Mohammed's teaching in theory precludes ordinary prostitution. However, in practice it is fairly common in Muslim countries, though by tradition it is forbidden; Muslim puritans have tried to suppress it in the past and are doing so today.

A moral code like that of Islam is not an exact guide to behavior, and Islam has been even more exposed than Christianity to waves of the most rigid puritanism, launched by fanatics, followed by periods of great laxity, in which sexual indulgence went to lengths undreamed of in the Koran. One of these periods is the sixteenth century, when the erotic manuals were in vogue, though long before this, twelfth-century Persian poet Omar Khayyám defied the Koranic prohibition and made a positive cult of wine bibbing. His most famous couplet was:

> Here with a loaf of bread beneath the bough,
> A glass of wine, a book of verse—and Thou.

This reads like an erotic picnic.

The constant struggle between permissiveness and austerity is unresolved. Asceticism is once more in the ascendant, and the present-day tide of puritanism, inspired by Muslim fundamentalists, aims at sweeping away all things Western, including not only bars and discotheques, but at times movie theaters and even restaurants. In Iran in the early 1980s the mullahs not only made laws against prostitution and adultery but even decreed that women should once more be enveloped in the lugubrious *chador*. The process for stoning adulterers (not prescribed in the Koran) was laid down in the minutest detail by Iran's fanatical divines. Offenders should be half buried in the earth, males from the hips and females from the breasts downward; the use of small stones was recommended, to ensure a slower death. So literally were the laws against exposure of the female body applied, even in the privacy of one's own garden, that snoopers who searched the houses of the remaining well-to-do for whiskey were also charged to make sure that their swimming pools were empty.

Iran, moreover, had no monopoly on the process of putting women back into their place. Only a foolhardy female would venture out in Pakistan during the early 1980s with bare head or bare arms. The Ideology Council, rewriting Pakistan's laws, approved the Islamic weighting of witnesses in legal cases, whereby two women count for one man. Women were banned from participating in spectator sports except in front of all-female audiences. In March 1982 the Women's Action Forum at least ventured to protest after a popular television commentator declared that the Koran allows wife-beating. The incident that led to the creation of the Women's Action Forum was the sentencing of a sixteen-year-old girl to a hundred lashes for adultery, since she was accused of living with her husband before she married him. The drive against sex out of wedlock reached a pitch where a newborn babe was stoned to death in Karachi. A priest cast the first stone. New legislation was contemplated under which a female prostitute, but not her customer, would be subject to the death penalty.

Erotica

For an outwardly austere society to produce erotic art and literature is anomalous if not incredible. Admittedly, the examples of Islamic erotica that survive today are few compared to the wealth of material from India, China, and Japan; nonetheless, these Islamic erotica show that in one of its more indulgent phases Islam brought forth an erotic literature startling in its blatancy. Sheikh Nefzaoui of Tunis, a sixteenth-century Arab author, wrote the celebrated *Perfumed Garden,* a prose sex manual interspersed with scraps of verse. The work had a checkered history; after completely disappearing, it was recovered by a French officer in 1850, though the first French edition was limited to thirty-five copies. Sir Richard Burton, when he died in 1890, left the first part translated into English, but his wife burned the section that dealt with homosexuality. Although the book refers only briefly to female homosexuality and to bestiality, it deals at inordinate length with every form of intercourse between male and female. Its section on male homosexuality is omitted from most Western versions. The author, whose chief patron was the bey of Tunis, was no stranger to the Indian sex manuals and lists the Indian coital positions, including one that in the Nefzaoui version could have been performed only by an acrobat of unusual dexterity: "The woman being stretched out on her back, the man sits down on her chest, with his back turned to her face, his knees turned forward and his toenails gripping the ground, he then raises her hips, arching her back until he has brought her vulva face to face with his member, which he then inserts, and thus gains his purpose." The sheikh wistfully added that he believed this position had been attained only in words.

Nefzaoui leaves little to the imagination; he stipulates the maximum and minimum length of the virile member best suited to satisfying a woman. He even prescribes ways for two very fat people with prominent stomachs to enjoy intercourse. Allowing for the most extraordinary contingencies, he adds a section for hunchbacks: "If a little woman is lying on her back, with a hump-backed man on her belly, he will look like the cover of a vase. On the other hand, if the woman is large, he will have the appearance of a carpenter's plane in action." The writer goes on to say that if the man and the woman are both humpbacked, her hump has to be enveloped in cushions; if the man has humps both on his back and chest, he has no choice but to renounce any embracing or clinging.

Muslims, in the limited periods when they were allowed, had

an eager appetite for erotic books bearing such titles as *The Book of Carnal Copulation* and *The Book of Exposition in the Science of Coition.*

A work of far greater eminence as a study of Islamic erotomania is the famous *Thousand and One Nights* (the so-called *Arabian Nights*). After an invocation to Allah the Merciful, a whole series of sexual adventures follow, involving all manner of people. As a single instance, one may quote the first story, in which the king's wife, the queen, is found stretched on her bed and embraced by a black slave, while the queen of a neighboring kingdom, not to be outdone, undresses in the presence of all her slaves and enjoys anal coitus with a huge African. The king put a stop to such orgies by beheading them all and as an afterthought ordered his vizier to bring him every night a young virgin, whom he ravished and killed at dawn.

The Harem

Harems certainly existed in Babylonian times in Mesopotamia, and archaeology even suggests their presence in embryonic form in that region as early as 3000 B.C. When the Persians conquered Babylonia in 539 B.C. they went much farther, and the *erderum* (Persian for harem) of Darius I (522–486 B.C.) was a vast establishment, housing countless secondary wives, concubines, and eunuchs, many of whom accompanied the great king on his campaigns.

Mohammed, though he made a number of marriages, neither invented nor promoted the harem, about which the Koran contains not a word. Hence, like the sex manuals, the harem is part of Islam's more permissive facet; it first appears in the courts of the khalifs of Damascus and Baghdad and thereafter spread throughout the entire Muslim world, where it became a status symbol; less exotic versions still exist today in a few countries. The splendors of the harems of Shiraz and Teheran are ecstatically praised by the poet Hafiz, while those of Cairo have been described by various nineteenth-century European visitors.

The Arabic word *harem* means "something that is forbidden" and applies not only to the place but also to the women who live in it. The harem is a very special kind of sanctuary whose inhabitants are deluxe prisoners, to be kept in suitable state in order that the master, when he visits them, may enjoy his pleasure to the full. Such luxury needs human ministrations and calls for a huge staff in which eunuchs play the leading role but that also required mistresses of the robe, craftsmen, jewelers, and doctors.

The Turks never bothered much about harems until they took Constantinople in A.D. 1453 and found the Byzantines enjoying them. Thereafter the Turks built up a gigantic organization, on a scale hitherto unknown. The secrets of the sultan's seraglio were tightly guarded, and the first recorded account comes from Domenico Hierosolimatano, court physician to Sultan Murad III (1574–95); by this time the number of girls in the royal harem had risen to twelve hundred. In the seventeenth century, the seraglio reputedly contained three thousand concubines who slept in dormitories, each containing one hundred. They were mostly foreigners captured abroad, though some Turkish girls entered the household of their own free will. All had to profess the Muslim faith. The atmosphere in some ways recalled that of a select English girls' school fifty years ago, full of high-spirited but well-disciplined young pupils. The difference lay in the sole reason why the girls were there; they were not taught to act as wives and mothers of an elite of empire builders but simply to give a good account of themselves if ever favored to share the bed of their master, a role that equally called for a rigorous upbringing. They also had lessons in dancing, singing, and cooking.

Unlike English schoolgirls, they practiced no sports. Turks did not care for women with boyish figures, preferring heavily built and big-breasted women; fattening food was therefore compulsory to produce the buxom physique. The diet, together with the habit of sitting on the floor cross-legged, produced an unwieldy type of female who could never walk properly on feet that became permanently crooked.

Discipline was fierce, and offenders were grimly chastised. Unruly inmates were eliminated by drowning in the Bosporus; for mere breaches of etiquette, an offender would be tied in a sack loaded with stones and cast from a barge towed into the channel. At times punishment gave way to sheer sadism, and Sultan Ibrahim I (1640–48) one day drowned his whole huge harem in this way, using relays of barges, just for the fun of collecting a new regiment of concubines. By a miracle one girl struggled out of her sack and lived to tell her tale in the salons of Paris.

The seraglio of the erotomaniac Ibrahim I became the scene of astounding orgies; the sultan would dart between the assembled odalisques; sometimes he was stark naked, at others swathed in furs, pretending to be a stallion, while the girls gamboled and whinnied on all fours like mares. The highest officers of state passed most of their time collecting sables, ambergris, and virgins for their master. His orgies involved acts of sadism inflicted on the youngest girls and of masochism, when the older members had to urinate on their master's body.

While Lady Mary Montague in the eighteenth century and Julia Pardoe in the nineteenth century have left vivid descriptions of the seraglio baths, relatively little was known of the sultan's harem until the fall of the Turkish Empire. Two English grandees, the Duke of Portland and Sir Robert Cotton, tried at the beginning of the nineteenth century to probe its secrets and offered the chief black eunuch half a million piasters to stage an orgy for them in the seraglio at a time when some of the younger girls were absent on vacation with the sultan. The chief eunuch thereupon proceeded to dress up all his black eunuchs as concubines and painted their faces white. Thus adorned, they were taken to a kiosk in a remote part of the seraglio garden; the Englishmen were ushered into the kiosk and told in solemn tones that the first confrontation of European males with odalisques was about to take place. The hoax ended in disaster when the floor gave way beneath the two noblemen after one eunuch had stepped on the springs that released a trap door concealed under a Persian rug; the visitors returned ignominiously to their yacht.

Little of much consequence was known of the sultan's harem until the deposition of Abdul Hanmid II in 1909. The Yildiz Palace, to which the court had moved, then housed 370 women and 127 eunuchs. There are many accounts of the dispersal, of which the best is that given by Francis McCullogh:

> One of the most mournful processions of the many mournful processions of fallen grandeur that passed through the streets during these days was one composed of the ladies from the ex-Sultan's Harem on their way from Yildiz to the Top-Kapu Palace (the Seraglio). These unfortunate ladies were of all ages between fifteen and fifty and so numerous that it took thirty-one carriages to convey them and their attendants. Some of them were sent back again to Yildiz. . . . Most of the ladies in the harems of the Turkish Sultans were Circassians, the Circassian girls being very much esteemed on account of their beauty and being consequently very expensive. . . . The Turkish Government telegraphed to the different Circassian villages in Anatolia, notifying them that every family which happened to have any of its female members in the ex-Sultan's Harem was at liberty to take them home, no matter whether the girls had been originally sold by their parents or had (as was the case in some instances) been torn from their homes by force.

As a result, a number of Circassian mountaineers came in their picturesque attire to Istanbul and were ushered into a hall filled with the ex-sultan's concubines, who were allowed to unveil themselves for the first time since they had reached puberty.

To satisfy the libido of a single autocrat was hardly a full-time occupation for hundreds if not thousands of odalisques. The sultan was less often a fiery stallion than an elderly man to whom the harem was little more than a drawing room in which he could relax. The Egyptian pashas, moreover, often were more attracted by boys, though they had to conform to the custom of keeping a female harem.

The eunuchs who attended the odalisques were unsatisfactory lovers, and the only alternative partners for the girls were their fellow odalisques, except in rare instances when baboons were reportedly roped in by enterprising concubines. Poet Fazil Bey, who wrote in the reign of Mahmud II (1808–39), tells in his *Book of Women* how the concubines would fall in love with one another, some taking the part of the male. To reach climax, the tongue, the candle, the banana, and the artificial phallus would be employed. To keep lesbianism within bounds, certain Muslim rulers forbade their girls to possess candles and served them bananas split into four parts to render them useless for the purpose.

Sex was not the only form of indulgence in the harem. Emmeline Lott was appointed governess to the children of the pasha of Egypt in the 1860s. She describes the vast consumption of gin in the harem; coffee and sweet liqueurs also were in abundance. All the women smoked like chimneys the entire day. The eunuchs joined in the seraglio sex games, whether or not they still possessed a penis and uncrushed testicles. They would lend themselves to any kind of perversion called for; if they refused, they were apt to be reported for other forms of improper conduct.

The Assyrians already used eunuchs in the ninth century B.C. to serve the king's concubines, and the Chinese emperors traditionally employed them for the same purpose. However, the great difference between the eunuchs of Constantinople and of Peking was that in China they were Chinese, whereas in Turkey they had to be foreign. Since the Koran forbids castration for believers, they were mostly slaves obtained in Egypt, Abyssinia, and central Africa. The Turks, to whom race and color otherwise meant little, were color-conscious in this respect and showed a strong preference for black eunuchs over white, who were more easily obtainable but who often proved delicate. Slave traders in the Sudan and elsewhere castrated their slaves for export and thereby made enormous profits, as eunuchs were more valuable than ordinary slaves.

Eunuchs who lose only their testicles but not their penis can have erections for a considerable time and can even enjoy sexual intercourse. However, the Turks, following the Byzantine custom, preferred those who had been fully emasculated. The seraglio doctors not only inspected the eunuchs on admission but also examined them every few years to make sure nothing had grown again.

Ambiguous Attitudes

People in the West often credit Islam with a penchant for pederasty, but the practice is not overtly condoned. The harem system, which consigned hordes of women to the households not only of the king, but also of the rich and powerful, was nonetheless conducive both to male and to female homosexuality. This was the obvious alternative both for the cloistered women of the harem and for those males left with too few wives, while prostitutes were in theory banned by Islamic law.

Islam absorbed, as it spread east and west, the remnants both of Hellenism and of the Persian Sassanid Empire and embraced peoples with a deep-rooted tradition of homosexuality. Unlike the Christians, the Muslims shunned any head-on clash with such tendencies, intensified by the seclusion of women and by the ban on fornication with unmarried girls. Condemnation by Muslim law-givers, conscious perhaps of a scarcity of alternatives, is far from absolute. The one passing mention of the subject in the Koran is obscure, in contrast with the utter damnation in the Christian Scriptures. The oft-cited passage in the Koran merely states: "And if two (men?) among you commit the crime, then punish them both." Unlike other offenses, no particular penalty is laid down. References in the Koran to Sodom and Gomorrah are a demonstration of God's power rather than as a castigation of pederasty. Certain authorities now deny that the passage quoted above refers to homosexuality at all, citing Muslim scholars who contend that the text has been misinterpreted and really lays down punishment not for men but for women who have committed indecencies mentioned immediately before the passage.

Moreover, from the purely material viewpoint, among Muslims homosexual acts, whether condemned or condoned, are not in the same class as the crime of adultery, for which harsh and specific punishments are named. Both adultery and fornication with unmarried females, who belonged to their parents, were offenses against property, infinitely graver than any misdemeanors between two males.

Sir Richard Burton (1821–90) included an account of homosexual love in his translation of *Arabian Nights*. Early in his life Burton, when serving as an officer in India, fell into disfavor with the authorities due to a report he was ordered to make by General Sir Charles Napier on Karachi, whose total population at the time was little more than a thousand. Burton discovered that this mere village supported no less than three brothels, offering not women but eunuchs and boys; the latter commanded double the price of the eunuchs. The report was sent to the government of Bombay, and as a result of his overly candid comments, Burton's military career was blighted. He thereafter wrote much about sexual customs but was forced to pull his punches to avoid giving further offense; he always referred to homosexuality as "Le Vice."

Burton did much to popularize the notion of Muslim males as engaged in perpetual pursuit of handsome boys. For him such predilections were typical of certain regions, and his key theory was the notion of what he called the Sotadic zone, which embraced the shores of the Mediterranean, whence it ran eastward to include Asia Minor, Mesopotamia, India, China, and Japan, finally extending into Oceania and parts of the New World. Within this zone Sotadic love was endemic and was treated as a mere "pecadillo," whereas races to the north and south of the zone looked upon the custom with disgust.

For Burton, Persia served as the perfect example of Sotadic activities among Muslims. He cites, among others, the governor of Bushire, who particularly fancied European youths; he would invite youngsters serving in the Bombay Marine Corps and ply them with liquor until they were insensible. The next morning his ingenuous guests would complain that the champagne left them with a curious irritation and soreness in the backside.

How seriously Burton took his own Sotadic theory is debatable, and no scholar accepts it today. Throughout the world, regardless of latitude, homosexual males can be divided roughly into two categories: those who indulge through choice and those, often youths on reaching puberty, who accept for a time this alternative for lack of others but who may expect in return some material reward. This second category is perhaps more in evidence in Islamic countries than in most others because of the strict seclusion of women and girls, which thereby gave added opportunity to confirmed pederasts. *Arabian Nights* includes several stories relating to Abu Nawas, a known homosexual who was regarded as one of the great poets of Islam during the

Abbasid period in Persia. In one of these stories, the poet set out to spend the night with one boy but ended up with three handsome youths who agreed to play the part of women for his benefit. In neighboring Afghanistan, homosexuality was even more favored, and boys in female garb were an indispensable part of a rich man's harem in the nineteenth century. The Afghans were commercial travellers on a large scale, and Burton relates how each caravan was accompanied by a number of these boys in women's attire, with rouged cheeks and long tresses; they were called traveling wives, and the "husbands" trudged patiently by their sides as they rode luxuriously on camels.

The Xanith of Oman

Today attitudes vary widely from one Muslim country to the next, in accordance with the political and social climate. While male as well as female prostitutes faced death in revolutionary Iran of the early 1980s, in some of the more traditional states of nearby Arabia they are treated with respect. This is well illustrated by a case that only recently came to light in the oil sheikhdom of Oman, giving rise to a lengthy and at times heated correspondence among scholars in *Man,* the journal of England's Royal Anthropological Society. In an article in this journal in 1977, Norwegian anthropologist Unni Wikan revealed the presence of a special category of transsexual male prostitutes in Oman, known as Xanith, who had escaped the notice of previous fieldworkers in that region. Wikan reported that in the coastal town of Sohar, with a population of three thousand adult males, these transsexuals numbered about sixty, or one in fifty of the adult male inhabitants; they acted in every respect as if they were women and were so treated by others. They were able, moreover, to move freely among women in purdah, to whom access was forbidden to any other males.

Wikan became aware of their existence almost by chance, when she went with a woman friend through a back street at some distance from the market; there they met an individual who talked like a man but was dressed in a pink *disdasha* (long tunic) and with whom her friend stopped to talk. Wikan was amazed, as no respectable woman in Oman talks to a man on the street.

At first Wikan thought her friend must have a secret lover, but the latter explained that, far from this being the case, the word *xanith* meant "effeminate" or "soft"; in the course of the next twenty minutes, Wikan's friend pointed out to her four more in all, equally dressed in pastel-colored disdashas. They walked with a swinging gait, were heavily made up, and reeked of perfume. Wikan's companion stated that most male servants, apart from slaves, were Xaniths, and that Xaniths were also freely available as male prostitutes. The Norwegian investigator suggests that they had not been mentioned in previous anthropological reports on the Middle East because the vast majority of fieldworkers were men, barred from any formal contact with women and therefore liable to miss the relevant clues.

The Xaniths fill a gap in the social life of Oman, which until 1971 remained a hermetically closed society with a strict rule of sexual segregation; Girls over thirteen were not merely veiled in public but also had to wear a kind of black mask over the face. The women today still live secluded lives and stay at home in the evening, while the men go to clubs and cafes. Officially there is no such thing as a female prostitute, and young non-Xanith boys who yield to homosexual approaches are apt to be punished. Female prostitutes in fact do exist, though they are hard to find and cost twenty Omani *reals,* as compared with one *real* for a Xanith transvestite.

Under such circumstances the Omani government seems to have adopted a laissez-faire attitude. Like the berdajes among the American Indians, people with such tendencies are merely reclassified as Xaniths and left in peace to pursue their career. They invariably play the passive role in intercourse; no stigma attaches to a man who seeks their company for sexual relations, and his *macho* identity is in no way impaired. No other problems arise from contact with a Xanith, who is his own master, whereas every woman is another man's property.

The journal *Man* received many letters on the subject from distinguished social anthropologists. A few questioned the accuracy of Wikan's report, but a more general criticism was her treatment of the Oman Xaniths as a unique phenomenon. Robert Brain quoted other examples, such as a 1971 report of the Nzemba tribe in Ghana, whose rich men liked to "marry" attractive youths; in Mombasa, on the coast of Kenya, a special category of males exists, known as Washogas. Like the Xaniths, they are passive homosexuals who offer their favors for money; they don women's clothing and are free to move among women. Other letters cited documented cases from the remoter parts of Turkey and Morocco, where a passive homosexual role was socially acceptable for youths but regarded as shameful in older men.

To such parallels of the Omani Xaniths in the Third World might be added the obvious example of the West today, where the homosexual option is freely available to all who seek it and where forms of homosexual coupling that might also be called "marriages" are quite frequent. The society of Oman, however, bears little comparison to the Western way of life, and its sexual pattern is totally different. The Xaniths are a closely defined group, set apart from other men, doing different work, and privileged to mingle freely with women; moreover, quite unlike the Western world, in places such as Oman, for single males homosexual intercourse may at times be the only outlet, since ordinary women are rigorously secluded, and the price of female prostitutes is prohibitive.

In general terms, such a wide range of sexual activities is forbidden to Muslims that it might be more accurate to call Islam less sex-positive than homosex-permissive. Conditions have varied greatly from one region to another throughout history, chiefly dependent on how far female prostitution may be tolerated. Reports are lacking as to how the young cope with their sex problems in countries where people are killed for prostitution.

The legend of the erotic East has been fostered in Western countries by *Arabian Nights* and other exotic accounts. But in reality, Islam was fully sex-positive in one sense only: For Mohammed, unlike the Christian divines, the sex act was not sordid but sublime, provided *only* that the partners abided by his book of rules. But these rules were so strict that they precluded many activities available, say, in China. For the Prophet, intercourse was commendable only within the confines of marriage, or with the privately owned concubines of the rich. Most other forms were a punishable offense. Admittedly, paradise was filled with willing houris, but a man first had to get there before he could savor its delights. For those who could not afford a string of wives and concubines, the openings were limited; and against anyone who tried to enrich his sex life in ways not favored by the Koran, the gates of the houri-filled paradise presumably remain barred.

Among the cultures of the world, Islam is to be noted for its rigidity in sexual customs more than for any laxity, since above all it stands for the supremacy of man over woman carried to extreme lengths. A symbol of this supremacy was the absolute stress placed on bridal virginity. This obsession led in turn to the encouragement in many Muslim countries of the barbarous practice of imposing chastity by means of female infibulation; as we have already seen, the custom is still widely favored. Islam was par excellence a conquering society, and its sexual customs were tailored to this end. In particular, the ban on the recruitment of local talent to serve as concubines and prostitutes acted as a spur to distant conquests. whose richest spoils were those enticing females, obtainable abroad but kept under lock and key in the warrior's own land. Moreover, the Muslim cult of war eliminated a number of males, thereby increasing the supply of females available to the survivors.

CHAPTER EIGHT

Sex for Sages

A Moral Principle

The Venetian traveler Marco Polo (1254–1325) was the first European to tell of the sexual mores of remote Cathay. While his account of the Sung emperor's court at Hanchow created a sensation in Europe, Marco Polo's hosts were even more astounded by some of his tales about the West. In particular, they ridiculed his assertion that Christian clerics urged sexual restraint upon their flock; they were shocked by his outlandish pretense that such divines practiced what they preached and were themselves sworn to celibacy, a condition the Chinese found obscene, especially in a holy man.

They were further unnerved by European modes of greeting when other visitors arrived. The common kiss on face or hand, which even the most bashful Christians might have exchanged, served in China as a direct prelude to greater intimacy. Hence the first Europeans who kissed each other publicly both horrified and fascinated their onlookers, who took it for granted that these traders were about to bare their genitals and treat their hosts to a shameless if bizarre display of erotic skills. The Chinese were inveterate voyeurs and would have treated the antics of alien exhibitionists as a form of entertainment.

From time immemorial, Chinese sages had taught that sexual abstinence was wicked and that for the good of his soul a man needed constant copulatjon with as many women as he could afford and preferably with several at a time. In this respect his subjects followed the example of their ruler, for the very survival of the cosmos depended on the king sleeping not with a single spouse but with an interminable series of partners in strict order of protocol. The need for change and variety was not a matter of taste; it was backed by moral principle defined in copious texts. To quote the *I-Ching*, one of the most important Tao manuals: "The constant intermingling of heaven and earth gives shape to all things. The sexual union of men and women gives life to all things."

Lovemaking was therefore an act of piety, while abstinence was a threat to the harmony of the universe. Sages who taught these doctrines spoke from personal experience. Unlike Christian clerics, their theories were based on practice, for in Taoist monasteries sexual techniques and disciplines were part of the daily curriculum. While knowledge of the religion of the earliest Chinese civilization, Shang, is limited, under the succeeding culture, Chou, Taoism began to spread from about 600 B.C. onward. As an overall view of the working of the cosmos, Tao embodies the basic beliefs of ancient Chinese thought, later enriched by the doctrines of Confucius and Buddha. Tao literally means "The Way" and hence also signifies "The Right Mode of Life." Fundamental to Taoism was Yin-Tao, "The Dark Hidden Way," which embraced its teaching on sexual intercourse.

Far from resting on shadowy notions open to many interpretations, Yin-Tao, as we shall see, was a dogma defined with precision in the lengthy sex manuals, of which the essence survives. They prescribe in exact terms first the cosmic principles that govern sexual union and also the best ways of performing the act. These beliefs and practices, first devised by the legendary Yellow Emperor, who supposedly reigned in about 2600 B.C., were still favored by Chinese seventeenth-century novelists and remained in force until China became a republic in 1912; they were shared by the two contradictory faiths of Tao and Confucius. The approach to sexual relations is thus remarkably consistent, and for nearly five thousand years sages taught that by sexual intercourse man achieved union with the cosmos, and that to achieve this happy state, he must learn as much as possible about the techniques of love.

One of the first emperors of the Han Dynasty (200 B.C.–A.D. 250) decided that too many of his subjects were neglecting this task and appointed special officials to draw up a list of unattached men over thirty and of women over twenty. Those on the register were ordered to consummate a union with the opposite sex before the following spring; the penalty for default was a hundred strokes of the lash, a rare instance of equal treatment of both sexes. Reportedly even the most inhibited preferred private if compulsory copulation to public flogging.

Basic to sexual dogma is the notion that the clouds are the earth's ova, which are fertilized by the rain, heaven's sperm. The aim of the Tao, or Way, is to maintain a balance between these two complementary forces, known as the *yin* (female) and *yang* (male). The yang is related to the sun, the sky, to light, and to fire, while the yin is associated with earth, moon, water, and shadow. Sexual union between man and woman is a replica of the interaction of the forces of nature, the fertilizing of the female earth by the male sky. Accordingly, since Tao was more philosophy than religion, sex in China, while not without its lighter side, was a pleasure but also a duty, integral to its whole ideology.

If the first aim of Tao sages was to establish the sex act as a cosmic force, their manuals also laid down the indispensable techniques that complied with this notion and by which the maximum personal benefits could also be derived from intercourse, in terms of good health and long life. Fulfillment of such aims was based on a singular precept unique to Chinese culture. Copulation carried out in the proper manner served as a stimulant to the yang force in men and to yin in women. The snag, however, lay in the precept, also taught by Tao, that when orgasm took place, the yang and yin were spent in the form of bodily effluents that were absorbed by the other partner to the act, to his or her great benefit. This belief led to the conclusion, both logical but strange in a male-dominated society, that a man could profit from intercourse only by avoiding orgasm: In this way he would strongly enhance his yang, replenished by the woman's effluents, while his own vital force remained intact.

Quality as well as quantity was demanded in a man's performance. As part of his yang-enriching technique, he must learn to prolong the time taken in coitus, but on no account must he attain orgasm; the longer the male member stayed inside the female partner, the greater the amount of vital force it would absorb.

Such theories, moreover, obliged the man to give each of his women, however humble her rank, the fullest satisfaction each time he slept with her, even though he himself could reach orgasm only on very specific occasions, governed by his age and by the time of year, the permitted frequency being reduced in winter. Masturbation was roundly condemned as a wanton waste of yang essence. Self-abuse was allowed only during prolonged absence from the company of women, when the semen, or yang, might become clogged within the body; it would then lose its potency and devitalize its possessor. Nocturnal emissions were believed to be caused by fox spirits that changed themselves from foxes into beautiful women to beguile men in their dreams and thus steal away part of their yang.

In a well-ordered Chinese household the master was therefore duty-bound to sleep with an endless series of lesser inmates, maidservants as well as concubines and secondary wives, without himself having an emission. Only as the final stage in this process would he then have coitus with his principal wife, whose offspring were his heirs and who would gain strength from her spouse's store of yang, massively enhanced through his amatory experiences with a whole string of partners, on whom he had not wasted a single drop. To absorb all the released yin of these women was both a physical and a spiritual exercise; the storage mechanism for a man's acquired yang was complex, and only by means of deep meditation could he pass it up the channel of his spine and collect it in his head, where it resided until spent on his senior spouse.

Comparable rules applied to religious recluses, who retired from the world and practiced dietary and other disciplines to attain longevity, with immortality as the ultimate goal. Taoist monks were among the most prolific of writers on sexual matters. Foremost among such disciplines were sexual experiments, not designed in their case to produce a strong heir but to discover the elixir of life with the help of copious drafts of yin, gained from female partners; of these a Taoist sage would need even larger numbers than the average layman, since one alone could supply a mere fraction of the required yin juice.

Such doctrines had patent drawbacks from the purely human point of view. In one of the many Chinese sex manuals, Peng-Tsu is questioned by the Yellow Emperor on the means to achieve immortality. Peng-Tsu replied: "It is very simple: the essential thing is to couple with a large number of young women but with only a single emission." The king's favorite then asks a rather pointed question: "If emission is to be avoided, where then lies the pleasure?" Peng-Tsu gave an equivocal reply: "When the sperm is emitted, the body feels tired . . . though one's pleasure is intense for a moment, in the end it is pleasure no longer. But if one makes love without an emission, one has abundant strength, the body is relaxed, and all the senses are alert. The calmer you are, the greater the delight. One can never have enough: How can that not be called a pleasure?" Voluptuaries in other countries might deny that Peng-Tsu's answer provides the perfect formula for satisfaction.

The yin-yang forces are represented in Chinese art by a number of symbols and even by complex hexagonal diagrams. The ubiquitous dragon, rampant and whiskered, conveys cosmic power and the vital essence of the Tao and is therefore masculine; on the other hand, the peach, with its deep cleft recalling the vulva, was a favorite feminine symbol. A Tengbird flying into a garden of peony flowers, or a dragon among swirling clouds indicated the union of the two sexes. Not only Tao employed such imagery; Buddhists and Confucianists in their own way used the same artistic traditions and pictorial language.

The Art of the Bedchamber

The Art of the Bedchamber, the term used to describe Chinese writings on sex, is first mentioned in a short explanatory note, dating from the second century B.C.:

> The Art of the Bedchamber constitutes the climax of human
> emotion; it encompasses the Supreme Way (Tao). Therefore,
> the Saint Kings of antiquity regulated man's outer pleasures in
> order to restrain his inner passions and made detailed rules for
> sexual intercourse. An old record says: "The ancients created
> sexual pleasure thereby to regulate all human affairs." If one
> regulates his sexual pleasure he will feel at peace and attain a
> high age. If, on the other hand, he abandons himself to its
> pleasure, disregarding the rules set forth in the above men-
> tioned treatises one will fall ill and harm one's very life.

Sex manuals had existed long before this brief note and described customs more than two thousand years older. Several
volumes known to have been produced during the Sui Dynasty
(A.D. 590–618) also have disappeared, together with many subsequent versions.

These manuals were very popular in the first millennium A.D.
In Tang Dynasty times (A.D. 618–906) certain earlier versions
were republished. The older handbooks thus remained in circulation, while new ones were added but were subsequently also
lost to posterity, though bibliographies still exist that list them
as treatises on medicine. The famous physician Sun Szu-mo had
in the seventh century written an important treatise titled *The
Healthy Sex Life.* Bibliographies record that it was reprinted
under the Sung Dynasty in 1066; a new edition of ninety-three
chapters was then produced as late as 1544 in Ming times, and
again in 1604. Another Taoist work dated 1566 contains fragments of older handbooks, including dialogues between the
mythical Yellow Emperor and the Plain Girl, first recorded in
writing two thousand years before.

Though so many texts have been lost, their essence has been
preserved. Copious extracts have been miraculously saved, not
in China but in Japanese medical works, published from the
tenth century onward. Tamba Yasuori was a Japanese physician
of Chinese descent; between A.D. 982 and 984 he compiled a
thirty-volume work, *Ishimpo (The Essence of Medical Prescription);* it
is the oldest extant Japanese work on medicine. Many Chinese
texts owe their survival to Yasuori's tomes, but of these the most
fascinating is the twenty-eighth, consisting of extracts from the

various versions of *The Art of the Bedchamber* current at the time. For nine hundred years Yasuori's work circulated only in manuscript, until in 1854 a magnificent block print was produced in Japan. He was a most conscientious scholar and scientist; he recorded the relevant passages exactly as he found them in the original manuscripts, not even correcting obvious errors. Later Japanese copyists of the *Ishimpo* showed the same scrupulous respect and as a result the 1854 text retained all the features of the Chinese originals, based on the exploits of the Yellow Emperor. Only in the twentieth century did a well-known scholar, Yeh Teh-hui, first republish the *Ars Amatoria* in China itself. Since all Chinese versions had disappeared, he used the Japanese text, from which he reconstructed five handbooks on sex, four of which are mentioned in the Sui Dynasty bibliography of A.D. 600; his fifth volume was the *Tung-hsüan-tzu,* or the *Ars Amatoria of Master Tung-hsüan.* R. H. van Gulik, leading authority on Chinese sexual customs, whose magnum opus *Sexual Life in Ancient China* includes many excerpts from these manuals, identified Tung-hsüan as a seventh-century scholar who derived his information from earlier Taoist sources. Tung-hsüan's attitude may be summed up in these words: "Of all things that make man prosper, none can be compared with sexual intercourse . . . those who miss its true meaning will die before their time."

Yeh received few thanks for re-creating these precious tomes. He set to work in 1903, and the completed block print was published in 1914, two years after the first revolution. However, Yeh's work was too much for the old-fashioned literati of the time, who were deeply offended. As a result, his reputation as a scholar was ruined. He was eventually murdered by bandits, but even such a tragic end failed to evoke much public sympathy. This was because, during the latter part of the Chi'ing, or Manchu, Dynasty (1644–1912), attitudes toward sex had changed radically, following the example of nineteenth-century Europe. In an excess of prudery, the Manchus banned sex manuals, and when van Gulik set to work on his masterly study he found that no serious commentaries on the subject were available either from Chinese sources or from Western books on China.

Yeh deduced that nearly all the old handbooks on sex had been divided into the following sections:

1. Introductory remarks on the cosmic significance of the sexual union, and its importance for the health of both partners.
2. A description of sexual play preliminary to the act.
3. The sexual act itself. The technique of coitus, including the various positions in which the act can be consummated.
4. The therapeutic aspect of the sexual act.
5. Sexual selection, prenatal care, and eugenics.
6. Various recipes and prescriptions for improving sexual performance.

His reconstructions follow this pattern, though they represent a mere fraction of the original total. The principal sexual manuals are stated in ancient texts to have covered eight rolls, whereas the twentieth-century version contained a single roll.

Van Gulik gives a full translation of the *Ars Amatoria of Master Tung-hsüan,* as reconstructed by Yeh. However, van Gulik decided that much of the text, including its spicier details, were unfit for print in any modern tongue and gave them instead in vernacular Latin; he thereby made them accessible only to scholars proficient in Latin, now mainly confined to Roman Catholic seminaries and English public schools. This peculiar convention was also followed by translators of the seventeenth-century Chinese erotic novels, with their pungent accounts of every conceivable deviation; in the 1930s many passages were considered fit to appear only in dog Latin, though they would not raise an eyebrow today.

Van Gulik's version of the sex manuals is accordingly an odd blend of English and Latin. Even in translating a passage on such a matter-of-fact subject as the signs of oncoming puberty in boys and girls, the growth of pubic hair is described in English, but the development of the sexual organs follows in the same paragraph with Latin renderings; for instance, the penis, for which one Chinese name is the Jade Stalk, becomes *Jaspius caulis.* (Other terms for the male member include the Positive

Peak, the Swelling Mushroom, the Turtle Head, and the Dragon Pillar.) In another passage from van Gulik, after a lively account, given in Latin, of the sexual act on the wedding night, including fellatio, the text reverts to English for its more prosaic sequel: "Afterwards they wipe their parts with the six girdles, and these are then placed in a basket."

The standard format of such manuscripts is based on dialogues between the mythical Yellow Emperor and his three sexual mentors, the Plain Girl, the Dark Girl, and the Elected Girl. Of these, the Plain Girl, Su Nu, is also a goddess of fertility, connected with rivers and lakes; in one version, she takes the form of a shell, one of the oldest Chinese fertility symbols. The second instructor of the Yellow Emperor, the Dark Girl, was equally versatile, since she is also credited with writing three books on military strategy; she acted not only as sexual consultant for the emperor but also as a source of arms, providing him with a pair of magic drums when he was about to tackle a particularly fearsome dragon.

These women exhorted their pupil to copy their own experiences since, being immortals, they had usurped the role of males. Having enjoyed coitus with cohorts of virgin boys, they reached the realm beyond old age and death; ordinary mortals were particularly warned against any contact with women of this kind.

Not unnaturally, since the sex life of the central figure, the Son of Heaven, was of such importance in Tao teaching as the key to cosmic harmony, it is described in its every detail in the manuals as a sequel to their discourse on yin and yang explained above. In Tao doctrine, the union of king and queen epitomizes the balance of positive and negative forces in the world. Since it was essential that the king should copulate with a large number of women before the act of procreation with his leading spouse, the status of such women had to be fixed with precision. In addition to their queen, emperors of the Han Dynasty had to have three consorts, nine wives of the second rank, twenty-seven wives of the third rank, and eighty-one concubines. These figures conform to the time-honored number magic. Odd numbers symbolized the positive forces of nature: three, being the first odd number after one, stood for male potency, and nine (three times three) represented the superabundance of sexual force. To multiply these magic numbers once more by three produces twenty-seven and eighty-one. According to the historian Ssu Ma-ch'ien, even the ruler of an early feudal state of the Yin Dynasty, Chou-hsin (1154–1122 B.C.), had an identical quota of consorts a thousand years before Han times. In addition, three thousand palace maids provided a permanent reserve for junketing, festivals, and displays of exhibitionism.

The sexual relations of the king and his many women was closely supervised by certain court ladies who enforced an arduous timetable; he had to cohabit with each one on specific calendar days and with a frequency dependent upon rank. Even the length of time he spent with each partner was regulated according to status. Royal coitus was recorded with special red calligraphy brushes, which in later periods created a genre of erotic literature called "Stories Written with the Red Brush."

Relations with women of lower rank not only had to precede those with the Queen and other consorts but also had to be more frequent to accumulate the maximum store of the yang forces from such unions. Copulation with the queen took place only once every month, after the ruler was replete with yang, thus offering the best chance of producing a strong and healthy heir.

Nonetheless, none of his successors could be expected to match the feats of the Yellow Emperor, whose marathon performance, as described in one text, involved copulation with twelve hundred women in a single year. At one point the Yellow Emperor, prostrated by his endeavors, put to the Plain Girl this preposterous question: "Now what if one decides to refrain entirely from sexual intercourse?" Her retort was uncompromising: "This is wrong. Heaven and earth have their opening and closing. Yang and yin develop from each other. Man is modeled after yang and yin and embodies the sequence of the four seasons. If one resolves to abstain from sexual intercourse, one's spirit will not develop, since the interchange of yang and yin will then come to a halt."

With the passage of time, the sexual relations of the emperor became the object of an ever more rigid protocol. The increasing number of his women created the need for an elaborate filing system, recording the date and hour of every successful sexual union, together with the dates of menstruation of his women and the first signs of any pregnancy. A text, *Notes of the Dressing Room,* dating from about A.D. 940, states that in the previous century every woman with whom the emperor had slept received an indelible stamp on her arm with the legend "Wind and Moon [meaning sexual dalliance] are forever new."

As a sequel to their treatment of the cosmic yin-yang forces and their prescriptions for imperial intercourse, the manuals deal copiously with sexual techniques applicable to both ruler and ruled. The scope is ample and the instructions explicit, but apart from the guiding precept of conserving yang by withholding semen, they contain little that is original.

In contrast with the countless variants of the Indian *Kamasutra,* thirty different coital positions are prescribed, mostly named after animals. At least one of these, the Dog of Early Autumn, in which male and female connect rear to rear, is more for the contortionist. Three of the thirty positions require the presence of a third party, a role usually filled by a servant, always available for such purposes in a well-ordered household. One of these threesome variants seems also to demand acrobatic skills on the part of the male performer; in the Paired Dance of the Female Phoenixes: "A man and two women, one lying on her back and one lying on her stomach. The one on her back raises her legs and the one on her stomach rides on top. Their two vaginas face one another. The man sits cross-legged, displaying his jade stalk and attacks the vaginas above and below." The man's role in this uneasy posture is eased by his avowed purpose of bringing the two women to climax while himself avoiding an emission.

Not only fellatio but also anal penetration was an approved form of intercourse, even with one's chief wife, and a man could obtain yin from this source just as well as from the vagina. And if male masturbation was strictly taboo as an extravagant waste of yang, in females it was ignored and at times even encouraged; it was feared that the numerous concubines of wealthy men, starved of alternatives, would seek devils for their pleasures if they did not masturbate frequently.

In addition to such technical aids, the handbooks offer copious instructions as to how the master of a house should conduct himself with his womenfolk. He should not, for instance, create jealousy by excessive attentions to any particular girl. His intercourse with a new recruit, or with a temporary favorite, should be carried out in the presence of others, who should be invited to take part in the act to avoid any hard feelings.

Tao and Confucius

Ostensibly the Chinese approach to sex was the product of only one of its several religions or philosophies, Tao. By an odd Chinese paradox, the same notions were shared by Confucianists, whose general philosophy was contradictory to Tao, and later by Buddhists.

Tao was a romantic protest against efficiency and sought a return to the simple life, a kind of golden age before the foundation of the state. Though sex-positive it was life-negative, praising nonaction above action. It was therefore under constant challenge by China's rulers, and at the beginning of the Christian era Han Dynasty emperors, though personally inclined to Tao, gave official favor to Confucianist principles. Whatever its personal appeal, Tao ran counter to their efforts to solve practical problems and to consolidate their power. In contrast, the doctrines of Confucius (559–471 B.C.) were efficient instruments for ruling an empire, since they lauded state service based on loyalty to the family and respect for one's ancestors.

Nonetheless, the flexible Chinese found no difficulty in reconciling the two faiths. The Taoist approach to sex not only retained its appeal but even won the active approval of Confucianists. The *I-Ching,* the *Book of Changes,* whose doctrines centered upon the interaction of yin and yang, was fully approved by Confucius himself:

> Why does a man after having reached his sixtieth year abstain from sexual intercourse? Because then he needs to nurture his growing weakness, and abstention then means that he treasures his life. The *Li-chi* says: "As long as a concubine has not yet reached the age of fifty, the husband shall copulate with her once every five days." This is also in order that he may help

her growing weakness. When a man has reached the age of seventy, this is the time of great debility. He can eat his fill only on meat, and if he sleeps alone he can not be warm. Therefore at that age he again starts having sexual intercourse.

Taoist sexual teaching continued to prevail until European ideas began to penetrate in the nineteenth century, culminating in the neo-Victorian puritanism of the Marxist revolution in 1950. However, long before this, Confucianist sages abandoned their master's permissive stance and drew up long lists of "merits and demerits," based on the need for moderation in sex as in other matters. One list awards fifty minus points, or demerits, for keeping too many concubines; a man also received ten demerit points for showing preference for one of his women over others. To look longingly after women in the street earned ten demerits, but for taking part in a frivolous play, the score was fifty. These penalties, however, were trivial in comparison with the cardinal sin for Confucianists, offense against parents or ancestors, which involved a penalty of one thousand points.

Buddhism first came to China from India in the first century A.D. and spread rapidly. Originally sex-negative in the extreme, Buddhism in China became a vehicle for exalting erotic pleasures and strongly supported *coitus reservatus,* the very basis of the yin-yang precept. Tantrism, derived from Buddhist doctrines, endowed sex with a mystic quality based on the belief that by union with the opposite sex a man could attain the attributes of the Buddha. Tantrism was a form of Buddhism that had found its way into China via Mongolia and Tibet, and emperors of the Mongol Dynasty (A.D. 1280–1368) even imported Buddhist monks to preside over sexual ceremonies. Coitus was prominent in Tantric imagery, and its deities often are depicted copulating with goddesses. For Tantric adepts, particularly monks and nuns, the road to salvation lay in copulation, in imitation of this divine pairing.

The Erotic Novel

In the seventeenth century A.D., as reprints of the manuals began to lose their appeal, their place was taken by erotic novels.

Both explicit and entertaining, they occupy a unique place in the world's erotic literature. An outstanding novel is the *Ch'in-Ping-mei*, both a literary masterpiece and a compendium of social custom; it was translated into English by Clement Egerton in 1939. As in van Gulik's rendering of *The Art of the Bedchamber*, the more salacious sexual scenes, with which this and other novels are studded, are translated not into English but into dog Latin; the English title is *Golden Lotus*, the name applied to Chinese women with the tiniest bound feet. Though written five centuries later, the scene of *Golden Lotus* is laid in the twelfth century, but the life and customs are those of the author's own time. If the format of the erotic novel is different, its sexual precepts follow the traditions of the Taoist manuals. *Golden Lotus* is essentially a Taoist cautionary tale; the hero is really a villain and a thief who dissipates his sexual reserves; he never conserves his semen, spending his precious yang in endless ejaculations. Not only the hero, but also Golden Lotus, the licentious girl who brings about his ruin, both come to a bad end: the hero dies of an overdose of an aphrodisiac, while Golden Lotus is killed by the brother of her husband, whom she poisoned.

Every conceivable variant of the sex act is described in intimate detail in the novel: fellatio, cunnilingus, and anal penetration are constant themes, while the hero, in addition to his other adventures, finds time for a homosexual affair with his page. A leading female character, called Porphyry in the English version, describes in expressive if basic Latin how "anal erotics were her favorite game, that she loved above all things *(Porphyria unum ludum super omnia amabat)*." She squeals *"mea vita, mea voluptas"* when the hero, Hsi Mên-Ching, excited her in this way, after she had taken a double dose of a love potion to increase her already insatiable appetites.

Other novels are also true to the precepts of the old manuals. A second work, *Chu-Lim-yeh-shih (Unofficial History of the Bamboo Garden)*, contains a carefully worked subplot whose aim is to instill their timeless lessons. The scene is laid even farther back, in A.D. 600. The beautiful Princess Su-ngo meets in a dream a Taoist adept who initiates her into the delights of intercourse. This dream launched Su-ngo on a career of lechery; she first seduces a young cousin who dies of exhaustion after endless indulgence with the heroine and her maid, to whom she had already taught the secrets of the Taoist manuals. She then marries, but her husband also dies of sexual prostration. After this she abandons herself to an interminable series of orgies in which her aging father-in-law plays a leading role; he proved to be a man of more stamina and survived the ordeal, only to be murdered by one of his sons.

Such novels provide a vivid and lively picture of sex life in the closing centuries of the Chinese Empire, describing certain customs that survived until 1950. The Western reader is struck, among other things, by the sublime indifference of adults to the presence of children, some below the age of puberty, as witnesses of their elders' lechery. These infant spectators were apt to cause havoc; sometimes they unwittingly betrayed clandestine affairs, with hideous consequences for those involved.

A prominent feature of the novels is the craze for artificially crushed female feet, repulsive to Western taste but tantalizing to the Chinese male. Whether to be regarded as fetish or fashion, the custom claimed women of all classes in the closing centuries of the empire, except for a few maidservants and peasants. Bandages, applied in early childhood, served to fold the toes and the front part of the foot downward; very painful at first, the deformity became more bearable as it finally set into the pattern of a hoof. This hooflike shape was given the romantic name of "Golden Lily" or "Golden Lotus," and another term for intercourse was then added to the colorful Taoist terminology—"A Walk Between the Golden Lilies." Such was the sexual significance of the fetish that a Chinese beauty would have felt far less ashamed if caught in an orgiastic act than if she inadvertently let a casual witness see her crushed feet, known as "lilies." Until forbidden in 1950, the mere sight of such crippled members could provoke a spontaneous male orgasm. Even ugly girls would fascinate admirers if their feet were small enough.

As far as one knows, no one has ever tried to explain in psychiatric terms this odd fixation, in contrast to the massive literature on genital mutilation. The Chinese, however, made such comparisons; in Lord Macartney's journal recording his stay in Peking at the end of the eighteenth century, he was told by a mandarin that deforming the feet was to a Chinese less strange than the foreign practice of cutting off parts of the penis during circumcision.

As in the Tao manuals, there is nothing private about sex in the erotic novels. Scenes are frequent in which a man or woman surreptitiously watches a couple having intercourse; if the voyeur is noticed, he or she might well be asked to join in the fun. Preferred forms of sex involved a number of participants, and performances of this kind were quite usual in any family with enough relations and domestic staff for the purpose. If the master of the house happened to be interrupted by a business caller, he would not dream of removing his penis from his partner of the moment while he talked of professional matters with the visitor.

In another novel of the period, *The Prayer Mat,* the leading protagonist of the sexual scenes, known as the Scholar, begins his day by copulating with his next-door neighbor, Scent Cloud, her aunt, Morning Flower, and her two girl cousins, whose husbands had gone off to Peking to take their civil-service exams. After a separate performance with each of the three girls, watched by the other two, he jumps into bed with all three and enjoys them simultaneously. Aunt Morning Flower then feels that she deserves a share of the action and carries off the Scholar to her house, where she tells how her first erotic experience was the sight of her impotent husband using an artificial phallus on a maidservant. In time her three nieces arrive in high spirits, bringing with them a couple of maids, both virgins. The Scholar sends for his two boy servants and a game is played with cards, each of which illustrates a different coital position; the players have to draw a card and perform the act illustrated.

One of Morning Flower's nieces, Priceless Pearl, took the top card. It showed a splendid picture of a man supported on his hands and feet, arched over the woman beneath him. His Jade Stem was shown to be gently touching her Pavilion Gate, and the position was called "Dragon-fly skimming the surface of the Pond." The meaning was clear, but when they hoisted the Scholar and Priceless Pearl onto the bed, he overplayed the part;

not content with a delicate dance within the Gateway, he proceeded to plunge into her Golden Gulley with a hundred thrusts.

By this time Aunt Morning Flower was trembling with excitement. But when her turn came, she went deathly pale; she had drawn the card called "Slave Girl Must Accept Anything," involving an act of sodomy performed upon a virgin. The three nieces were convulsed with laughter, but insisted that the rules of the game forbade her to draw another card instead. Three pairs of hands seized her and forced her to bend over a chair; at the sight of her exposed posterior, the Scholar went wild with joy. When he tried to insert his Jade Stem into what seemed an impossibly small orifice, Aunt Morning Flower screamed as if she were being murdered. After five unsuccessful assaults by the Scholar, the girls showered the target area with spittle and pushed the Scholar hard from behind; the aunt's screams began to suggest pleasure as well as pain as the performance was successfully concluded. The poor woman spent three days in bed to recover from this unwonted performance, but thereafter she joined in a whole series of orgies, which continued for two months. Like *Golden Lotus,* this novel offers a cautionary lesson on the perils of overindulgence. The Scholar, ashamed at his excesses, dies after cutting off his own penis.

The novels often refer to manuals of a simpler kind, known as "Pillow Books," designed for use before, or during intervals in, intercourse. These were portfolios or paintings illustrating a whole range of postures, accompanied by explanatory texts. A passage in *Golden Lotus* mentions their use: "On the twelfth or thirteenth day of the ninth month, there was a full moon. Chen Ching-chi was shaking the already flowering marsh mallows when Plum Blossom [a maid] rushed up to him and took him to Golden Lotus' apartments. Golden Lotus greeted him at the door, squeezed his hand and drew him into the bedroom, where all three sat down. Plum Blossom served wine and sweets. Golden Lotus snuggled up to Chen as the cups passed from hand to hand. After a while Golden Lotus became rather intoxicated. She began to cast ingratiating and lascivious side-glances at Chen. Then all three undressed and started to study the twenty-four postures of the Spring Series. They proceeded to try them out on the bed." Chen's energy began to flag: " 'Plum Blossom,' cried Golden Lotus to the maid, 'push him from behind if he gets tired.' " In addition to these Pillow Books, the traditional manuals were often accompanied by woodcut illustrations, but as yet no set of these has been published alongside a translated text.

The Chinese Hetairai

The erotic scenes in the novels mainly take place in the home, though brothels are also described, and courtesans are often mentioned. Prostitution in China has a very long history, and as early as 650 B.C. Emperor Kwan Chung assigned a special quarter of his capital as a residence for whores, though not until about a thousand years later do the records first mention brothels licensed by the state for use by the general public.

Accounts of prostitution have a monotonous similarity the world over; brothels in one place offer the same merchandise as in another and vary mainly in petty details: the prices charged, the taxes levied, or the ways of procuring girls. Of more special interest in China are the high-class courtesans, whose social standing bears comparison with the Greek hetairai. Several courtesans are the heroines of literary works, and one even achieved fame as a poetess: Yu Hsuan-chi, who lived in the eighth century A.D., came from a wealthy family but was disinherited by her father because she wrote verses with lascivious undertones. When he died, she promptly registered as a prostitute and soon became notorious for her wit and beauty. Another venal poetess, Hsueh-Tau, lived about a century later; after achieving fame both as poetess and prostitute, she eventually became a Taoist nun but without altogether abandoning her previous calling. (Buddhist and Taoist convents often made a good income by supplying food and wine to guests who had designs upon the nuns; such pleasures were tax-free, since the nuns were not required to register as prostitutes and no state dues were levied on money paid for their favors.)

High-class courtesans were skilled dancers and singers; they were also expert conversationalists. Marco Polo, writing of thirteenth-century Hanchow, not only describes the vast concourse of ordinary prostitutes but also stresses that the skills of the highest class were not confined to the bedchamber, since they could adapt their style of conversation to their hearer to captivate strangers. No aspirant could sleep with a courtesan without a long period of courtship. Van Gulik even suggests that, due to the burden of marital duties to wives and concubines imposed upon the rich, they sought the company of courtesans not for intercourse but as a means of escape from the dreary round of sexual obligations. Courtesans could also act as companions for wealthy travelers, who normally left their household womenfolk at home; if they did copulate with them, their sexual metabolism would suffer no harm; because this type of sex lay outside the range of conjugal relations, the sex manuals ignore the subject, and considerations of yin and yang simply did not arise.

The poorer people did not have the means to patronize houses where courtesans wrote poems, played chess, or sang to the guests. The lowest class of prostitutes, known as *yu chi,* or "wildfowl," existed to serve the populace. In the hopes of getting higher prices, they might propose novel techniques unknown to their clients' wives. Cheap brothels were usually situated in dilapidated houses; the outside walls often had no windows but were pierced with holes at eye level to allow people to see naked women sitting in lascivious postures on straw mats. Customers would choose a girl, and their performance could then be watched by passersby, who often had to line up to take a peep. These hovels are mentioned in erotic novels, whose characters sometimes went there to enjoy an evening of slumming in marked contrast to their own more genteel surroundings.

During imperial China's final decadence, when Westerners were present in force, prostitution flourished as never before to satisfy this new class of customer. A government survey published in the 1920s reported that in the major cities one in 325 inhabitants was then a prostitute. In Shanghai the proportion was higher; when under foreign control it possessed 633 registered brothels with 4,575 inmates, out of a total population of

665,000. As a means of advertising their wares, male attendants in brothels would carry the choicest specimens through the streets in early evening; some even advertised in local newspapers. Recruitment was conducted by purchase of children from their parents, or by kidnaping.

Cut Sleeve

Some brothels also catered to homosexual tastes. In the Chinese view, no one should condemn an act because it was different, but only if it was harmful. Puritanism and asceticism in the Christian sense were unknown until recent times in East Asia, and in China no one would have thought to censure homosexual acts on ethical grounds; they would be condemned only if carried to such excess that conjugal duties were neglected, physical health impaired, or, above all, if the expense was out of proportion to the pleasure. For the need to preserve one's yang essence, relations between males conveniently presented no problem. The two partners spent none of their priceless yang, because if both ejaculated, the result was not a loss but merely an exchange. Expense was a more valid objection to homosexuality, since relations with boys tended to cost more than with "flower girls." Male partners were plentiful, but they often charged more because they could claim to be better company than the average girl, since they were better educated. The Chinese suffered from the same problem as the highly intellectual Greeks: They were bored by the company of their women who, unlike the boys, had no conversation.

Homosexuality, therefore, as in Greece, served more as an alternative than as a substitute for heterosexual relations; in both societies it was a sacred duty to one's ancestors to beget male children. Though widely accepted, homosexuality was never exalted to the status it enjoyed in Greece. Nonetheless, from early times it received imperial sanction; in the *Chan-Kuo*, a compilation of the third century B.C., a story translated under the title "The Catamite and the Fish" tells of the ruler of Wei and his boy lover. While the two were fishing together the boy lamented the existence of as many handsome creatures who sought his master's favors as there were fish in the sea; the king, to reassure his favorite, decreed that henceforth no one was to speak of other beauties in his presence.

The great historian Ssu Ma-ch'ien, who wrote in the second century B.C., devoted a section of his history of the contemporary Han Dynasty to biographies of the rulers' favorites, listing the catamites of four emperors of that century. Though devoid of political talents, they became a power behind their masters' thrones. Due in part to the role they played in politics, these boy lovers were arrayed as officials with gold pheasant caps and gem-studded girdles; they powdered and rouged their cheeks.

> Neither Chi nor Hung had any particular talent or ability: Both won prominence simply by their looks and graces. Day and night they were by the ruler's side, and all the high ministers were obliged to apply to them when they wished to speak to the emperor. As a result, all the palace attendants at the court of the Emperor Hui took to wearing caps with gaudy feathers and sashes of seashells and to painting their faces, transforming themselves into a veritable host of Chis and Hungs.

The last emperor of the first Han Dynasty, Ai-ti (6 B.C.–A.D. 2), had many favorites. The best-known, Tung-hsien, was the hero of the "cut sleeves" incident. The ruler was sharing his bed with Tung, who fell asleep lying across his master's sleeve; the emperor was forced to get up to deal with a political emergency; reluctant to disturb his sleeping partner, he cut off his sleeve, and the term *tuan-hsui,* "cut sleeve," then became a euphemism for homosexuality in Chinese literature.

After the fall of the Han Dynasty, historians mention male favorites less often, although a number of emperors had relations with boy actors whom they maintained at their court. In the Chinese theater men played the female as well as the male parts. Like female impersonators in the West today, many of these actors were homosexual. According to one account, custom demanded that masters in the acting school deflower their pupils in a peculiar manner. At school the youngest would be placed at the bottom of the class; they sat on benches to which were fixed a number of round wooden pegs of different sizes. As the pupil advanced in seniority, he would insert an increasingly big peg into his anus, until he was ready to graduate. Chinese homosexual novels became popular; perhaps the most famous, translated as *Precious Mirror for Gazing at Flowers,* was published for the first time in 1856. All the characters are men, whose passions are described in the tenderest terms. The story ends on a pathetic note when the hero bids farewell to his lover. He has decided to give up his former delights and plans to have an organ grafted from a dog in order better to satisfy female partners. The greatest of all Chinese novels, *The Dream of the Red Chamber,* also contains homosexual incidents.

Homosexuality at times reached such proportions that measures were taken to combat excesses. During the Northern Sung Dynasty (A.D. 960–1127) so many boys were making a living as male prostitutes that a ban was proclaimed; offenders were to receive one hundred blows with a bamboo cane and a heavy fine. The law had little effect, since during the subsequent Southern Sung Dynasty (1127–1279) cohorts of male prostitutes walked the streets, often dressed as women, and even founded their own guild.

Lesbianism flourished in China, as in so many lands where polygamy was carried to extremes, leaving countless women unsatisfied for months on end by sex-sated husbands, with no other recourse than their fellow wives and concubines. In addition to wholly lesbian novels, *The Dream of the Red Chamber* contains more references to female than to male homosexuality. In one passage a man hears two girls "playing chess" in the next room, a term used for intercourse with one's own sex; in that context their remarks are quite explicit:

> There was more tittering. Then came a voice, speaking quite clearly. "It's your move now. Why don't you move?" Sounds like real chess, he thought. He wondered with whom Spring Breeze was playing. He hadn't recognised the other's voice. Then Spring Breeze started talking again. "Go on, then! We take it in turns, don't we? First you, then me. Steady now, gently does it!" There was silence for a few moments. Then the other girl gave a sort of sighing moan. "Oh, that's done me!" She added in a low, pleading tone: "I say , don't go any

further with that pawn of yours!" Spring Breeze answered coolly: "Don't count on that. You may not like it, but I do!" The other retorted, laughing now: "Right! We'll soon see about that!" So far as he could make out, she recovered command of the game and with a few brilliant moves got the advancing piece into trouble and captured it. "That's what we call pulling off boots in chess!"

For Lesbian lovemaking, elaborate aids existed. Van Gulik refers, in English, to a double olisbos, a short-ribbed stick of wood or ivory, before reverting to Latin to describe how, fixed to the body of one of the two female partners, it enabled her to play the man's part while she herself was stimulated by the opposite extremity.

Women who lived in such restricted circumstances also at times sought satisfaction from eunuchs. Until the sixth century A.D. castration had ranked as a punishment, and war captives also were sometimes gelded. The original methods of surgery were crude, and the mortality rate was high. Gradually the Chinese evolved a safer technique, of which we have several nineteenth-century Western accounts. By this time eunuch-making was a specialized hereditary profession, whose fees were high. Strict rules governed the process, which by law had to be voluntary. Applicants were numerous, since many important offices in the palace were open only to eunuchs, and a man who was prepared to sacrifice his private parts could reap rich rewards.

Before the operation the eunuch-maker would approach the patient and ask him whether he felt that he might later regret the operation; if he showed the slightest hesitancy, it was not performed. Due to problems of bladder control that often followed, a patient was forbidden to drink water for three days after his genitals had been removed and was therefore apt to suffer greater agonies from thirst than from any other aftereffects. The eunuch had to preserve his pickled penis and testicles in a container, to be shown at intervals as he advanced up the ranks of the palace hierarchy. They were buried in his grave so that his masculinity might be restored in the next world.

Although a eunuch could not become emperor, many were dedicated and powerful servants of the throne, and several ended as virtual dictator. They continued to be employed until 1924, when the last Ch'ing emperor was driven from his palace, where he had continued to live after the 1912 revolution, surrounded by his eunuchs; estimates of the number of eunuchs in China at that time amount to as many as one hundred thousand. Among the most powerful of modern times was An Te-hai, chief eunuch to Dowager Empress Tzu Hsu, who reigned for many decades until her death in 1908. One of his main duties was to distract a series of feeble crown princes with a superabundance of concubines so that effective rule remained in the hands of the old empress. Part of An's task was to find outstandingly virile soldiers for his mistress's own pleasure and to organize palace orgies; these debauches were spectacular pageants staged by the chief eunuch, who was himself a talented actor.

A Means of Grace

The Chinese had the mental agility to exalt sex to become a means of grace while exploiting it as a form of pleasure. Precepts first preached five thousand years ago showed such staying power that they were respected until the eclipse of the empire. More than a mere life-force, yin-yang are integral to the Chinese world view, based more on philosophy than faith. In a sense, yin-yang are not simply part of Tao, the Way; they *are* the Tao. Confucianist teaching was centered upon the good of the state, while Taoist sought individual salvation. But in their approach to the erotic, the Chinese were able to reconcile the two creeds; the head could follow one belief, the heart the other.

Every culture has its heroes. The Greeks, themselves a sex-positive people, idealized Achilles, the fallen warrior. The Chinese Empire revered the Yellow Emperor, famed for prodigious feats performed not on the battlefield but in the bedchamber.

But intercourse, raised to be a pillar of the state philosophy, became—at least in theory—oversystematized, and one is sometimes left wondering what Chinese sex life was like in practice. Was a mandarin in fact condemned to an endless marathon of titillation with every concubine and kitchen maid? To the outside observer the yin-yang principle appears as an eccentric fad, and coitus prescribed by the manuals as sex play more than erotic fulfillment. For the man, orgasm was a rare luxury, while such techniques, if the Hite report on female sexuality is to be believed, would offer the woman a mere simulacrum of satisfaction.

The novels of the last few centuries of the empire may offer a truer picture of what really happened; describing in detail many options absent from the manuals, they succeed in adding a fun element to sex, now expunged with a vengeance from the annals of the Peoples' Republic.

Paradoxically, teaching in sex-positive China, like Christian attitudes to Eros, suggests a divergence between theory and practice. The tedious sexual timetable devised by the sages is an open invitation to evasion; moreover, their theories leave convenient loopholes, of which the most obvious is exemption from the fetters of yin-yang of homosexual intercourse and relations with prostitutes.

Nonetheless, the mere fact that the basic philosophy of China should even try to impose such an exhausting career of coitus interruptus on the well-to-do reinforces the belief that sexual practices are more a matter of training than of instinct. Whether in India, ancient Greece, Peru, China, or even Europe, studies show that people can be conditioned to regard almost anything as either normal or outlandish, as moral or depraved. If institutionalized homosexuality was a bulwark of the Greek city-state, it produced fear and revulsion in the minds of nineteenth-century Englishmen, who idealized Greece. Chinese manuals not merely advocated but even imposed sexual practices that still rank as a felony in other lands.

Taoist teachers treated sex as the key to a state of harmony, both cosmic and human. But by a *tour de force* without precedent, this mental conditioning was obliterated by the Peoples' Republic. If the Manchu emperors at times favored restraint, the new rulers were relentless puritans. The performance is all the more astonishing because while sexual mores tend to follow set patterns in each culture, these are not instilled in a year or a day, like tricks taught to laboratory rats; they emerge slowly by a process of social evolution that subtly serves the goals of the society in question.

It defies reason to explain how a whole system, basic to Chinese culture, can be erased like a tape from a computer, now reprogrammed to support alien and antiquated forms of prudery. By the oddest *volte-face* of modern times, China embraced the sanctimonious standards of those nineteenth-century Christians whose predatory incursions supposedly paved the way for the Revolution.

Sex was one of the first aspects of the old China to attract the attention of the new masters. In 1950, barely a year after their victory, the marriage law of the Peoples' Republic was passed. It outlawed all extramarital intercourse, treated as a social danger and classified as a form of rape. Based on this law, the Shanghai Court of Justice ruled that intercourse between unmarried people was a felony, defined as "feudal sexual behavior." Even more draconian was the clause against unwed couples living together, and in very recent instances offenders have been sent to remote reeducational camps, from which they would be lucky to emerge alive.

In a book published in Hong Kong but giving the Communist government point of view, premarital intercourse is listed in the index under the heading "Sexual license and abuse." Private life is subjected to official dogma on a scale unknown since Calvin's Geneva. As an example, the same book quotes a Party directive that anyone who falls in love with a partner who was undesirable, from the Party point of view, should accept the Party's advice and sacrifice the love. Marriage among revolutionary cadres is to be preferred. Another pamphlet, issued in 1963 and still widely used, makes it clear that no one is supposed to have intercourse before the age of twenty-five. The more obvious alternative, masturbation, can be avoided by establishing "correct Communist attitudes." Animal contact, the last refuge of the medieval peasant and, conceivably, for lack of others, of the young revolutionary, is not mentioned.

No one can say how far such precepts are followed to the letter. Nor can one foresee to what extent a seemingly outlandish experiment will take root on alien soil. Although it may

be possible to impose sexual patterns over countless generations, time alone will show whether such a process can be thus
foreshortened and whether age-long urges can be stilled over-
night.

Form and Decorum

No account of the *Ars Amatoria* of China would be complete
without mention of Japan, whose present-day sex life, unlike
China's, retains many vestiges of former traditions. In some
respects Japanese customs in the past resembled those of China.
The emphasis was also on harmony and order, attainable in
Japan by aesthetic perfection in all things and by the strictest
adherence to form and to decorum. Following the introduction
of Chinese learning in the sixth century A.D., the notions of yin
and yang became popular; in A.D. 675 a special council was
established to advise the government on yin and yang lore. As
we have seen, it was the physician Tamba Yasuori whose Japanese version saved the Chinese sex manuals for posterity. Tantrism also spread from China to Japan, where the linking of
erotics with religion became even closer. The Tachikawa, a Tantric sect, practiced sexual rites at mass gatherings and went to
such extremes that it was banned by the government in the
fourteenth century. However, it continued in secret, and traces
of its doctrine survive. A few Tachikawa texts have been published, and other documents today remain hidden in Japanese
monasteries, sealed and marked "Not to be opened."

The Japanese had their own sex manuals; unlike the Chinese
texts, they taught their readers how to derive the maximum
pleasure from the sex act but did not pretend to propound a way
of life or a philosophy. In the seventeenth century these books,
known as Shunga, became popular in Japan; in place of the
crude diagrams of sex handbooks now in vogue in the West, they
were illustrated by creative artists.

The Shunga books shared the Chinese view of sex as an aid
to health and longevity. Quality in performance was stressed
more than quantity; the preface to Sugimura's Shunga book *The
Best of All Pleasures* counsels moderation: "Excesses, in general,

are the root of illness and foreshorten life; this is even more the case with iniquitous appetites in sex. The great will destroy their nation; the lesser will lose their homes and ruin their lives. Moderation should be the rule of all things." The Shunga format survived into the twentieth century, and in the 1930s department stores often would include a volume in the corner of a chest of drawers sent to a prospective bride.

Long before Shunga came into fashion, erotic scrolls were produced, though no originals exist. The first of these cited by a literary source is called "The Phallic Contest" and was formerly kept in the Toji Temple in Kyoto, the main shrine of the Shinjon sect. Its text was written by a Shinjon abbot, Joken, in the twelfth century, though the earliest version was older; devoted in part to the delights of the orgy, it also touches on the lighter sides of intercourse; the comic element is even more in evidence in "The Fart Battle," only partly erotic in nature, since its central theme is a ribald account of a "wind-breaking" contest between two groups of imperial courtiers. "The Fart Battle" and "The Phallic Contest" came to form a pair, since they jointly won first prize at a picture contest held by Emperor Kameyama in about A.D. 1270. "The Brushwood Fence" scroll is more wholly sexual and ends by demonstrating a series of coital positions, with voluptuous illustrations. The original was presented by her aunt to Princess Kenreimon-in when she was betrothed to Emperor Takakura in 1172.

These scrolls treat coitus as merely the final act in a courtly ceremonial that was integral to the art of lovemaking. Compared with the many coital positions shown in Indian and even Chinese manuals, their choice was restricted and varied little from the "normal" Western postures. The keynote in Japan was elegance. Oral techniques were used sparingly to avoid loss of decorum. Formal deference also prevented the female from turning her back on her partner, and this eliminated many alternatives that were so popular in China. Great stress was placed on prolonging the sex act. This lengthy performance must on no account be marred by any ruffling of the woman's coiffure, the supreme source of feminine attraction. The arrangement of the hair was not just a superficial adornment but had a deep erotic significance hard for Westerners to apprehend. Such arrangements are praised in countless texts and illustrations as the woman's "glowing crown." Professional courtesans learned special techniques to make sure that even after the most ardent embraces not a hair fell out of place.

The Japanese have always had a genius for organization, and they aimed to offer the greatest physical pleasure in a way that combined efficiency with elegance. Arising out of this obsession with efficiency, organized or commercial sex in Japan has an original quality less evident in behavior within the family unit, which in the past tended to follow Chinese patterns.

By a curious paradox the geisha, inseparably linked to commercial sex in the minds of foreigners, is by tradition more entertainer than lover. This has not changed, and the principal geisha houses of today are richly endowed and some own priceless real estate in big cities. Geisha parties are now the preserve of big business, for the benefit of its best customers. Friends have described to me these functions, whose cost to the hosts is stratospheric; their tedium is relieved only by the fact that they start at 6:00 P.M., soon after offices have closed, and end early. The geishas, like the Greek courtesans, are supposed to converse with guests on their favorite topic and amuse them with parlor games but not to sleep with them; each has her own rich protector, who has an exclusive claim on her favors. In contrast, the brothels of former times have been replaced by innumerable bars and strip-tease joints, where countless "hostesses" (who have absolutely nothing to do with the geisha houses) are readily available.

Her high status as a gifted, expert, and lavishly paid entertainer is best described in a geisha's own words to a German inquirer some fifty years ago: "Ladies can be divided into two categories. There are those who, like ourselves, earn a living by the independent exercise of a profession and there are those who are wholly subordinate to the other sex. The latter include both married women and prostitutes. I have heard that in the West, prostitutes are less respected than they should be . . . there is really no difference between them and a wife. Neither has chosen, of her own free will, to be what she is. The former deserves credit for submitting good humoredly to a whole series of husbands night after night and the other for doing exactly the same with a partner whom she also, like the first, did not select. In each case her father made the choice for her and drew the resultant profits. I am glad I am neither. I am grateful to my father for arranging my training as a geisha." She goes on to explain that the father had borrowed five hundred yen from a geisha house and established the girl there as security for the debt. He was thus able to buy a big shop while his daughter was taught literature, dancing, and perfect manners. Thereafter she had smart clothes and good pocket money, while her sisters were far less well off. When she went to spend her vacations with her family, everyone in the village treated her with deference.

The geisha tradition is not very ancient, and they are first heard of in the mideighteenth century in Kyoto and Osaka; originally many geishas were male (called *otoka geisha* in Japanese). Both male and female geishas were originally closely linked to brothels, for whom they would seek patrons, though their own function was not mainly sexual.

The traditional brothel system conformed to the Japanese dual passion for decorum and for organization. When the Tokugawa government first transferred the capital to Tokyo (then called Edo), brothels were scattered all over the city. But the keepers petitioned the government for a special quarter of their own, which was duly established in 1617 in the ward of Yoshiwara. Originally there were five classes of brothels, and in the two lowest the women were displayed in cages in the street. In 1882 this was forbidden, and instead their photographs were pinned up outside the door. The establishments were subject to strict government regulations, which fixed the price for each category, together with the tax and even the form of invoices to be used. According to a report written in 1899 on Yoshiwara, in the previous year the 40,208 registered brothels underwent a total of 134,100 police inspections.

The terms of sale of a young girl to a brothel or teahouse were tightly controlled. According to Article 20 of a law of 1896: "In the treatment of the girls, the brothel owner must be fair and decent, and he should do all in his power to lead them back to a more virtuous way of life and to prevent that they should continue to earn their living in so dishonorable way." The wording of this law serves to illustrate the incipient effects of Western moralizing in the non-Western world, since it is at complete variance with the traditional Japanese notion that the brothel girl, far from leading a "dishonorable" life, was held (as, say, in ancient Rome) to fulfill a most commendable social function; she had been performing this task in the brothel district of Yoshiwara since 1617, satisfying, among others, the bodily needs of innumerable government servants. By the 1890s, not only the girls but also the customers were closely supervised. Another regulation stipulates: "Brothel owners must keep two books, Book A and Book B. In Book A all arrivals at the house must be recorded. In Book B the names, addresses, professions, ages, behavior, and dress of each visitor is to be noted. Each time that a new book is begun, the old book must be examined by the appropriate police officers. The old books must be preserved for five years."

Before Westernization was completed, for a respectable official such visits, far from being censurable, were praiseworthy if not indispensable. It was held that intercourse solely with one's own spouse could not complete a man's sex education, since the teahouse inmates possessed talents unknown to the ordinary wife. Prostitution therefore served as a form of instruction, necessary to a man who wanted to satisfy his own wife. The girls not only were versed in the ceremonial and formal preliminaries, inseparable from the sex act in even the meanest establishments; they also were so skilled in the arts of intercourse that the girl, not her partner, would take the lead in choosing postures. She therefore had two main duties: to learn the required techniques and then how to convey them in a delicate fashion to her customer.

Rigorous schooling was required for the purpose; when a female child was sold by her parents to one of the countless Yoshiwara establishments, her education in the arts of love began immediately. Known as a *kamuro,* she would be assigned as serving girl and assistant to one of the adult girls; before

being initiated into the arts of love she was taught flower arrangement, music, and dancing. Her introduction to intercourse
was a ceremonial occasion. According to custom, she had the
right to choose her first partner; the brothel owner would try
tactfully to arrange that her choice fell on a rich customer who
would defray the cost of the accompanying feast, which he himself otherwise had to bear.

This well-ordered system served the needs of the commercial
and official classes of Edo; however, the samurai, the military
hierarchy who were dominant in Japan from about 1200 until
the Meiji revolution in 1868, at times sought other outlets. As
in most of Asia, homosexuality had never been a punishable
offense in Japan; the spread of Buddhism from about A.D. 600
gave it added respectibility, since the relationship between older
monks and novices combined tutorial cares with sensual satisfaction.

The samurai spent their lives in endless campaigns, in which,
unaccompanied by women, they formed attachments with
younger men, and sodomy was at times regarded as a more
manly means of satisfaction than coitus with delicately trained
females. In many samurai houses the women lived apart from
the men; the domestic services for the male quarters, such as the
tea ceremony and flower arrangement, often came to be performed by boys dressed as girls. These "pages" not only yielded
to their masters' sexual demands but even relieved them of the
burdensome duty of satisfying their wives.

Stories about love between members of the samurai class
(generally an elder and a younger) recall those of Greek com-
rades-in-arms. For several centuries the custom was widespread
in Japan, and many knights would seek out a youth who should
be worthy of him and with whom he could form a blood brother-
hood. Knights would easily become involved in an affair of jealousy and even fight duels on behalf of the beloved. The younger
partners were called *kosho*, and such attachments often are described in Japanese literature. For instance, Ihara Saikaka, a
seventeenth-century novelist, in his first novel, *The Man Who
Spent His Life in Lovemaking*, tells of a bisexual hero who roamed
around the country making love to thousands of women and

hundreds of boys. One of his novels, *The Mirror of Manly Love,* treats of purely homosexual relations, both between master and pupil in Buddhist monasteries and more particularly between samurai warriors and young men to whom they gave their favor and protection.

CHAPTER NINE

Erotic India

An Age-long Tradition

The sexual act, lauded by Chinese philosophers, was extolled with fervor by Indian mystics. Signs of an erotic cult already appear in the Mohenjodaro civilization, which flourished in the Indus Valley between 2500 and 1000 B.C. Figurines of bejeweled mother goddesses are at times pregnant, at others they nurse an infant. Ithyphallic images anticipate the Hindu cult of Shiva, whose symbol was to be the erect penis; conical stones already represent the *linga,* as the phallus was later called.

Indian religion was permeated by sex. Regarded in the Christian West as a necessary evil, in India sex was wrapped in magic and mystery. Basic to Hinduism is the view that sexuality is holy and that the sexual afflatus in men and animals is the outward sign of the gods' presence within each being. Human intercourse is the mere repetition of a divine action.

The earliest Hindu scriptures, the Vedas, mainly dating from the second millennium B.C., describe the Creation in erotic terms: "In the beginning was desire, which was the primal germ of the mind." One of the earliest Vedas, the Rig Veda, refers to the Golden Germ from which all creation sprang. Parts of the

White Yadur Veda relate to coitus; in one section, a series of dialogues between Vedic priests and their female partners deals with this subject in explicit detail. The Upanishads from the first millennium B.C. are even more open. The Brihadaranyaka Upanishad, dating from somewhere around 500 B.C., is the first to set out in specific terms the sacred nature of intercourse: "Her lap is a sacrificial altar; her skin a soma press; the two lips of the vulva are the fire in the middle. Verily, the world of him who practices sexual intercourse knowing this, is as great as the world of him who performs the great strength-libation sacrifice."

The greatest deity, Shiva, is god of both destruction and regeneration. In this second role, his emblem is the phallus. In Shiva temples the principal idol is a mound-shaped stone symbolic of the divine copulation, seen as the very cornerstone of the universe. Many Hindu temples portray every conceivable sexual activity and are filled with erotic carvings. Not only the cult of Shiva but also that of the great Krishna is founded on love in its carnal sense. Myths based on the youth of Krishna dwell upon his relations with cowgirls, with whom he ceaselessly mates. One such scene takes place in a forest, where the god plays the flute surrounded by country maidens, each enraptured by the fantasy that the young god is dancing and then making love with her alone. Krishna was said to have married 16,108 wives who bore him 180,008 sons. In many paintings he, as the incarnate god, is shown enjoying a wide range of erotic delights. Homosexual congress rarely features, but he occasionally appears in the embrace of a female monkey.

Linga

A compulsive trait of Indian religion is its obsessive cult of the phallus; known as the linga, it is not merely a divine symbol but a divinity in its own right. The word linga derives from the earliest term for the digging stick, which served as a primitive plow; both phallus and digging stick were instruments of insemination. Not only is the phallic cult recognizable in the early Indus civilization; the Aryan invaders, who overran India from the north in about 2000 B.C., at first treated with contempt these "penis-worshipers" among the original inhabitants. This resistance to the cult, however, was short-lived, and the newcomers soon became its most ardent votaries.

Linga-worship today takes many forms, centered upon images in stone, earth, metal, and wood. Lingas carved with symbolic devices still are used in rituals in which both men and women take part. Many were observed by early European visitors. A 17th-century account tells of a ceremony in the town of Ganjam in which a huge image of the god Gopalsami was carried through the streets in a coach covered with pictures of copulating gods and goddesses. An attendant on the coach held a stick carved in the shape of a phallus between the idol's legs; virgins and childless women paid homage to the stick.

Another aspect of phallus worship at this time was a female display of devotion to Shiva by kissing in public the genitals of naked strolling priests. These fakirs would show not the slightest twinge of emotion at this gesture; had they done so they would have been held to ridicule. When the statue of the god himself was exhibited in the temple, instead of giving a mere kiss of adoration, the female acolyte would receive his erect member into her mouth.

There are many legends about the origins of linga worship, linked to the story of the first day of the Creation, when the two gods Brahma and Vishnu sprang forth into being out of nonbeing. Both gods, bewildered by their sudden appearance, started questioning each other about their origin, to establish precedence, when they noticed beside them a resplendent linga of such huge dimensions that neither its top nor its bottom could be seen, and so they set about investigating it. Vishnu assumed the form of a boar to dive into the primal ocean to get at the base, and Brahma turned himself into a swan to fly to the top. Though Vishnu dove deep, he could find no base to the linga and reluctantly returned to the surface of the water to find Brahma waiting for him with news of his success in reaching the top. On this basis Brahma asked Vishnu to agree that he was the superior creation, but at that instant Shiva, the owner of the linga, appeared. He questioned Brahma about the top of the

239

linga, and when Brahma proved ignorant, it was evident he had not reached the top. Both Brahma and Vishnu were then forced to admit that the linga was infinite—lower than the deep and higher than the heavens—and both offered to do homage to it and to urge man to do likewise.

The linga mythology is linked to that of fire. When the giant version seen by Brahma and Vishnu eventually fell to earth, it became like fire and caused conflagrations wherever it penetrated. Only by worshiping it with flowers and perfumes could it be tamed. The phallic cult was a vital element in the marriage ceremony; according to ancient tradition a tiny gold plaque that resembled a fig tree and symbolized the linga was tied around the bride's neck. In the eighteenth century Roman Catholic missionaries tried to substitute the cross for this token; due to the resistance of their converts, the linga symbol survived, but with a cross engraved upon it. Wedding songs still used today call on bride and bridegroom in intimate physical detail to practice throughout their lives the gods' act of love and, true to this celestial command, to copulate both for pleasure and for procreation.

As we shall later see, in erotic literature the linga reigned supreme. In the sex manuals, whether a lover is true or false, young and beautiful, or fat and forty are mere trifles beside the vital question as to the length and breadth of his member.

Members of a special Hindu sect, known as Lingayats are dedicated to the exclusive worship of the linga as the symbol of the god Shiva-tatva. The sect was founded by Basava (A.D. 1125–1170), a Brahman from southern India who became the prime minister of the king of Kalyana. His career came to a sad end. Accused of embezzlement by the king, he plotted his master's murder. Pursued by the king's son, he drowned himself in a well. By an odd paradox, these worshipers of the human genitalia deny to themselves the pleasures of sex: They lead ascetic lives; they are strict vegetarians and shun liquor and even tobacco.

Tantra

Far more vital to the story of Indian sex life than these bizarre penis-worshipers are the followers of the various Tantric sects.

They are the leading proponents of the cult of the erotic that is intrinsic to Hinduism as a whole. The notion of mystical sexuality, present in earlier scriptures, both Buddhist and Hindu, found its fullest expression in Tantrism, which embraced both religions. Though its origins are unknown, the movement reached it peak between A.D. 700 and 1200; a large part of its scriptures consist of dialogues between Shiva and his wife, Parvati. In the Tantras the more austere teachings of the Buddha, traditionally asexual, are turned upside down, and in the Guhya-Samaja Tantra he indulges in acts of serial debauchery with a cohort of females. The Tantric sects envisage a summit of sensuality endowed with a magic essence beyond the reach of ordinary mortals; even relations with a virgin, or with one's own sister or mother, fall short of the ultimate requirement. The sex act, no longer a mere means of procreation, is a beacon pointing the way to salvation; according to this comforting doctrine, heaven was the reward, not for abstinence, but for indulgence. Only by copulation can a man obtain true knowledge of the One, the Brahma.

Pairing, the origin of being, the root of the world, is raised to the status of a rite, the key to enlightenment. Hence certain sects imposed regular congress even between monks and nuns. In search of the Absolute, the man pictures himself as the male deity who transfigures his partner so that she becomes the Sakti, his divine female counterpart. The essence of Tantra is this union of male and female energy, a union that is both mental and physical. Due adoration cannot be paid to the mother goddess unless a man has sexual intercourse with a woman, as representing the Sakti, or female energy. Moreover, no merit is gained unless the female partner is a married woman. Any man who worships the goddess without having intercourse is among the lowest of beings.

These carnal acts of homage were preceded by periods of mental discipline that included meditation on the *yoni* (vulva) of a virgin or of a married woman. Such lascivious precepts were subject to one limitation: frequent emission by the male, as in China, was thought to be dangerous; it was to be averted either by periods of total abstinence or by the use of yogic techniques to avoid the spilling of semen in coitus. It seems from a passage in the *Brihadaranyaka Upanishad* that the tendency to suppress male orgasm was very ancient. This act of continence was symbolized by nude figures of gods and saints with flaccid linga, known as "down penis." A pendulous member is to be seen on the famous statue of the Jain saint Gomatesvara. Jainism, like Tantrism, teaches that sexual concourse is the gateway to salvation but always insists that over-indulgence is a weakness and an evil.

Tantrism fostered the notion that there were two kinds of semen, male and female. The male element was concentrated in the head, behind the throat, and in the female in the vulva. The two elements could be brought together by *coitus reservatus,* which, again as in China, was thought to draw them up the spinal column, converting them into a form of radiant energy that ascends into the head. This circulation within the male body of both elements of semen re-created for an instant the primeval hermaphrodite, the Great One, who was both male and female.

Tantric sexuality was by no means confined to intercourse between two individuals. At secret meetings of certain sects known as Saktis, a naked woman, the wife of the chief priest, sat in the middle of a "holy circle" composed of men and women seated at random, without regard for caste or kinship. After a liberal feast each man becomes for a time Shiva, and each woman his spouse, Durga, and all copulated freely, disregarding even the incest taboo. Other sects of sexual mystics went even farther and held true orgies on certain nights in the crypts of their pagodas. Participants, including husbands and wives from nearby villages, would fling themselves like maniacs at total strangers.

Kamasutra

Indian erotic literature is unique both in volume and content. According to legend, the art of lovemaking in every form was first codified in a work of a hundred thousand chapters by the god Prajipat. This mammoth manual was condensed into a mere thousand chapters by Nandi, Shiva's bull, with added refinements based on his personal observations of the god's own

mastery of technique when coupling with his wife, Parvati. Even
Nandi's version was too voluminous for ordinary mortals, and
the Sonkha sages, who wrote at length on Vedic ritual, further
reduced the work to three hundred chapters; finally it was condensed into 150 chapters by Babhravya, founder of India's
greatest school for sexology.

None of these books now exists, and the earliest and most
authoritative version that survived is the *Kamasutra,* written by
Vatsayana, probably in about A.D. 400. According to tradition,
Vatsayana was a celibate and a stern ascetic whose recompilation
did not rest on personal experience. The *Kamasutra* deals more
with sexual congress for pleasure than for magic ends; it covers
every conceivable aspect of the topic. Of supreme importance
is the setting for the act. Copulation should never occur in a holy
place, nor in a roadside inn frequented by travelers. The ideal
type of house is minutely described, including such petty details
as the need for a spittoon to be placed near the bed, since vapors
and phlegm generated during coitus were venomous and had to
be expectorated.

The *Kamasutra* is not for poor lovers; it insists that a whole
series of rooms be set aside for courting, which also demanded
a garden of ample dimensions. Flower beds must be decorously
arranged, a point to which long passages are devoted. An item-
ized inventory of the required furniture and fittings is given.

> The articles . . . in the master's apartment, are two couches
> with beds, soft and comfortable and spotlessly white, sinking
> in the middle, and having rests for the head and feet at the top
> and the bottom. At the head of his bed is a Kurcha-sthana, a
> stand or perhaps a niche for placing an image of the deity that
> he worships . . . besides, at the head there is also an elevated
> shelf serving the purposes of a table whereon are placed arti-
> cles necessary for his toilet in the early dawn, namely, fragrant
> ointment such as sandal-paste, a garland of flowers, small pots
> containing bees' wax and sweet perfumes, the skin of the
> Matulunga or the citron fruit for perfuming the mouth and
> also betel-leaves prepared with spices and scents.

Promising conversational gambits are offered at extreme
length, starting with a reticent approach to put the woman at her

ease, followed by more intimate talk as a means of inflaming her passions. The *Kamasutra* devotes thirty-four sutras to the kiss alone. The author describes three kinds of kisses to indicate respect, three kinds to be used for informal occasions, two in which the lower lip is employed, four using both lips, three inside the mouth, six on other parts of the body, and there are also six to eight miscellaneous kisses. The kiss involves the use of the lips, tongue, and teeth, and its variations run through the whole gamut, from the gentle pressure of the mouth, the hard pressure with closed or open lips, sucking, and *damssna* (biting). The term *prahanana* (combat) is reserved for "love combat," and lovemaking is frequently described as a refined form of battle. The man attacks, the woman resists, and by means of the subtle interplay of advance and retreat, assault and defense, passion explodes and the final result is a delightful victory for both parties.

Bites and scratches and even blows are essential parts of the love battle. To quote the *Kamasutra* text:

> Thus, nail marks may be shaped like a crescent, circle, lotus, tiger's claw, etc.; and the various fingers employed to make them and the parts of the body best suited for each type of mark are set forth. The left hand is preferred for inflicting such marks, and nails cut into jagged edges like a saw-blade are said to afford the keenest thrills. Teeth marks are also named, like "spot-bit," "coral-chain," "elephant-tusk," "broken-cloud," and so forth. All these require skill in execution and can only be perfected through practice.

Many other kinds of bites and scratches are minutely described, the number varying from eight to twelve of each kind. When it comes to blows, mallets, scissors, needles, and pincers are recommended to assist the process, but they must be used in the precise manner laid down. The book cites as a warning the story of a king of the Chola country who killed a courtesan by striking her in the bosom in a manner not prescribed.

Last but not least, an endless choice of coital postures is given, amounting to a total of 729 variants. A single pair cannot possibly try them all, since many are for the benefit of specific couples, depending on the peculiarities of their genitals. The postures are named after the cow, the mule, the donkey, and countless other animals, whose characteristic sounds may be imitated during coitus to enhance enjoyment.

Finally, the whole love drama must be suitably rounded off. The text insists that after the act the lovers go to different washrooms, behaving as if they were strangers and avoiding each other's glances. On return from their ablutions their shyness disappears and they sit together on the terrace, and while enjoying the cool air, eat sweetmeats, drink milk (this is especially recommended) or mutton broth, followed by fried meats, fruit juices and fruit, and share betel leaves. They finally go to sleep but on different beds from that on which they had congress, as tradition forbids sleeping on the coital couch. The ideal time taken for the whole act from the woman's arrival at the house to the postcoital sleep is one *yama* (three hours).

Vatsayana's true hero is the wealthy man-about-town with few commitments and unlimited leisure, devoted to the pursuit of pleasure. The tone throughout is both cool and tender. The author accepts but never labors the basic Hindu premise that the coupling of male and female is emblematic of the union of the human with the divine. He advises the rich youth on the best way to lead a life of sexual pleasure, on the assumption that he will later go on to be a good father and husband, or even a sage, severed from the joys of the world.

The *Kamasutra* is not confined to ordinary intercourse between couples. Lengthy treatises deal with group union, oral congress, sodomy, flagellation, and bestiality. There are also hints for courtesans and eunuchs and long lists of aphrodisiacs for those whose powers are failing. As in all Hindu teaching on sex, the *Kamasutra* places limitations on the pursuit of pleasure. Women are not to be enjoyed either in the cold season, or in very hot weather. A wide range of females must be shunned at all costs, including lepers, lunatics, ones who reveal secrets, and those of very dark complexion.

Next in importance to the *Kamasutra* is the *Rati Rahasya* of Koka Pandit, a scholar who lived in the eleventh century A.D. Unlike the saintly Vatsayana, Koka Pandit was a man of the world who practiced what he preached and could draw on a wealth of personal experience when he wrote of the art of love. The *Rati Rahasya* is accordingly a more down-to-earth manual; while the *Kamasutra* aims at perfection, the *Rati Rahasya* serves as a factual handbook on lovemaking and coition, with a classification of female types, methods of union, and postures of sex. Pandit's work was popular with Muslims as well as Hindus and paved the way for another famous sex manual, *The Theatre of the Love God* by Kalyanamalla, a Hindu who served a Muslim nobleman and whose work was translated into the languages of many Muslim countries.

Temple Art

The flamboyant temple art of India is inspired by the love life of the gods. Though erotic figurines from the Indus Valley are over four thousand years old, the superb sculptures that adorn so many temples were first carved in the sixth century A.D. and belong to a tradition that survived for about a thousand years; it offers a rich repository of Hindu iconography, with a strong emphasis on the physical act of love, both human and divine. Some of the finest carvings adorned the immense wheeled chariots called "cars," built on the same pattern as the temples, with towering canopies and spires. They were used to carry the images of the gods on feast-day processions. Many of their wooden posts and panels display love scenes similar to those of the temples themselves. Both temples and cars have survived mainly in southern India, since most were destroyed in the North by Muslim invaders shocked by such exuberant displays.

The sculptures show a broad range of sexual activities. Sometimes couples are illustrated, but commonly three or more participants appear. In some scenes, orthodox copulation occurs, but many depict fellatio, cunnilingus, and anal coitus. Invariably those who take part appear to be utterly self-absorbed and do not face the beholder as, for instance, in Christian icons. The men often carry weapons, indicating that they are gods or heroes; goddesses always have outsize and perfectly spherical breasts. The many dancing figures in the friezes illustrate the close connection between dancing and eroticism.

Temple carvings fall into three main categories: simple figures, mainly female; couples; and more complex groupings. In all three varieties, the girls, like the modern pinup, display a conventionally idealized beauty, with full breasts and broad thighs; the vulva are often clearly illustrated. When single figures, both male and female, are shown masturbating, their faces express a delight far more intense than that of any copulating couple. The repertoire of coital postures is limited by the tradition that a divine pair cannot be shown lying down. In one instance, however, the male partner stands on his head, and two women perform acts of contortion of a kind recommended in the sex manuals but impossible to any but the most skilled acrobats. No conceivable variant on the sex act is too exotic to merit illustration; one anonymous painting of unknown age depicts a pair of lovers in full intercourse on the back of an elephant, while the man at the same time contrives to aim at a tiger with his bow and arrow. Some group scenes show a man copulating with a girl, who in turn practices fellatio on another man with an outsize penis. However, more often one man appears with several women; this is a more logical combination, since the *devadasis*, or temple prostitutes, always had two female apprentices or novices in attendance; moreover, a grouping of one man and five females offers the canonical formula for perfect sexual enjoyment and is found again and again in the later temple carvings.

While this one-to-five combination is frequent, some scenes go farther and illustrate the orgiastic aspects of Hindu sexuality. For instance, the great festival of the goddess Vesanti ended in a saturnalia in which children of both sexes ran riot and even incest was allowed. Such scenes were not only painted in friezes but even enacted in realistic detail by actors and actresses on portable stages. Though not shown in temple art, in erotic performances of a more secular nature, as described in the *Kamasutra*, children under the age of puberty would be used to fan the partners, who took no more notice of them than they would of a modern electric appliance.

Konarak, also known as the Black Pagoda, a colossal temple in Orissa, offers the most famous display of erotic carvings, of which its walls are encrusted with hundreds dedicated to the sun god Surya; the greatest temple of love ever built, it was abandoned in about A.D. 1230. Shiva's many temples are rich in such scenes; the god himself is often represented merely by a stone model of his sexual organ. But the walls of these shrines are covered by a seething mass of smiling figures of both sexes, enjoying to the utmost one of the inexhaustible range of alternatives recommended by the sex manuals. The beholders of such scenes, when they themselves copulated, knew that they were the incarnate followers of these blissful gods.

In these and other temples, the erotic scenes appear mainly on the outer rather than the inner shrines. This led certain Western scholars to suggest that the purpose was to allow the worshiper to give free vent to his imagination outside the building, which he would then enter, cleansed of lascivious thoughts. This notion, however, plainly stems from the Western-Christian view of intercourse as obscene and is totally alien to Hindu traditions. It cannot be repeated too often that Hindus, far from treating sexual indulgence as an impediment to holy living, on the contrary regard it as a precondition.

Caste-consciousness

In a society that was both male-dominated and sex-positive, the well-to-do male demanded variety, and polygamy was certainly practiced in wealthy families in Vatsayana's day. Princes and kings in particular claimed the privilege of possessing a crowded harem. Equally, however, it was not unknown for a rich man to have only one spouse, and the *Kamasutra* mentions a Prince Nanda who was so devoted to his first wife that he would take no other. In India the caste system placed certain limitations on plural marriage; in many instances even casual intercourse with a woman of lower caste was strictly banned, and passages in the Hindu Scriptures consigned to hell any man who lay with a slave woman. High-caste men who sought low-caste women were at times subject to the death penalty; the offense of a man who had relations with a partner of higher caste than his own was even graver; if he was not killed, as an alternative penalty his penis was cut off. If a high-caste woman demeaned herself with a man beneath her station, her head would be shaven, her body smeared with butter, and she would then be led naked along the street, mounted on a donkey, its color depending on the caste to which she had sunk, the lowest color of all being black.

As in so many regions, education was a male privilege; due to their ignorance and lack of conversation, women were apt to be treated by men more as possessions than as companions. The low esteem in which most wives were held is illustrated by the practice, already favored in Babylon, of mortgaging wives and daughters to moneylenders with the strict proviso that they could be pledged only to members of their own caste, as a guarantee for debts contracted. Also, in cases of some dispute or obligation, where money was not the issue, wives and female relatives could be simply handed over to the other party, who had the right to treat them as human chattels, to be released only when the obligation to him had been fulfilled.

The cruelest and most striking demonstration of the utter subjection of Hindu wives, as a form of expendable property, was the practice of suttee, the immolation of the woman on her husband's funeral pyre. The duty of the wife to accompany her spouse on his journey to the next world did not originate in India. Excavations of the Royal Cemetery of Ur show that in about 2800 B.C. numerous females, probably secondary wives and concubines, were buried with their royal master, though no certainty exists that his principal wife met the same fate. Suttee was also an ancient practice in China, where it survived even longer than in India; while earlier graves suggest that the custom was yet older, historical records from the last centuries before the Christian era show that by then the practice of burying concubines with kings was fully established. The Chinese firmly believed that his wives remained the property of a dead man and logic demanded their sacrifice as an act of devotion, and sometimes even daughters ended their lives on the death of their father. Barely a century ago, public hanging was the most usual form of suttee practiced by Chinese widows, accompanied by ceremonies so elaborate that only the wealthy could afford them. To die in such a way was treated as a privilege; wives of deceased husbands had to seek formal permission from the authorities, who often turned down their request.

Suttee, derived from *sati* (chaste woman), has a long history in India. It was found in the Punjab by Alexander the Great in 326 B.C.; the first Indian text to mention the subject was written in A.D. 316. By A.D. 400, widow-burning had come into vogue, above all in Bengal, whose literature is lavish in its praise; it continued to gain such popularity that the great sixteenth-century lawgiver Raghunandar recommended suttee to every widow without reserve. From the eighteenth century onward, eyewitness accounts by British officers record lurid and heart-rending scenes. Lengthy rituals accompanied the act; the husband's family took every precaution to make sure the wife could not escape if the ropes binding her to her spouse's body were broken by the heat of the funeral pyre; relatives, armed with fire-resistant green poles, were ready if necessary to push her back into the flames. The eldest son normally lit the pyre on which his mother died. Suttee knew no age limits; records show that in 1820 a four-year-old child-wife was burned in this way, while another woman aged 104 years staggered onto her husband's pyre.

The custom became ever more widespread in Bengal until eventually the British—always loath to interfere with Hindu practices—were driven to take action by the outcry that arose in England. Hitherto they had not dared to do so for fear of a mutiny among their Indian troops, such was the force of Indian public opinion in favor of suttee. As a first step toward a total ban, the authorities introduced a system of permits for suttee; a minimum age was enforced, and a police officer had to be present at the ceremony to ensure that the act was voluntary. Wife-burning could thereafter take place only on the outskirts of Calcutta. Not until 1829 was the practice officially forbidden by Lord William Bentinck, a governor general who was prepared to take risks. The crisis that inevitably followed came to a head in 1833 on the death of the rajah of Ahmadnagar. His son defied the ban and had already burned five of his father's wives when the British intervened; fighting ensued and matters were settled only after artillery reinforcements had been sent for.

Threatened with heavy guns, the new rajah promised not to burn any more of his father's concubines and, on behalf of himself and his children, to renounce suttee forever.

The gruesome custom deserves mention as a proof of the utter subjection of women in India, China and many other civilized societies, a subjection as unthinkable among more primitive tribes as in Western society today. Things had been different in India in earliest times. A woman of a higher caste could then divorce her husband if she wearied of him; if a Brahman, she thereafter had the right to enter a temple, where she served men of her class as a temple prostitute. The *Rig Veda* (cir. 1400 B.C.) makes no mention of child marriage, but the custom gradually crept in, and by about A.D. 1000 the proper age for a girl's marriage was held to be between the ages of eight and twelve. It was thought that if a girl was unmarried when she reached puberty, her father had failed in his duty toward her; she could then resort to the otherwise unsocial custom of choosing a husband for herself. To have an adult unmarried daughter in the house would be a source of shame and humiliation both for her and her parents.

Child brides were not normally deflowered by their husbands; the custom of ceremonial defloration gradually took hold and a sixteenth-century Portuguese visitor, Duarte Barbosa, tells how this act was performed on a ten-year-old girl by means of a stone linga. Husbands were grateful for this service; the belief was widespread that blood flowing from the ruptured hymen might harm the bridegroom.

If suttee symbolized the subjection of wife to husband, by a strange paradox India also possessed a tradition of polyandry, whereby a woman would take several husbands. This tradition was a legacy from a more primitive past; it survived among hill tribes, such as the Todas, until very recent times and is still found in the Himalayan region on the remote northeastern frontier. Polyandry, while not recommended by Hinduism as a whole, nonetheless occurs in its mythology. The Mahaburata, a vast collection of myths, folk tales, and legends of the early Vedic gods, written between the fourth century B.C. and the fourth century A.D., does not praise polyandry; however, the heroine of the epic, Draupali, a princess of divine descent, has the five Pandava brothers for her spouses. Another center of polyandry was Malibur; among certain castes, property descended in the female line, and a woman would take several husbands who had no rights of ownership but who could claim access to her person and to her home and could live off her land. The notion of polyandry is inspired by the figure of the mother goddess who personifies both fertility and sexual desire and is present in the many scenes in Indian art that represent the goddess as the erotic focus of a masculine group and that seem to derive from polyandrous habits of thought in earlier times.

Devadasis

Sanskrit, from which modern Hindu derives, has 330 synonyms for the word "prostitute" to cover the whole hierarchy of the profession—ranging from royal concubines and the courtesans of high society, to ordinary streetwalkers and common harlots. Collectively called pleasure girls, they are described by dozens of epithets, such as "melon-breasted," "mountain-bosomed," "hip-shaking," "lotus-scented," and even "fish-fragranced."

At the very summit of the profession stand the *devadasis,* or temple prostitutes. The scriptures are lavish in their praise of a man who would devote part of his wealth to the purchase of girls for temple service; one text assigns a special place in heaven to a noble who had acquired a bevy of girls for a solar shrine.

As early as the seventh century A.D., a Chinese visitor found hordes of dancing girls at the temple of the sun god at Multan. When King Rajaraja built the great temple of Tanjora in the tenth century, he endowed it with four hundred devadasis; their duties, apart from satisfying male worshipers, were light; they had to dance twice a day, fan the idol with Tibetan oxtails, and sing before it when carried in procession.

Temple prostitution, instituted in Babylonia and practiced in ancient Greece, was carried in India to greater lengths than ever before. Couples often would donate their first child, if a daughter, as a gift to the god. Piety was not their only motive, since many parents wanted to be rid of female offspring, for whom they would otherwise have to provide lavish and even ruinous sums as a dowry to obtain a husband of the right caste; dedication to a temple thus was an alternative to infanticide as a means of absorbing surplus female offspring.

The devadasis' training started at the age of eight, when they would be formally married to the image of the god Krishna, or to a sword, symbolic of that deity; Krishna, as the young and beautiful lover, was the personal god of the temple girls. After marriage, the girl was ritually deflowered by a priest; in some cases she was made to sit astride a stone linga or the member of some ithyphallic deity; occasionally a privileged worshiper was allowed to perform the task. Thereafter they were systematically trained by priests and Brahmins in dancing and erotic skills.

The devadasis were honored and even envied for their accomplishments. Worshipers visited the temples to enjoy their conversation as well as their caresses. For many centuries devadasis and high-class courtesans were the only females in India to receive the semblance of an education; part of their rigorous training was being taught to read. Hence, when Christian missionaries started schools for Indian girls, people naturally presumed that the pupils of these establishments were being trained as prostitutes dedicated to some Christian deity. Literacy was still held to be disreputable for married women; the belief was widespread in the higher castes that the husband might die if his wife should read a book, or even hold a pen in her fingers.

Almost equal in status to the devadasis were the various classes of courtesans. Foremost among these were the king's girls *(raja-kanya);* paid on a comparable scale to the king's ministers, they were selected not only for their beauty but also for their other accomplishments. Far from being hidden from view, like the inmates of a Turkish harem, their status was openly recognized. They attended certain state ceremonies, and on occasion, when a rajah wanted to pay special honors to a visitor to his domain, he would send his courtesans in a body to meet the traveler at the city gates.

Next in importance to the king's girls were the *ganikas,* whose status was comparable to that of the Greek hetairai. Like the Japanese geishas, they often had a single patron or protector. These courtesans were trained to provide companionship both in and out of bed. Their intellectual attainments were not limited to reading and writing; they were taught to cultivate all the arts, and some even competed with poets in composing extemporary verse. They were paid enormous sums for their services, and the story is told of one who charged her lover five thousand gold pieces for a single hour of her company. So important had they become in Vatsayana's time that he wrote: "A public woman, endowed with a good disposition, beauty, and other winning qualities, and also well versed and proficient in the sixty-four arts of love, obtains the name of *ganika,* or public woman of high quality, and receives a seat of honour in the assemblage of men. She is moreover always respected by the king, praised by learned men, and her favour sought by all—an object of universal regard."

Another sexologist, Kshemendra, describes in his *Kalisava* the sixty-four arts of love to be learned by the ganika. They include the art of perspiring, of cheating, of striking, of pretending to be poor, of boasting of former lovers, and of simulating virginity. The ganika must learn to know the disposition of her lover from his changes of temper, manner, and facial expression. In the last resort, if she finds that his affections are waning, she should attempt to lay her hands on his most valuable possessions without his becoming aware of her intentions. Some of the *Kalisava*'s down-to-earth maxims may perhaps have lost much in their effectiveness, since the prospective male victim was equally free to study its catalog of ruses and stratagems, which surely served to put him on his guard.

This strictly mercenary attitude of the typical courtesan is confirmed by many accounts; she would employ agents and dependents who had access to fashionable society and who could contact men who were rich and leisured. Ganikas used people of a different type to manage their finances and help them to retain the wealth they earned from their exorbitant charges. Well-placed officers of state were also important clients, with whom contacts had to be made through clever but needy procurers, such as petty police officers, clerks in law courts, jesters, and even florists. On no account should a courtesan offer herself openly for sale. It was the task of her agents and intermediaries to enumerate her talents but without giving the impression that they were engaged in a "hard sale" of their patroness.

The Hermaphrodite Ideal

Like other sex-positive religions, Hinduism sanctioned many alternatives to standard forms of heterosexual coitus. The erotic manuals, as we have seen, discuss at length oral-genital contact; the *Kamasutra*'s lengthy discourse on the subject begins with a description of eunuchs who put on women's clothes and who, for lack of a vagina, used their mouths to make a living as courtesans. The text reports that eunuchs who dressed as males also tried to touch the linga of men, and if they found them erect, engaged in oral-genital contact, described step by step as an elaborate, eightfold process. Tantric writings are even more specific and define twelve stages in the process. Practiced as a religious ritual, it was believed that if a worshiper achieved orgasm in this way, the vital powers of the organ and of its activated semen could be absorbed by a third party present by introducing the left-hand ring finger into the worshiper's rectum throughout the performance. In many parts of India, sex play with eunuchs served as a kind of curtain raiser to coitus with a woman. An old or semiimpotent man, before his female partner was due to appear, would summon to his house a eunuch who would shampoo him and rub his body to rouse him to a suitable pitch of excitement.

Fellatio was sanctioned by the gods, and in certain cases it conveyed special powers on those who indulged. According to legend, Shiva's seed was ejected into the mouth of the fire god, Agni, and transferred by him to the womb of the goddess Parvati, who thus gave birth to the great war god, Karttikeya. As a variant on this theme, when a man and a woman, assuming opposite positions, practiced at the same time fellatio and cunnilingus, a magic circle of great potency was thought to be created by the presence of another woman, who thrust her finger into the rectum of the female partner.

To anal copulation magic qualities were also attributed. The animation of the rectal center was supposed to energize a man's artistic, poetic, and mystical faculties. Opinions on this point were nonetheless divided; many authorities praised the habit, while certain doubters voiced the fear that males who favored the practice would be reborn impotent. Tantric and other sects engaged in mystic concentration on the anus, into which they introduced wooden plugs as an aid to meditation, while in other rituals they practiced digital insertion; such acts were based on yogic disciplines and on the belief in a close correspondence between the anus and certain higher centers of the body.

As part of the cult of anal intercourse, male homosexuality was at times not merely tolerated but even encouraged. In this instance also, however, opinions were divided, and a text from the fourth century B.C. advocates a specific fine for male homosexual intercourse; a smaller penalty was proposed for lesbian contacts. Such penalties were mild compared with those for certain other transgressions; the most heinous offense for a man was to seduce his guru's wife. Offenders would be made to embrace the red-hot image of a woman; alternatively, after their genitals had been cut off, they would be made to walk until they fell dead.

Attitudes toward homosexuality were tempered by the fact that, in Hindu tradition, the dividing line between the sexes tended to be blurred. The hermaphrodite condition was an ideal to be pursued rather than a deformity to be pitied. According to Tantric doctrine, the Supreme Being is both male and female, with the qualities of both genders. Hinduism, anticipating perhaps certain biological and psychiatric concepts of our time, taught that every man and woman embodied elements both male and female. The only difference was that in a man the masculine qualities exceeded the feminine, while the reverse applied to a woman. In each individual a conflict existed between the male principle and the female principle, which could be stilled only for brief periods during intercourse, when both partners merged into the Absolute, itself of no defined gender.

Shiva, in sculpture and painting, sometimes is shown with female organs on his left side and male organs on his right side (precisely, as we have seen, as can occur occasionally in real life). In many legends, a male god took on female form; the great Vishnu transformed himself into a ravishing beauty called Mohini to settle a dispute between gods and demons. Shiva was so bewitched by Mohini's glamor that he besought Vishnu to resume his female form; the two gods had intercourse and Mohini, alias Vishnu, gave birth to Harihara, a hermaphrodite deity.

The Sakhibhava sect revered this somewhat transsexual Vishnu as the greatest god; only Krishna was truly male, while every other creature was inherently female and subject to his pleasures. Female followers of the sect offered their favors freely, convinced that Krishna himself took part in the act. Male followers also dressed as women and affected female movements and behavior, with the avowed aim of becoming the god's sexual partner.

In addition to mythical stories of sex change, India's literature contains many accounts of transvestism, usually on the part of men who dress and behave as women. The god Samba, son of Krishna, a notorious drunkard and glutton, would dress as a pregnant woman and go about mocking the other gods. As Sambali, his name became a synonym for eunuch. Arjuna, the manly hero of the *Bhagavad-Gita,* pretended to be a eunuch, dressed as a woman, and taught the young daughter of King Virata how to dance and sing.

Masturbation, if not blessed by the gods, was never discouraged. As an aid to satisfaction, an odd device was used called a *viyoni* (without yoni), which was made of wood and cloth and shaped like a vulva, with a yoni-shaped aperture; used mainly in fertility rites, it was lined with leaves and other vegetable matter. Artificial phalli were employed by both males and females; the stone lingas in many temples served not only to deflower virgins but also were used by barren wives, who sat on them in the hope that Shiva's own image would make them fertile. For erotic purposes a wide range of fruit and vegetables was recommended to young females, including radishes, bananas, and even the bulbous eggplant. Other artificial phalli were made of candle wax, wood, bone, and metal; many writers on sexual topics urged men to use them to stimulate their partner before intercourse.

The almost inexhaustible range of aids to sexual stimulation included special attachments to the penis made of gold, silver, copper, iron, zinc, lead, or wood, dependent upon the economic status of the user. Usually made in two parts, they fitted around the penis like a glove. Designed as a form of stiffener, they enabled a man—in theory, at least—to satisfy his partner regardless of old age or impotence. Painful methods of enlarging the penis also were recommended; the *Kamasutra,* for instance, suggests that a man should rub his linga with the bristles of certain insects that live in trees, then cover it with oil; this treatment would cause it to become inflamed and swell. If the correct procedures were followed, the member, after healing, would remain longer for the rest of his life.

In some parts of India, men were encouraged to perforate the penis, like the lobes of the ears for earrings, to enjoy the greatest pleasure. Others sewed tiny bells of gold, silver, or bronze, again depending on income, into the foreskin. This also caused the organ to swell and heightened the satisfaction of the female partner.

Hindu tolerance was at times even extended to bestiality. Sexual contacts between animals and humans appeared frequently in temple sculpture. Tantrism often portrayed the man as a rabbit, bull, or horse, and the woman as a doe, mare, or she-elephant. Such representations are not pure symbolism, since animals were thought to be more sensuous than humans, and various yogic disciplines aimed at giving a man the virility of a beast and the ability to copulate with animals. The notion that all desire is holy set no limits to such forms of indulgence, which were described even in the scriptures. In Hindu mythology, Mallika, wife of the divine Prasenajt, satisfied her lust with a pet dog, while her husband copulated with a goat.

In certain Tantric sects no holds were barred and even necrophilia was not excluded. In the so-called black ritual, the adept sits astride a male corpse, which he animates by occult means;

the body twitches and turns, its tongue protrudes, its penis becomes erect and eventually ejaculates.

The Victorian Raj

Long before the arrival of the British, a reaction had set in against the eroticism of ancient India. The Muslim invaders of northern India obliterated most of the sculpture of that region. Moghul Emperor Aurangzeb is said to have destroyed over two hundred temples in a single year. Priapic statues were smashed everywhere and even simple nudes, such as the stone figures of Jain saints at Gwalior, were deprived of their penises. In the following centuries Western visitors were equally shocked at the temple art that survived in the South. Abbé Dubois, who wandered around South India from 1792 to 1823, wrote of the ubiquitous lingas of Shiva as "obscene symbols, the very names of which, among civilized nations, are an insult to decency."

Though they sought to reject other aspects of Western teaching, the leaders who achieved Indian independence were indelibly stamped with the moral attitudes of Victorian England. Despite such reservations on the part of its new rulers, however, vestiges of ancient practices survive. The devadasis were already banned in Bombay in 1934. Nonetheless, a United Press report, printed in the *Bangkok Times* in August 1981, told the story of a child dedicated at birth to the goddess Ranuka; she was one of an estimated five thousand girls who still serve that goddess. The same report asserts that occasionally parents also dedicate their sons to Ranuka; forced to become transvestites, known as *jogretes,* they wrap their bodies in saris, wear bangles, and adopt a female hairstyle. At a recent conference of devadasis in Nipani City, in the southern state of Karnataka, a *jograta* told listeners that he had completed his high school studies when his parents dedicated him to the goddess. He told the audience of devadasis and reporters: "I am not angry with my parents, or unhappy, because I'm doing what the goddess wants me to do." One young and pretty woman, who identified herself only as "baby," told the conference that she was picked to be a devadasi when still in her mother's womb. All sorts of men in the temple made

love to her: "good men, bad men, beggars, and even thieves."
They paid whatever they could afford.

Priests still use devious methods to persuade parents to dedicate their daughters, sometimes inventing deathbed confessions
in which a dying relative begs that a girl from the family must
serve Ranuka. However, opposition to such survivals of past
customs is increasing, and among the devadasis themselves a
militant group, the Phule equality organization, was founded in
1975. It has since been lobbying the state governments of Karnataka and of Maharashtra (where Bombay is located) to enforce
the Bombay Devadasi Act of 1934. The act not only renders
both parents who dedicate a girl, as well as priests, liable for
prosecution; ironically, the girl herself, if over eighteen years
old, also can be fined. ·

Another ancient tradition that survives in some places is linga-
worship, and many phallic images of Shiva still are used in
temples today. Art forms of the recent past are rich in love
scenes, but their faintly erotic sentimentality is based more on
fantasy than on real life.

Like the brothels and the devadasis, child marriage, such a
characteristic feature of bygone India, was already under attack
before the end of the British raj but has been very slow to
disappear. Child wives numbered six million in 1921 and five
million in 1931; but in 1961 it was officially stated that there was
not a single known case of a married girl under ten years of age,
though there were still four million between the ages of ten and
fifteen. Such claims, however, are hardly substantiated by a
Press Trust of India report of May 17, 1983, that a few days
previous to this, on a day known as Akhateej, considered lucky
for marriage, more than ten thousand children, many of them
babies in their parents' arms, had been married to prearranged
mates. In the area around Ajmer, 230 miles southwest of Delhi,
an average of fifty to sixty child weddings were performed annually in each village.

Sex and Salvation

In India sex-positive attitudes were carried to their ultimate
conclusion. Scarcely a single variant, or "vice," could be named

that was not merely accepted but even praised, if not by one sect, then by another, as practiced by the gods themselves. Throughout the non-Christian world an active sex life tends to be favored by the prevailing philosophy or religion. Hinduism goes farther and treats sex not merely as desirable but even as indispensable for individual salvation; as a consequence, no other region is so rich in erotic art and literature. Equally, no other civilization was so imbued with the spirit of mysticism; true to the precept that in each culture the sexual code harmonized with its basic tenets, in India, unlike China, sex assumed a mystical quality; union with the divine, an intensely spiritual experience, becomes identified with human intercourse.

Whereas the Chinese sought longevity and harmony in this world, for Indians sex was a means of salvation in the next. Nonetheless, even in a society that offered a rich variety of options to its members, freedom always was subject to certain limitations, fairly typical of every culture except contemporary Western society. The sanctity of marriage was never undermined by the endless range of alternatives offered by sex manuals. The notion that a woman should die on her husband's funeral pyre, a ceremony in which her children played a major role, stresses the absolute cohesion of the family unit ruled by the father. Nowhere was the contrast more stark between the adoration of the great mother goddess, under a variety of names, and the abject subjection of women to their spouses.

CHAPTER TEN

East and West

Patterns of Behavior

The first part of this book was devoted to tribal peoples, where a fairly constant theme was teenage fornication, widely approved and sometimes imposed. For married people the rules were stricter. Nonetheless, in many places wives as well as husbands had alternative outlets: wife-lending to honored guests; female copulation with young novices; and even festive orgies in which few holds were barred.

Equally, most but not all primitive cultures accepted that some people had homosexual leanings. This concession took different forms: The American Indian made a virtue of necessity, and those who showed early transsexual tendencies were formally made to adopt the female state and become bardajes.

While the world's higher civilizations, starting about five thousand years ago, were in most things so unlike, with respect to sex they all cast off certain tribal habits while retaining others. Starting in Mesopotamia, marriage was no longer governed by mere custom but by written law; there and elsewhere formal codes ostensibly confirmed the rights not only of men but also of women; however, in practice the great lawgivers of the Near

East, from Hammurabi in 1800 B.C. to Mohammed in A.D. 600, legalized female enslavement. Higher civilizations sanctified private property, of which women were merely one form. Tribal wife-lending or wife-sharing was outlawed as infringing on such rights. Bridal virginity became an obsession, since no man would invest in a tangible asset, in the form of a wife, who had already lavished her favors on all and sundry.

Equally, states and empires were more circumspect in dealing with homosexuals, though they were seldom actively persecuted. While wife-stealing was everywhere a capital offense, only in Europe were equal penalties applied to sodomy, even with one's own spouse.

Notwithstanding such common traits, differences between the world's civilizations in their approach to sex have been seen to be basic. Arguments have ceaselessly raged as to how far individual behavior is the product of heredity or environment, though this nurture vs. nature controversy has become increasingly sterile as both elements are accepted as vital.

However, where whole societies rather than individuals are concerned, the discussion remains more lively. Harvard Professor Edward Wilson can justly claim to be the founder of sociobiology, which studies the relationship between inherited genes and the conduct of whole groups. His original work on the subject, *Sociobiology,* published in 1975, was based on the habits of birds and baboons, whose well-defined modes of behavior he simply extended to man by applying the same genetic logic to the variations among his many cultures. In his latest book, *Genes, Mind and Culture,* published in 1982, Professor Wilson is less adamant that civilization is the outcome of a certain combination of genes. The theory was anathema to many, and Wilson's first book caused an uproar in academic circles, among whom his second work also found little favor; noted Cambridge anthropologist Edmund Leach has described it as "just bunk."

Inherited genes obviously play some part in group behavior; Wilson, however, argues that they alone lead people to opt for a given range of choices in forms of conduct that, taken collectively, go to form a human culture. His reasoning rests upon a formidable and, to the layman, bewildering array of mathematical data.

Many anthropologists treat as sacrilege the notion that "behavioral genes" are the determinant factors in the customs of peoples separated for many thousands of years, such as, say, American Indians and Africans. Such theories, not wholly alien to the spirit of *Mein Kampf,* contrast starkly with those of another Harvard psychologist, Burrhus Skinner, who sees group (as well as individual) behavior as the product of environment and studies how it operates. Skinner's behaviorism plays down the role of genes in the process. Wilson may rightly insist that in animals, and even in human beings, certain phobias may be innate, though in previous chapters it has been accepted that the incest "phobia" is more a self-imposed rule, designed as a safeguard to society. But it surely defies all reason to try to explain in terms of genes why, for instance, Christians favor monogamy and Muslims polygamy simply because such reasoning, couched in scientific language, can be applied to the mating habits of a few animal species. Why, for instance (to take an example divorced from sex) did the Samoans formerly devour their sacrificial victims, while to their fellow Polynesians, the Tahitians, the idea of eating such victims would have been revolting?

The factors that blend to form the genius of a given culture are hard to define. Sexual behavior, undoubtedly a key element, has been consistently found throughout our study to conform to the true essence of that culture. This precept has been applied to overall patterns of sexual behavior but has not been stretched to a point where every custom, however trivial, is seen as a vital cogwheel in the mechanism of a given society, as once proposed by Malinowski's theory of functionalism.

Nonetheless, it does seem that the human mind can be programmed to view a given sexual custom in terms ranging from adulation to abhorrence; one need only recall that celibacy or abstinence, treated as the very summit of virtue by Christendom, ranked as sheer depravity in China; sodomy and fellatio, enjoyed by the gods and praised by the Scriptures in India, became a felony in many Western nations.

Sexual behavior seems therefore to be less a product of the genes of a given group than a response to its guiding principles. The general tenor of its sexual code conformed to India's dedication to mysticism. The Chinese Empire was grounded in philosophy, to which the sexual ethics of the yin-yang principle were fundamental. Islam, impelled by the urge to conquer infidels, rewarded its conquerors with the right to acquire foreign concubines. In Greece the institutionalized man-boy relationship served as a backbone to the tiny armies that protected the city-state, the basis of society.

Odd Man Out

It might be argued that the Christian West is the odd man out, with a sexual code of conduct that runs counter to its true essence. At first sight, it seems preposterous that the heirs of Rome could opt for such a sex-negative code of morals. The cause is to be sought not in genes but in history. Christian attitudes derived from a special set of circumstances; Christianity adopted extreme asceticism less in obedience to its founder's teachings than as a bid for support in face of competition from other self-denying and sex-denying creeds, offering spiritual solace to people whose material world was collapsing. Such precepts were not designed to uphold a rising civilization like, say, Taoism in China or Islam in Arabia, but served rather as a substitute for the discredited values of a crumbling order.

While the Church, once officially recognized, promptly discarded its founder's dedication to poverty, it clung to sexual asceticism (which he had not stressed) as a disciplinary weapon in a disintegrating society, for Christianity did not long serve as an effective buttress to the existing authority: The Church itself became all that remained of civilization at a time when clerics were the only people who could read and write.

In the later Middle Ages and early Renaissance, learning ceased to be a Church monopoly and a new and more secular civilization gradually arose; such sex-negative doctrines then became less help than hindrance to what was no longer a priest-ridden relic of the ancient World but a dynamic and ebullient society. As time went by, they came to be increasingly ignored, or circumvented.

Its sex-negative creed has often been presented as the very mainspring of Western culture and therefore vital to its needs;

in contrast to the lascivious Oriental, debilitated by indulgence, Western man, according to this notion, devoted his pent-up energies to nobler ends, and his civilization triumphed over all others. The theories of J. D. Unwin, outlined in a previous chapter, typify the notion that success is the preserve of the abstemious, granted to those societies that banned premarital relations and enforced the strictest monogamy on married couples. But such views, advanced as late as the 1930s, overlook the triumphs, whether material or moral, of, say, Islam or China. On a more strictly materialistic level, the staggering achievements of present-day Japan are those of a people who are the reverse of sex-starved. Only in revolutionary China has sexual repression reached a level recalling that of the early Christian Church. Not only is extramarital sex a felony there, but also marriage is officially presented, as among early Christians, as a kind of spiritual meeting of minds consecrated to the same cause, with procreation as a very secondary motivation. But this repression followed a period of moral collapse in China, comparable to that of the late Roman Empire, and signs are not absent of a cultural eclipse as far-reaching in scale as that of Europe during the succeeding Dark Ages.

The rise of Western civilization involved more a revolt against sex-negative attitudes than their acceptance; asceticism of a rather different kind, however, did answer some of the needs of its latter-day industrial phase. Unlike, say, in ancient China or India, Christian attitudes to sex have oscillated between periods of repression followed by others of tolerance. A new wave of repression, emblematic of the rise of the Protestant bourgeoisie began in the seventeenth century and continued into the nineteenth century. The flesh became once more the root of all evil. Notwithstanding an interval of tolerance in the eighteenth century, sex then began to take on a new dimension. Governments no longer were dealing with peoples but with populations; procreation, and therefore sexual relations, became a basic factor in the new age. By the nineteenth century, Protestant Christianity became inseparable from the work ethic; this process stressed the need for more children, born in wedlock, to man the factories. The fulfillment of this demand implied duty and not pleasure, a notion alien to the work imperative. As part of this process, ribaldry was banned and a conspiracy of silence expelled sex from everyday reality; all forms of sexuality that were not reproductive—within the legal framework of marriage—were proscribed and all nonprocreative acts outlawed, an attitude recalling that of St. Augustine, even if the motives were not identical.

Michel Foucault in a few revealing passages in the first volume of his *History of Sexuality,* first published in 1976, challenges certain aspects of the standard version of Victorian sexual repression. In the first place, if the orderly procreation of more children was its main purpose, it is hard to explain why the ruling elite first imposed such restraints upon themselves while the working classes for a long time escaped the full deployment of Victorian morality.

Foucault argues that sex was not exactly brushed under the carpet; it was simply treated in a different way, a theme for learned discussion but not for jocular banter. The *ars erotica* of previous societies was replaced by a new *scientia sexualis.* The subject was medicalized: the sexuality of children came under close scrutiny, together with that of mad people and criminals. Sex became a matter of health and sanitation, and scarcely a physical disturbance was not laid at its door, whether stuttering among children or paralysis among the elderly. The effects of a healthy, or unhealthy, sex life had an ineluctable effect on future generations, and shortcomings would lead to the birth of homosexuals, exhibitionists, and other perverts. Intercourse during pregnancy, for instance, was even thought to produce epileptic children.

The dire perils of masturbation attracted special attention. The new science of sex developed a bizarre fixation about onanism as the root of all evil. Since Old Testament times masturbation had not been a major target for moralists until in 1710 an anonymous English clergyman-turned-quack doctor published his shattering indictment *Onania, or the Heinous Sin of Self-Pollution.* The book unleashed a pitiless war of attrition against this innocuous outlet: *The New Orleans Medical Journal,* for instance, in 1855 quoted an eminent French doctor as stating that neither the plague, nor war, nor smallpox had proved more disastrous for humanity than the habit of masturbation.

Sodomy also came under closer scrutiny; it was no longer simply a felony, such as, say, stealing sheep. Instead, the homosexual became a species, to be studied like any other, if only for the purpose of his eradication, or cure. This investigation naturally reinforced social controls. In England, any act of "gross indecency between males" (but not between females), even in private, was first in 1885 made a misdemeanor, punishable by two years' hard labor, while sodomy was defined as a felony, incurring penal servitude for life. This was the product of an extra clause, known as the Labouchere Amendment, tacked on to a House of Commons bill raising the age of consent for female prostitutes from twelve to sixteen years.

Industrial society, a new phenomenon in world history, accordingly also produced a sexuality that conformed to its basic imperatives. Repression was only one facet; there was no fundamental refusal to recognize the dynamics of sex but rather a striving to formulate scientific truths on the subject. In 1857, only twenty years after Queen Victoria had ascended the throne, Dr. William Acton published his *Functions and Disorders of the Reproductive Organs.* This authoritative text was not only strongly anti-onanist but also in effect antifeminist. For Acton, in intercourse the woman was merely the passive instrument from which the man evoked music, a comparison that was later to attract acid comments from Margaret Mead and other feminists.

Opposing Trends

The sexual revolution of the 1960s and 1970s is at least in part a delayed reaction to the teachings of earlier psychiatrists and sexologists. In a few respects but not in others, it represents a reversion to practices common in tribal society, some of which may be almost as old as *Homo sapiens* himself. In part this reversion may be coincidental, even if it accords with the precepts of anthropologists who lauded the seemingly stress-free ways of remote islanders.

The approach to sex of the modern teenager in advanced

societies is not quite that of the Trobriander. Premarital sex, widely accepted, is performed in relative privacy. It is not a formal institution, and the bachelors' house has been replaced by the automobile, used as a kind of mobile bed. The greater modern tolerance of deviant, or atypical, acts prevailed in most tribal societies and in many non-Western higher civilizations. Today the problem is different because modern society no longer makes the same sharp distinctions between the *macho* male and the defenseless female. Not only do men and women dress more alike than before, but also both go out to work and often do the same jobs. A more androgynous approach to life, in ancient Greece an artistic ideal, has now become an established fact.

Modern marriage has less claim to be regarded as a reversion to tribal patterns. Virginity is no longer mandatory and the rules of the game may be more relaxed, but the emphasis is still on monogamy, and infidelity remains the commonest motive for divorce. While Muslim males could marry four wives simultaneously, the Western trend is now toward serial monogamy, in which pairing with a new partner presupposes separation from the old. Wife-lending, as known to tribal society, and even group sex have been frequently tried but without becoming generalized.

The modern Western approach to sex, having absorbed certain non-Western traits but not others, acts in turn as a potent force for change in many parts of the world; however, its dominance is far from absolute, and it has provoked sharp reactions, particularly among Marxists and Muslims. Communist countries were among the first to use women for jobs that had always been a male monopoly. But Western commercialization of sex was, in terms of Marxist dogma, a challenge to be resisted at all costs. Where ancient customs have been swept away, they have been replaced by a Western-type puritanism that relates to a bygone era; in China today any notion of a sexual, as opposed to a social, revolution is as alien as it would have been to Karl Marx himself or to Queen Victoria. The Soviet Union has not gone to quite such extreme lengths in brushing sex under a Victorian carpet; nevertheless, there are no Western-style pinups, no newspaper scandals, and the sexual restraints imposed on Soviet films are unbelievable when judged by our standards. A typical theme of TV movies has been described as "Boy Loves Girl Loves Tractor." A wayward young man on a collective farm woos a devoted Party member; she consents to marry him only after he has changed his ways and become an exemplary citizen who exceeds his quota as a tractor driver. Notwithstanding all its criticism of the "moral decadence" of the West, the Soviet Union's immunity from its influences is more apparent than real; the divorce rate has risen rapidly, and *Pravda* announced in 1980 that a third of all marriages there ended in the first year. Even the Pill, made in Hungary, is now on sale.

In the modern totalitarian state, the Party apparatus is able to exercise an iron control over every facet of its citizens' lives, including sex. The situation is different in the more loosely organized societies of the Third World, most of whom have fewer defenses against the lure of Western "moral decadence." Nonetheless, this encroachment is now subject to impassioned counterattack inspired by Islam in a wide spectrum of non-Communist countries. Stark rejection is now spreading from its original stongholds, such as Iran, to far-flung outposts of Islam in Algeria and Indonesia. Fundamentalist Muslims now condemn not only such obvious sinks of Western iniquity as discos and bars but even object to restaurants and to innocent gadgets such as wristwatches.

By a bizarre paradox, however, if Western permissiveness is taboo, Western technology is supreme and now serves outlandish sexual customs, such as female circumcision, practiced mainly by animists and Muslims. Dr. Fran P. Hosken, who edited the 1977 report on the subject, pointed out in a recent letter to the *London Economist* that both infibulation and clitoridectomy are now commonly performed in hospitals, for which they are an invaluable source of revenue, and have become a most lucrative proposition for physicians, often trained in the West. The male head of a family now can be certain that he can sell to the highest bidder on the marriage market a girl whose virgin state is guaranteed, not by a witch doctor, but by the graduate of a Western university.

Larger numbers of girls still suffer the same tribulations under nonclinical conditions, and the number of women affected is estimated at between twenty million and seventy-five million. In September 1982, fourteen girls in Kenya died in the process, and as a result, President Daniel arap Moi decreed a nationwide ban on female circumcision, though his predecessor, Jomo Kenyatta, had upheld the custom as a symbol of nationalist resistance to colonialism (the British had wanted to impose a ban, but had not dared to enforce it). President Moi's law was specifically drafted to include missionary hospitals, both Catholic and Protestant, that had by implication practiced genital mutilation. Moi is the first African statesman to take this bold stand; when the matter was raised at the United Nations Women's Conference in 1980 by foreign delegates, they were shouted down by Africans, outraged at what they took as a racial slur.

The Turn of the Wheel

Like most upheavals, the sexual revolution of the 1960s and 1970s was the product of stresses that had been building up for many decades; it is perhaps surprising that such forces had not exploded a generation earlier and that many of the older taboos survived for so long.

In the early years of this century Freud had already withdrawn sex from the confines of the bedroom and put it under the microscope. The writings of Havelock Ellis, a near contemporary of Freud, were almost as prolific. As early as 1897, in his book *Sexual Inversion,* Ellis relates how white rats turn to homosexuality when deprived of females, the weaker rats playing the passive role. He even extended his studies to birds and observed how the male of a tropical species, *Machetes pugnax,* would often resort to intercourse with his own sex due to the extreme coyness of the female. Based on observations in the Berlin Zoological Gardens, he reported that no animal was more "depraved" than the pigeon, among whom members of the same sex would not merely indulge in occasional relations, but even pair off for several months. In reporting these discoveries, he anticipated by eighty years a report of *Time* magazine of December 12, 1977, describing the homosexual pairing of female gulls on islands off the coast of California, information that was still described as "astounding."

Havelock Ellis was the first to admit that many of his findings were based on yet earlier research by a number of distinguished nineteenth-century sexologists, such as Richard von Krafft-Ebing (1840–1902), whose greatest service, according to Ellis, was "the clinical enthusiasm with which he approached the study of sexual perversions." Krafft-Ebing's *Psychopathia Sexualis,* published in 1886, was an immense success and ran to many editions. Freud was less eager to give credit to his precursors; at times he posed as a beleaguered hero who thought up psychoanalysis all by himself; nonetheless, his theory of infant sexuality, which so deeply disturbed his contemporaries, was advanced by German sexologist Albert Moll decades before Freud hit upon the subject. Moll, however, took a nineteenth-century view of masturbation and in one of his works illustrated devices that could be fitted over male or female genitals, like little suits of armor with locks attached, to frustrate such temptations.

Like Freud, Havelock Ellis also produced hostile reactions. The first volume of his monumental *Studies in the Psychology of Sex,* originally published under the title *Sexual Inversion,* was in 1898 declared to be a "lewd wicked bawdy scandalous and obscene libel" by an English court, which ordered its seizure and destruction. On the strength of this, in the United States the book promptly became a blockbuster. The work of such pioneers produced only gradual results, and even half a century later many people were severely shocked by statistics given in the Kinsey reports showing the frequency of practices still regarded as perverted.

However, once the revolution finally burst its bounds, changes were rapid. Little, for instance, did those venerable doctors who blasted the evils of onanism dream that a hundred years later guidelines for the staff of a hostel for mentally handicapped adults, published by the London borough of Hounslow in 1982, would urge that the patients be given instructions on how to masturbate, and information on homosexuality. The state itself, far from suppressing abnormalities, now panders to every variant and even pays the check. The *Vancouver Sun* of August 11, 1979, reported a sex-change operation performed on a convicted murderer, Sheldon William Ball (henceforth Shelley Ball), an inmate of the maximum-security institute of Edmonton. It was stated that the decision was made from "the purely humanitarian point of view."

Nonetheless, however dramatic the revolution, lip service is still lavished on older conventions: Women still show a certain preference for tales of romantic fiction, implying a longing for sentimental attachment of a safe and traditional kind. Far from envying, say, the Australian aboriginal female, with her complex relationships with several men at a time, for the average woman monogamy is still the ideal; divorce merely marks a change from a lifelong union to a form of serial monogamy. For some men also the changes seem illusory. One individual was quoted in *The Hite Report on Male Sexuality* as saying, "The sexual revolution is maddening because there is still no more sex for me— but the media say everyone else is having it."

Even premarital sex falls somewhat short of the universal pattern of the South Seas. However widespread, its impact often is regional; Jonathan Gathorne-Hardy, in his book *Marriage, Love, Sex and Divorce,* tells how girls of the northern part of the London borough of Fulham say, "We all have lovers," while those of South Fulham say they can't do this.

Moreover, supporters of sexual reaction are active and can claim certain results. Organizations such as the Coalition for Better Television in the United States monitor every minute of prime-time TV to call on the networks to purge their programs of anything overtly sexual.

The New Right U.S. senator from Alabama, Jeremiah Denton, has sponsored a proposal designed, at a cost of $30 million, to establish a network of high-school shops to instruct teenagers in what he describes as "the one foolproof contraceptive, chastity." A powerful ally to the countercrusaders against the revolution is the dramatic spread of herpes, in which the wider acceptance of oral sex has played a part. Sex for pleasure entails new hazards, and married philanderers tend to be particularly wary, since the ravages of the complaint, though far from fatal, cannot be concealed from outraged spouses. New and more devastating maladies are now being traced to indiscriminate sex.

Family Problems

In recent years the bonds of marriage in the more advanced nations have been loosened to an extent never recorded in human history in East or West. In ancient Rome, a similar trend was mainly confined to the upper class; when the poet Juvenal describes women who had eight different husbands in five years, he is writing of the rich.

The percentage of marriages that end in divorce has doubled in the past decade and now exceeds 40 percent in the United States and 30 percent in Great Britain. The reasons for the explosion in the divorce rate are far from clear, though women's liberation, and the fact that two thirds of all wives now work outside their home, is an obvious factor. Other causes are not hard to find. Marriage therapists and sociologists ever since the 1930s have sharply criticized the fixation on romantic love, which gives rise to expectations that no marriage can fulfill and causes partners to make exorbitant demands on each other.

To this snare of the eternal idyll a new burden has been added, the quest for "personal fulfillment" in marriage. To the frenzy of everlasting romance is now joined this new catchphrase, upholding each partner's claim to "enrichment" and to the realization in marriage of his or her "deep potential." A third destructive force is the demand for total sexual satisfaction. Much of *The Hite Report: A Nationwide Study on Female Sexuality* is devoted to female orgasm, but it concludes that many women achieve this more successfully through masturbation than through intercourse. Judged purely from this standpoint, an electric vibrator can offer a woman more than a wedding ring.

Not only has the institution of marriage thus become more fragile, its very nature also has been transformed. Until recent times, marriage even in the West was based on the idea of the wife being a form of property. But among other factors, the female-headed household has destroyed this notion. In 1950 the number of families with children headed by women was 8 percent of the total; in the latest census, the number has risen to the astonishing figure of over 60 percent.

Hence, not only the nature of marriage but also its purpose has changed. Males in Western society are increasingly tending to feel it is not their responsibility to nurture children. Equally, many women no longer believe it is necessary to raise children within the framework of a family headed by two parents. But once the formerly sacred task of procreation is cast aside and marriage is focused simply on sex and companionship, the role of the wife becomes more comparable to that of a Chinese courtesan.

Child-psychiatrists are divided on the effects of this situation, which is hard to quantify. Everyone, of course, agrees that children are better off in a stable home, but no consensus exists as to just *how* injurious are the effects of a broken home. On the one hand, certain experts minimize the damage. Dr. E. E. LeMasters, professor of social work at the University of Wisconsin, condemns "parental determinism," whereby everything that happens to human beings when they become adults is blamed on their parents. Others question the role of parents in child-rearing; psychologist David Cooper in *The Death of the Family* brands the nuclear family as oppressive; for Cooper it instills too many social controls on a child, "Who is taught not how to survive in a society but how to submit to it."

Child-psychologist Hilary Anderson diametrically opposes this viewpoint when she writes that divorce for a child can be just as devastating as cancer for an adult. The undue proportion of convicted delinquents who come from broken homes may in part derive from their economic disadvantages; for whatever their differences on other aspects of the problem, psychiatrists and sociologists agree as to the disastrous economic consequences of divorce in most cases. In 1977, of the nine million American children living in one-parent families, 62 percent fell below the poverty line, as compared with 12 percent of all families. Among other ordeals facing the children of divorce are a built-in antipathy to their parents' new spouses and a frequent tendency of parents to use their children as pawns, whether as spies to inform on their ex-partner or as victims of a tug-of-war in which the child is urged to side with himself or herself against the other. These adult jealousies make life unbearable for children, who otherwise are often perfectly capable of adjusting to parents' divorce and even to new lovers *provided* the facts are adequately explained to them.

Today the family in the Western world faces an uncertain future. As social psychologist Urie Bronfenbrenner dramatically puts it: "American families and their children are in trouble. Trouble so deep and pervasive as to threaten the future of our nation." He writes of the national neglect of children and of a society whose pressures downgrade the role of parents and prevent them from doing what is needed to serve as guide, companion, and friend of their children. Nowadays, in the parents' absence, their educational role is usurped by television, which the average American child watches for between two and four hours per day. By the age of sixteen he or she can be expected to have spent between twelve thousand and fifteen thousand hours in front of the TV set, or the equivalent of twenty-four hours per day for fifteen to twenty-four months. This flickering member of the family unit now occupies more waking hours of a child's life than parents or schools.

This crisis in the Western family is a long-term problem; it was already discussed in American magazines in the late nineteenth century, and between 1870 and 1920 the number of divorces in the United States increased fifteen fold. The origins of the decline are even remoter; over the past two hundred years the family has yielded, mainly to the state, most of its previous functions; it is no longer the principal place of learning for the child, and religious life no longer stems from the hearth. The vital economic ties that held a family together were severed when it ceased to be a business partnership in which all cooperated, once the fathers began to work in factories far from home. It retains only the function of providing a haven, a place of rest, often of a rather transient kind.

Sociologists, who sometimes display a talent for telling us in academic language simple facts that we already know, harp on the modern tendency, not only for the father but also for the mother, to work outside the home—to a point where by the mid-1970s only in a third of two-parent families was the husband the sole breadwinner. However, what is easily forgotten is that since time immemorial and until the industrial age, women were not confined to household chores and child-rearing, but as part of the family division of labor performed many essential tasks, such as tending its plot of land and making its clothes and even its crockery.

This study is not basically devoted to the changing sexual patterns of the West, on which a vast literature exists. Of greater concern in our context is the interrelationship between such changes and the customs of the rest of the world among peoples whose culture may still be regarded as partly non-Western. As a possible alternative answer to the problems of the West, sociologists and psychiatrists have frequently pointed to the very different systems that prevail elsewhere. In most Third World nations today the nuclear family, consisting of only parents and children, is the exception rather than the rule, and the one-parent family is much rarer. Even in Mexico, more exposed to Western influences than many others, a household almost inevitably contains, in addition to parents and children, other individuals, such as grandparents, uncles, aunts, cousins, and occasional lodgers. The notion that aging parents should be left to fend for themselves in separate dwellings is almost unheard of there. To quote a specific case, an old people's home donated to Mexico City in the 1960s was a dismal failure and was used to house only a minimal residue of octogenarians, entirely without living relatives, who otherwise would automatically have cared for them.

The system of the extended family has obvious and inestimable advantages; since everyone contributes something to the needs of the group, it functions in practice and does wonders in relieving the miseries and tensions of poorer countries. Only a utopian, however, can believe that the extended family can suddenly be reintroduced into the richer nations. Slowly but surely, as part of the elusive search for individual "fulfillment," the notion has taken root in the richer countries that the young married must be left on their own and that the presence of the proverbial mother-in-law, let alone of aunts, uncles, and cousins, will wreck the idyllic romance that nowadays, without their presence, founders anyway in 40 percent of all cases in the United States. Moreover, in the Third World also, the universal drive to industrialize endangers the system, since it uproots people from their place of origin. At a time when the extended family is already endangered in the Third World, it is surely useless to suppose that it can be reestablished in the United States and Europe.

Given the determination of most married women to seek work outside their homes the second alternative most commonly put forward is a network of child-care units that would fill the breach. Practiced on a large scale in the Soviet Union, whose inefficient economy creates an insatiable demand for female labor, it might be termed the Soviet solution. A comparable system has been favored for centuries by the English gentry, who still consign their children to boarding schools from the tender age of eight.

In the Western world, much has been achieved in child care —for instance, in Japan and Scandinavia. But American governments are reluctant spenders on infant centers, as sociologists never cease to complain. In 1972, for instance, President Richard Nixon vetoed a major program of legislation devoted to this end. In a country where, unlike the Soviet Union, parents want a choice between different forms of center, these tend to be costly, and the point can easily be reached where the expense absorbs much of the mother's extra earnings.

As a third possible solution, when in 1977 Kenneth Keniston headed a Carnegie Corporation study on children and the family, he argued that work rather than the family should be reshaped to fit the needs of modern life. It is sometimes further suggested that the electronic era will so revolutionize work that it will reunite the family. Much of society would then consist of a kind of "cottage industry" in which all members of the nuclear family would sit cozily together, the parents earning their living and the children doing their studies in a roomful of computer terminals. But this solution remains a futurist's dream and in any case would function equally efficiently in a female-headed household; like child-care units, it offers no complete answer to the problems of the immediate future.

The ease with which divorce is obtained in Western countries has come to be taken for granted as sheer common sense. But the fact remains that with the partial (and ominous) exception of the late Roman Empire, every human culture has previously numbered among its highest goals the cohesion of the family unit and the prevention of its ruin. Surely Urie Bronfenbrenner hardly exaggerates in viewing the very fabric of modern society as threatened by failure in that respect.

Sociologists ceaselessly point to the defects of current divorce laws and to their potential damage to children. Law reform lies far beyond our scope, and one can only reaffirm emphatically that the present state of affairs would have been unthinkable both in tribal society and in any other higher civilization; it certainly does not prevail today among, say, Muslims or Hindus, not so much due to any inferior status of women, as to concern for the welfare of the young. Whatever the future may hold, the evidence of the past raises doubts as to how long a situation can exist under which the most solemn contract that a human being can make, that of uniting with a partner for the ultimate purpose of bringing other beings into the world, of forming, guiding, and educating them, is so often cast aside. People constantly enter into simpler commitments—say, to buy houses, cars, or even electric gadgets. Such contracts usually are honored, and the percentage of default is low, because the penalties for such default fall squarely on the shoulders of those who made them. But in the case of marriage, some of the worst consequences can be shrugged off onto third parties, the children.

Traditional marriage and family life, whatever their shortcomings, seem likely to survive, even if they no longer command the same prestige among men and women as the only way to conduct their relations. In attitudes to sex and to family life, the pace of change surely will not slacken; in the process, the West hopefully will not turn a blind eye to the lessons to be learned from other cultures, past and present. Examples taken from diminutive South Sea islands, once fashionable, may be less relevant. But in many nations of the modern Third World, situated in regions that brought forth great cultures of the past, ruling parties may be steeped in corruption, the economy reduced to a shambles, and poverty rendered endemic; yet the astonishing fact remains that in such societies, where all else fails, the family, usually embracing many individuals, is a going concern, the key to survival amid a sea of trouble.

If the return to something more like the extended family is at present an ideal rather than an immediate reality, certain lessons have at least been learned from the non-Western world. Not only is teenage promiscuity more widely accepted as a legacy from tribal society; in addition, the general concept of sex for pleasure and not merely for procreation, taken for granted in other higher civilizations, has surely come to stay; this current recognition that men and women may currently expect to enjoy a wider range of sexual options than previously admitted is probably neither reversible nor harmful.

Other useful lessons from non-Christian societies have been partly or totally ignored. One practice of other civilizations that has so far been only partially adopted by the West is a wholly realistic attitude toward homosexuality. The process of gay liberation is far from complete, and in *The Second American Revolution* Gore Vidal observes that "Jews, Blacks and homosexualists are despised by the Christian and Communist majorities of East and West." A more wholehearted acceptance would surely enable homosexuals to distinguish themselves in a much wider range of activities and thereby make a greater contribution to society as a whole.

The most vital lesson that still remains to be learned from other societies than our own is the need for greater tolerance within the family unit and a greater readiness on the part of both spouses to adopt a more open approach to marriage. If people would only face the fact that a large proportion of humans have certain promiscuous tendencies, then a redefinement of marriage in this sense becomes not only an obvious but even an essential need as offering the best solution to family problems.

Tribal societies, as we have seen, often provided well-defined secondary outlets for both partners to a marriage. All higher civilizations, except for our own, freely admitted the

281

man's right to alternative partners; in the West, this right had in the past been tacitly accepted in the most sophisticated circles, as, say, among the French and at times even the English aristocracy.

Surely in our society, obsessed with equal rights, this worldwide concession to human frailty, far from being denied to men, should logically be extended to women as part of the concept of equality of the sexes. Instead, the bourgeois concept of marriage survives in the West, and in the case of the average couple, with obvious exceptions, even the most casual straying from the path of fidelity is a pretext for divorce. Men in particular are still apt to be outraged at the thought that their wives might indulge in extramarital activities. We are still far from the ancient Chinese notion that any form of sexual conduct between or among two or more individuals was acceptable provided it did not actively harm any third party.

Marital constancy in the past was less a product of law than of religious faith expressed in the most solemn vow, a breach of which would consign the offender to lasting damnation. But nowadays, freed from such terrors, people are more inclined to follow the dictates of the devil and yield to temptations basic to human nature. Absolute fidelity then becomes a total anachronism and it is surely not too much to hope that, in the ever-changing sexual panorama of today, if marriage remains the rule, tolerant but once-and-for-all pairing will come to be preferred by most to serial monogamy as the logical outcome of the sexual revolution. Until marriage is redefined in this sense and the acceptance of alternative outlets for both partners is more willingly accepted, the revolution will not be complete.

To this the most obvious objection lies in the fact that other causes for marital instability exist when partners fall out not because of infidelity but because they just don't want to live together anymore. But different forms of intolerance are also present in at least some of such cases. Sociologists and psychologists of the future perhaps will lay less stress on the ideal of individual "fulfillment" for a particular human being, regardless of the interests of others, and will call to mind the universal lesson, less lightly set aside in the non-Western world, that man is a social animal; solutions devised for the moral enrichment of each separate person will falter if they disregard the good of the community, of which the family and marriage, perhaps of a more open kind, have not ceased to be the mainstays.

Bibliography

ALLGROVE, George. *Love in the East.* London: Anthony Gibbs and Phillips, 1962.

ARBOLEDA, Manuel G. "Depictions of Homoerotic Activities in Moche Ceramic Art" (paper presented at the XLIII International Congress of Americanists, Vancouver, 1979).

BANE, Mary Jo. "Marital Disruption and the Lives of Children." *Journal of Social Issues,* Vol. 32, No. 1 (1976).

BAUMANN, Hermann. *Das Doppelte Geschlecht.* Berlin: Dietrich Riemer, 1955.

BEAUVOIR, Simone de. *Le Deuxième Sexe, les Faits et les Mythes.* Paris: Gallimard, 1949.

BECKER, J.E. de. *The Nightless City, or the History of the Yoshiwara Yukwaku.* London: Probsthain, 1899.

BEGLER, Elsie B. "Sex, Status and Authority in Egalitarian Society." *American Anthropologist,* Vol. 80 (1978).

BENEDICT, Ruth. *Patterns of Culture.* Boston: Houghton Mifflin, 1934.

BERNDT, Ronald M. and Catherine H. *Sexual Behaviour in Western Arnhem Land.* New York: Viking Fund, 1951.

BETTELHEIM, Bruno. *Symbolic Wounds: Puberty Rites and the Envious Male.* New York: Collier Books, 1962.

BLAINE, Graham B. *Are Parents Bad for Children?* New York: Coward, McCann & Geoghegan, 1973.

BEURDELEY, Michel. *The Clouds and the Rain: The Art of Love in China.* London: Hammond & Hammond, 1969.

BLOCH, Iwan. *Anthropological Studies in the Strange Sexual Practices of All Races in All Ages.* New York: Anthropological Press, 1933.

BOUSQUET, G.H. *L'éthique Sexuelle de l'Islam.* Paris: Maisonneuve et Larose, 1966.

BRASCH, R. *How Did Sex Begin?* Sydney, N.S.W.: Angus & Robertson, 1973.

BRONFENBRENNER, Urie. *Who Cares for American Children?* New York: Simon & Schuster, 1972.

BRUSENDORFF, Ove, and Paul Hennigson. *A History of Eroticism.* New York: Lyle Stuart, 1963.

BRYK, Felix. *Neger-Eros.* Berlin: Marcus and Webersverlag, 1928.

BULLOUGH, Vernon L. *The History of Prostitution.* New York: University Books, 1964.

————. *Sexual Variance in Society and History.* New York: John Wiley & Sons, 1976.

BURTON, Sir Richard. *The Erotic Traveler.* New York: G. P. Putnam's Sons, 1967.

CALVERTON, V.F. and S.D. Schmalhausen, eds. *Sex in Civilization.* London: Allen & Unwin, 1929.

CARPENTER, Edward. *Intermediate Types Among Primitive Folk.* London: Allen & Unwin, 1929.

CHACLADAR, H.C. *Social Life in Ancient India: A Study in Vatsayana's* Kamasutra. Calcutta: Siesil Gupta, 1954.

CHARNAY, Jean-Paul. *Islamic Culture and Socio-Economic Change.* Leiden: E.J. Brill, 1971.

CHERLIN, Andrew. "Remarriage as an Incomplete Institution." *American Journal of Sociology,* Vol. 84 (1978).

CHIN PING MEI. *The Golden Lotus,* trans. C. Egerton. London: 1939.

CLEUGH, James. *Love Locked Out.* New York: Crown, 1964.

————. *A History of Oriental Orgies.* New York: Crown, 1968.

COLE, William Graham, *Sex and Love in the Bible.* London: Hodder & Stoughton, 1960.

COOPER, David. *The Death of the Family.* New York: Random House, 1970.

CZAJA, Michael. *Gods of Myth and Stone: Phallicism in Japanese Folk Religion.* New York: Weatherhill, 1974.

DAHLBERG, Frances, ed. *Woman the Gatherer.* New Haven, Conn.: Yale University Press, 1981.

DANIELSSON, Bengdt. *Love in the South Seas.* New York: Reynal, 1956.

DAWSON, Warren R. *The Custom of Couvade.* Manchester: Manchester University Press, 1929.

Bibliography

DEGLER, Carl N. *At Odds: The Women and the Family in America from the Revolution to the Present.* New York and Oxford: Oxford University Press, 1980.

DEVEREUX, Georges. "The Sexual Life of the Mohave Indians: An Interpretation in Terms of Social Psychology." M.S. Dissertation, University of California at Berkeley, 1936.

————. "Institutionalized Homosexuality of the Mohave Indians." *Human Biology,* Vol. 9 (1937).

————. "Incest Among the Mohave Indians." *Psychoanalytic Quarterly,* Vol. 8 (1939).

————. "Mohave Indian Autoerotic Behavior." *Psychoanalytic Review,* Vol. 37 (1950).

————. "Cultural and Characterological Traits of the Mohave Related to the Anal Stage of Psychosexual Development." *Psychoanalytic Quarterly,* Vol. 20 (1951).

————. *A Study of Abortion in Primitive Societies.* New York: International Universities Press, 1976.

DÍAZ DEL CASTILLO, Bernal. *Historia de las Indias de Nueva España.* Garden City, N.Y.: Doubleday, 1956.

DOVER, Sir Kenneth. *Greek Homosexuality.* Cambridge, Mass.: Harvard University Press, 1978.

DUFFY, J. "Masturbation and Clitoridectomy." *Journal of the American Medical Association,* Vol. 186 (1963).

DURKHEIM, Emile. *Incest: The Nature and Origin of the Taboo.* New York: Lyle Stuart, 1963.

EDWARDES, Allen. *The Jewel in the Lotus.* New York, Julian Press 1959.

ELLIS, Havelock, *Studies in the Psychology of Sex,* 6 vols. Philadelphia: F.A. Davies, 1926.

Encyclopedia of Religion and Ethics, ed. James Hastings, 13 vols. New York: Charles Scribner's Sons, 1951.

ENGLISCH, Paul. *Sittengeschichte des Orients.* Berlin: Kiepenheuerverlag, 1932.

FEATHERSTONE, Joseph. "Family Matters." *Harvard Educational Review,* Vol. 49 (1979).

FEHLINGER, H. *The Sexual Life of Primitive Peoples.* London: A. & C. Black, 1921.

FERRERO, Guglielmo. *The Women of the Caesars.* New York: G. P. Putnam's Sons, 1925.

FISHER, Helen E. *The Sex Contract: The Evolution of Human Behavior* New York: William Morrow, 1982.

FLACELIÈRE, Robert. *Love in Ancient Greece.* London: Frederic Muller, 1962.

FORD, Clennan S., and Frank A. Beach. *Patterns of Sexual Behavior.* New York: Harper & Brothers, 1952.

FOUCAULT, Michel. *The History of Sexuality*, Vol. I. New York: Pantheon Books, 1978.

FRAZER, Sir James. *The Golden Bough*, abr. ed. London: Macmillan, 1922.

FREUD, Sigmund. *Totem and Tabu*. London: Hogarth Press, 1913.

FÜRSTAUER, Johann. *Eros im Alten Orient*. Stuttgart: Güntherverlag, 1965.

GATHORNE-HARDY, Jonathan. *Marriage, Love, Sex and Divorce*. New York: Summit Books, 1981.

GIFFORD, E.W. "The Kamia of Imperial Valley." Bureau of American Ethnology, *Bulletin* No. 197 (1931).

GOLDBERG, Ben Zion. *The Sacred Fire: The Story of Sex and Religion*. New York: Horace Liveright, 1932.

GORDON, Pierre. *L'Initiation Sexuelle et l'Evolution Religieuse*. Paris: Presses Universitaires de France, 1946.

GREEN, Richard, and John Money, eds. *Transsexualism and Sex Reassignment*. Baltimore: The Johns Hopkins Press, 1968.

GROOT, J.J.J.M. de. *The Religious System of Ancient China*. Leiden: E. Brill, 1894.

GUERRA, Francisco. *The Pre-Columbian Mind*. London and New York: Seminar Press, 1971.

GULIK, R.H. van. *Sexual Life in Ancient China*. Leiden: E. Brill, 1961.

HENRIQUES, Fernando. *Prostitution and Society*. London: MacGibbon & Kee, 1962.

HITE, Shere. *The Hite Report: A Nationwide Study of Female Sexuality*. New York: Dell, 1976.

————. *The Hite Report on Male Sexuality*. New York: Alfred A. Knopf, 1981.

HOSKEN, Fran P. *The Hosken Report: Genital and Sexual Mutilation of Females*. Lexington, Mass: Women's International Network News, 1979.

HOWARD, Clifford. *Sex Worship: An Exposition of the Phallic Origins of Religion*. Chicago: Chicago Medical Book Company, 1917.

HUNG LOU MENG. *The Dream of the Red Chamber*. New York: Pantheon Books, 1958.

HUNT, Morton. *Sexual Behavior in the 1970s*. New York: Playboy Press, 1974.

HUNTSMAN, Judith, and Mervyn McLean, eds. Special Issue on Incest Prohibitions in Micronesia and Polynesia, *Journal of the Polynesian Society*, Vol. 85 (1976).

JENKYNS, Richard. *The Victorians and Ancient Greece*. Cambridge, Mass: Harvard University Press, 1980.

JOHANSON, Donald, and Lucy Maitland Edey. *The Beginnings of Humankind*. New York: Simon & Schuster, 1981.

Bibliography

KAPP HOWE, Louise, ed. *The Future of the Family.* New York: Simon & Schuster, 1972.

KAUFMANN DOIG, Federico. *Sexual Behavior in Ancient Peru.* Lima: Kompaktos, 1979.

KENISTON, Kenneth, and the Carnegie Council on Children. *All Our Children.* New York: Harcourt Brace Jovanovich, 1977.

KIEFER, Otto. *Sexual Life in Ancient Rome.* London: Routledge & Kegan Paul, 1934.

KIRKUP, James. *Japan Behind the Fan.* London: J.M. Dent, 1970.

KOHLER, Joseph. *On the Prehistory of Marriage.* Chicago: University of Chicago Press, 1975.

KROEBER, A.L. *The Handbook of the Indians of California.* Los Angeles: Californian Book Company, 1953.

LANDIN, Judson T. "The Trauma of Children when the Parents Divorce." *Marriage and Family Living,* Vol. 22 (1960).

LEACH, Edmund. "Sins or Rules?" *New Society,* Vol. 27 (1963).

LÉVI-STRAUSS, Claude. *Elementary Structures of Kinship.* Boston: Beacon Press, 1969.

LEWINSOHN, Richard. *A History of Sexual Customs.* New York: Harper & Brothers, 1958.

LICHT, Hans. *Sexual Life in Ancient Greece.* London: Routledge & Kegan Paul, 1932.

LORENTZ, Konrad. *On Aggression.* New York: Harcourt, Brace & World, 1966.

LOSA, Antonio. *Raizes Judaico-Cristas do Islamismo.* Brazil: Braga, 1963.

MACE, David and Vera. *The Soviet Family.* Garden City, N.Y.: Doubleday, 1963.

MAIR, George. *The Sex Book Digest.* New York: William Morrow, 1982.

MALINOWSKI, Bronislaw. *The Sexual Life of Savages: An Ethnographic Account of Courtship, Marriage, and Family Life Among the Natives of the Trobriand Islands, British New Guinea.* New York: Harcourt, Brace, 1923.

———. *Sex and Repression in Savage Society.* London: Routledge & Kegan Paul, 1927.

———. *Sex, Culture and Myth.* New York: Harcourt, Brace & World, 1962.

———. *A Diary in the Strict Sense of the Word.* New York: Harcourt, Brace & World, 1967.

MARSHALL, Donald S., and Robert C. Suggs, eds. *Human Sexual Behavior: Variations in the Ethnographic Spectrum.* New York: Basic Books, 1971.

MEAD, Margaret. *Coming of Age in Samoa.* New York: William Morrow, 1928.

———. *Sex and Temperament in Three Primitive Societies.* New York: William Morrow, 1935.

MEIJER, M.J. *Marriage Law and Policy in the Chinese People's Republic.* Hong Kong: Hong Kong University Press, 1971.

MEYER, Johann Jakob. *Sexual Life in Ancient India.* New York: E.P. Dutton, 1930.

MONTAGU, Ashley. *Sex, Man and Society.* New York: G.P. Putnam's Sons, 1969. *Coming into Being Among the Australian Aborigines.* London: Routledge & Kegan Paul, 1937.

MOOKERJI, Radha Kamud. *Hindu Civilization.* Bombay: Bharatiya Vidya Bhavan, 1950.

NEFZAWI, Sheik. *The Perfumed Garden,* trans. Sir Richard Burton. London: Neville Spearman, 1963.

PARRINDER, Geoffrey. *Sex in the World's Religions.* London: Sheldon Press, 1980.

PARTRIDGE, Burgo. *A History of Orgies.* London: Anthony Blond, 1958; New York: Boronga Books, 1960.

PEDRALS, Denis-Pierre de. *La Vie Sexuelle en Afrique Noire.* Paris: Payot, 1950.

PENZER, N.M. *The Harem.* London: George Harrap, 1936.

PUNEKAR, S.D., and Kamala Rao. *A Study of Prostitution in Bombay.* Bombay and Calcutta: Lavani, 1962.

RAWSON, Philip. *Erotic Art of the East.* London: George Weidenfeld & Nicolson, 1973.

REINHARD, David W. "The Reaction of Adolescent Boys and Girls to the Divorce of their Parents." *Journal of Clinical Child Psychology,* Vol. 6 (1977).

RENTOUL, Alex C. "Physical Paternity and the Trobrianders." *Man,* Vol. 31 (1931).

RIVERS, W.H.R. *The Todas.* London: Macmillan, 1906.

SAHAGÚN, Fray Bernardino de. *Florentine Codex: General History of the Things of New Spain,* 12 vols. Santa Fe, N.M.: The School of American Research and the University of Utah, 1950–63.

SCHLESINGER, Benjamin. *The One-Parent Family.* Toronto: University of Toronto Press, 1978.

SCOTT, George Ryley. *Curious Customs of Sex and Marriage.* London: Torchstream Books, 1953.

——. *Phallic Worship.* London: Torchstream Books, 1933.

SINGER, June. *Androgyny: Towards a New Theory of Sexuality.* London: Routledge & Kegan Paul, 1977.

SORENSEN, Robert C. *Adolescent Sexuality in Contemporary America.* New York: World Publishing, 1973.

Bibliography

SPENCER, Baldwin and F.J. Gillen. *The Native Tribes of Central Australasia.* London: Macmillan, 1899.

SUGGS, Robert C. *Marquesan Sexual Behavior.* London: Constable, 1966.

TABET, Paola. "Les Mains, Les Outils, Les Armes." *L'Homme,* Vol. 19 (1979).

TANNER, Nancy Makepeace. *On Becoming Human.* Cambridge: Cambridge University Press, 1981.

THOMAS, Northcote W. *Kinship Organizations and Group Marriage.* Cambridge. Cambridge University Press, 1906.

THOMAS, Paul. *Kama Kalpa, or the Hindu Act of Love* Bombay: D.B. Taraporevala, 1960.

TORQUEMADA, Fray Juan de. *Monarquía Indiana,* 3 vols. Mexico City: Editorial Chavez Hayhoe, 1943–44.

TÜLLMANN, Adolf. *Das Liebesleben der Naturvölker.* Stuttgart: Hanns Güntherverlag, 1961.

UNWIN, J.D. *Sexual Regulations and Human Behaviour.* London: Williams & Norgate, 1933.

———. *Sex and Culture.* London: Oxford University Press, 1934.

VELLAY, Charles. *Le Culte et les Fêtes d'Adonis-Thammouz dans L'Orient Antique* Paris: Ernest Leroux, 1901.

WALKER, Benjamin. *Hindu World: An Encyclopedic Study of Hinduism,* 2 vols London: George Allen & Unwin, 1968.

WESTERMARCK, Edward. *The History of Human Marriage.* London: Macmillan, 1901.

———. *The Origin and Development of the Moral Ideas.* London: Macmillan, 1906.

WILSON, Glenn. *The Coolidge Effect: An Evolutionary Account of Human Sexuality.* New York: William Morrow, 1982.

Woo Chan Cheng. *L'Erotologie de la Chine.* Paris: Bibliothèque Internationale d'Erotologie, 1963.

Index

Index

INDEX

Index

INDEX

Index

Martyr, Peter, 88–89, 90
Masturbation
  ancient Egypt and, 139
  ancient Greece and, 156–157
  China and, 206, 213, 228
  Christianity and, 268–269, 273
  female orgasm and, 275
  India and, 257–258
  Judaism and, 174
  North American Indians and, 96
  the Polynesians and, 64
Matriarchies, 11, 24, 60, 135
Mbuti Pygmies, 25
Mead, Margaret, 43, 73–75, 269
Meiji revolution (1868), 234
Mesopotamia, 118, 122, 123, 124, 127,
  128–133, 148, 170, 263–264
Messalina, 166–167
Michelangelo, 183
Middle Ages, 182–183, 266
Mirror of Manly Love, The (Saikaka), 235
Missionaries, 33–34, 55, 69–72, 75, 86
Moche civilization (Peru), 109–113
Mohammed, 185–188, 191, 200–201,
  264
Mohaves, the, 92–101
Mohenjodaro civilization (India), 237
Moll, Albert, 273
Mongol Dynasty, 215
Monkeys, 14, 16, 18, 82–83, 127
Monogamy, 125
  ancient Egypt and, 136
  Christianity and, 184–185
  gorillas and, 22
  the Polynesians and, 68
  serial, 270
Montagu, M.F. Ashley, 42
Montague, Lady Mary, 193
Morgan, Lewis Henry, 11, 13, 24
Mortimer, George, 80
Moses, 171, 177, 185
Murngin, the, 27
Muslem fundamentalism, 188–189, 196

Nandi, the, 47–48
Napier, Sir Charles, 196
"Natural History of the Incas" (de
  Oviedo), 89
Natural selection, 20–21

Navaho, the, 92
Necrophilia, 258–259
Nefertiti, 136, 140
Nefzaoui of Tunis, Sheikh, 190
Neo-Platonism, 155, 176, 179
New Orleans Medical Journal, The, 268–269
Nocturnal emissions, 206
North American Indians, 87, 91–103,
  263
Notes of the Dressing Room, 213
Nuclear family, 276, 278
Nudity, 175
Nuñez de Balboa, Vasco, 88–89
Nut (mother goddess), 134

Oedipus complex, 36, 49, 81
Omaha Indians, 87
Oman, 198–200
Onan, 172, 173
Orangutans, 14
Orgiastic ceremonies, 37, 157, 159
Orpheus, 149
Orphism, 175–176
Osiris, 134, 136, 137–138
Oviedo, Fernandez de, 89–90

Paiderasteia, 149–155
Pakistan, 189
Papuans, the, 43, 48
Parvati, 161, 241, 243, 255
Paul, St., 169, 175, 176–181, 185
Pederasty, 144
  ancient Greece and, 149–155
  Christianity and, 178–179
  Judaism and, 174, 178–179
Peking man, 23–24
Penis envy, 50
Pericles, 146, 147
Peruvian National Museum of
  Anthropology, 111
Phaedrus (Plato), 155
Phaido of Elis, 152–153
Phallicism, 50, 107, 121, 127–128
  ancient Egypt and, 137–138
  ancient Greece and, 158–159
  ancient Rome and, 165
  India and, 138, 238–240, 260
Pharaonic circumcision, 47
Philip III of Spain, King, 183

297

INDEX

Index